AMERICA FOR SALE

As we stand by and watch, foreign investors are buying up U.S. assets—from major banks and brokerage firms to public infrastructure such as highways. We are on our way to a European Union–type North American common market and a one-world government.

What can we do to stop it?

- Demand state legislatures enforce employment laws and deny benefits to illegal immigrants
- Repeal NAFTA and pull out of the WTO to replace those "free trade" agreements with "fair trade" agreements
- Pass laws limiting foreign investors to minority ownership in U.S. banks, brokerage firms, and infrastructure projects
- Change U.S. tax incentives to reward corporations that bring jobs back to America

Jerome Corsi's brilliant book outlines an immediate course of action. Together, we can protect our independent and self-governing nation and preserve our economic power and military strength.

> "Dr. Corsi shines a light on issues that no working man or woman can afford to ignore."
>
> —James P. Hoffa, General President, International Brotherhood of Teamsters

This title is available from Simon & Schuster Audio and as an eBook

AMERICA
for SALE

FIGHTING THE NEW WORLD ORDER,

SURVIVING A GLOBAL DEPRESSION,

and

PRESERVING U.S.A. SOVEREIGNTY

JEROME R. CORSI, PH.D.

THRESHOLD
EDITIONS

New York London Toronto Sydney

For those who endured the economic hardships
of the Great Depression of the 1930s without losing
their faith in the free enterprise system and a
sovereign United States of America

Threshold Editions
A Division of Simon & Schuster, Inc.
1230 Avenue of the Americas
New York, NY 10020

First Threshold Editions trade paperback edition October 2010

THRESHOLD EDITIONS and colophon are trademarks
of Simon & Schuster, Inc.

For information about special discounts for bulk purchases,
please contact Simon & Schuster Special Sales at 1-866-506-1949
or business@simonandschuster.com.

The Simon & Schuster Speakers Bureau can bring authors to your live event.
For more information or to book an event contact the Simon & Schuster
Speakers Bureau at 1-866-248-3049 or visit our website at
www.simonspeakers.com.

Designed by Elliott Beard

Manufactured in the United States of America

10   9   8   7   6   5   4   3   2   1

ISBN 978-1-4391-5477-9
ISBN 978-1-4391-5478-6 (pbk)
ISBN 978-1-4391-6687-1 (ebook)

CONTENTS

PREFACE

A Transformational Crisis

Never let a serious crisis go to waste. What I mean by that is it's an opportunity to do things you couldn't do before.
—White House chief of staff Rahm Emanuel, November 2008[1]

Never waste a good crisis.
—Secretary of State Hillary Clinton, March 2009[2]

The global economic recession that began in December 2008 has resulted in a meltdown of U.S. financial institutions unlike any seen since the Great Depression of the 1930s. What follows are three vignettes that offer a first impression of how the economic crisis was manipulated into a vehicle to push the U.S. economy further in the direction of government control. The ultimate agenda of the globalists managing the economic crisis, in the presidential administrations of both George W. Bush and Barack Obama, has been to use the crisis as an opportunity to push the U.S. private-enterprise economy further in the direction of a government-managed economy.

In 2009, prominent economic and political figures, such as those cited in these three short snapshots, have been remarkably open about their intent to manipulate the economic crisis as a "transitional crisis" useful to advance their globalist goals.

1. WORLD ECONOMIC FORUM
DAVOS, SWITZERLAND
JANUARY—FEBRUARY 2009

A call to utilize the current global economic crisis as a panic in which governments worldwide could transform national economies into a truly global economy emerged from the World Economic Forum during its 2009 meeting in Davos, Switzerland.

The call came from none other than Klaus Schwab, the founder of the Davos forum. Schwab told CNN in a televised interview from Davos that "the current global economic slowdown is a 'transformational crisis' that should be utilized to shape a 'new world.'"[3] The statement was shocking because it suggested that even if elite economists and world leaders did not cause the global economic recession in order to produce a global new world order, they were being advised to manipulate the global economic crisis for that purpose.

"Above all else this is a crisis of confidence," Schwab said. "To restore confidence you have to establish signposts that the world after the crisis will be different. We have to create a new world and that is what Davos 2009 will be all about—serving society."

As if to underscore Schwab's dramatic conclusions, several economists used the 2009 Davos forum as a platform on which to proclaim that the dimensions of the world economic downturn reflected an unprecedented collapse of economic activity around the globe. The message was clear: the dramatic meltdown demanded solutions never before contemplated.

Nouriel Roubini, a professor at New York University's Stern School of Business, was interviewed live by CNBC from Davos on January 27, 2009. Roubini declared before a national audience that the global banking system was "effectively insolvent." The possibility that the worldwide banking system was bankrupt was shocking, suggesting the asset crisis in the United States had by the beginning of 2009 spread across the globe. Roubini, who is a frequent guest on syndicated financial news shows, was adding to his reputation as "Dr. Doom," a reputation Roubini earned for his typically gloomy but often accurate forecasts.

Roubini estimated that the worldwide crisis in bad bank assets would extend far beyond the collateralized-mortgage-obligation problem caused by subprime loans, to include bad loans in consumer credit cards, car loans, and student loans, as well as commercial loans that have been packaged into securities sold to banks and brokerage firms. Roubini es-

CONTENTS

timated the toxic assets would total $3.6 trillion, about half of which he believed was held by U.S. banks and brokerage firms.

Roubini's estimate was shocking, especially since the U.S. Congress had allocated only $700 billion in two tranches of the Troubled Asset Relief Program, or TARP, funds to resolve the bank-asset problem, the largest bank bailout voted by Congress in U.S. history. If the true magnitude of the bank toxic-asset problem had to be measured in the trillions, then the TARP funds, admittedly huge, would be insufficient to solve it. Should bank toxic assets measure into the trillions of dollars, then solving the problem with $700 billion in TARP funds would be like trying to put out a fire raging in a New York skyscraper with a pail and a garden hose.

Roubini called on the Obama administration to employ a "Swedish solution," in which the U.S. government would nationalize troubled banks, not just investing bailout cash but also taking over, giving management control to U.S. government bureaucrats. In the early 1990s, Sweden nationalized banks, but only after the banks had taken the losses.

Also interviewed by CNBC from Davos, Joseph Stiglitz, a Columbia University economics professor and 2001 Nobel laureate who advised the incoming Obama administration during its transition, expressed his concerns that the U.S. Treasury and the Federal Reserve had used TARP funds to overpay for bad assets. "The private sector would not touch these bad assets with a ten-foot pole," Stiglitz said. "It's not clear we have here a good deal for the taxpayers."

Arguing that "taxpayers have provided capital, but have received no control," Stiglitz also contended the U.S. government should begin nationalizing the banks under the Swedish plan, where the private owners of the banks would first take the losses for the bad assets and the government would nationalize the banks at a much lower share price, as a result of the private liquidation of troubled assets. He reasoned that economic incentives dictated that private bank managers, if left in place after TARP funds were injected without government control, would "have incentives to pay themselves bonuses, to pay shareholders dividends, and to use bailout funds to make acquisitions."

"We need to run these banks for our interest," Stiglitz said, arguing the Obama administration should move quickly to nationalize banks receiving bailout funds. "The government could not do worse than the banks themselves have done," he observed, insisting TARP bailouts made no sense unless the government ended up controlling the banks. "You can call it 'conserving the banks,' if you want to use a nice term,"

Stiglitz said, conceding his willingness to package his intent in a euphemism designed to obscure the true purpose of government taking over the banks. "But right now the government is paying too much for bad bank assets and ending up with no real control. It's not clear it's a good deal for the taxpayers."

Economist Christopher Wood explained the "Swedish solution" in an influential *Financial Times* op-ed he published in January 2009.[4] Wood argued that because the TARP program had failed to follow the Swedish model, the U.S. government simply poured the first tranche of $350 billion in TARP bailout money into banks and brokerage firms without requiring the banks to write down their bad assets first and without the government taking majority control over the bailed-out banks.

Wood observed that bank and brokerage firm bailouts in the United States and Great Britain had resulted in "a weird hybrid of public and private sector," in which the government was gaining increasing equity stakes in the bailed-out banks, such that "what is happening is nationalization by stealth." Wood pointed to the November 2008 government bailout of Citigroup, in which the U.S. government put more money in the financial services conglomerate than the entire market capitalization of the company on the day the deal was announced; still, the taxpayer got only a 7.8 percent equity stake and the incumbent management was allowed to stay in place.

Under the Swedish model, the troubled banks were nationalized, with shareholders wiped out in the process. The managements of the banks were replaced and depositors were fully protected. Wood preferred the Swedish model because under TARP "too many banks are being rewarded for failure." Wood stressed that a "crucial principle of the Swedish model is that the banks were forced to write down their assets to market and take the hit to their equity before the recapitalization began." Under TARP, the asset portfolios of the troubled banks remained burdened with billions of dollars in toxic assets despite the massive infusion of funds. "The ultimate endgame in countries such as the U.S. and Britain is still likely to be full-scale nationalization of most of the banking system, as the logic of such action finally becomes overwhelming."

"Another point about nationalization, as in the Swedish model," Wood wrote, "is that it allows the government to separate the bad assets from banks' balance sheets and place them in one big 'bad bank.' " In writing this, Wood prefigured what was soon to become a major initiative of the Obama administration, namely, that the toxic assets in bank and brokerage-firm portfolios be sold off to a "bad bank" so that the "good banks" could now function as private-sector businesses managed by "old-fashioned commercial bankers." Wood neglected to mention that for the "good bank/bad bank" scenario to work, the government would have to buy the toxic assets from banks at nearly their full face value, not their currently dramatically reduced market value. The taxpayer, in other words, gets stuck with the workout problem of trying to recover whatever value can be recovered from the toxic assets sold into the bad bank.

Wood's good bank/bad bank solution gained attention as the unprecedented magnitude of bank toxic assets became apparent to economists worldwide.

2. HENRY KISSINGER AFFIRMS CALL FOR "NEW WORLD ORDER"—PROPOSES GLOBALISM TO SOLVE CURRENT WORLD ECONOMIC CRISIS

Former secretary of state Henry Kissinger reaffirmed his call for the incoming Obama administration to use the current financial crisis to create a "new world order" in a commentary piece for the *International Herald Tribune*.[5]

Kissinger's commentary made it clear that globalists intended to utilize the current global financial meltdown to advance globalism. In developing his call for action, Kissinger also made clear that his view of globalism involves a lessening of American power and influence in order to elevate other less advantaged countries' participation in the global economy.

"The economic world has been globalized," Kissinger proclaimed. "Its institutions have a global reach and have operated by maxims that assumed a self-regulating global market." Kissinger warned against individual countries taking action through national political institutions to cushion the shock of the current financial decline with a view to ameliorating their domestic economies.

Rather than focus on domestic politics, Kissinger said the solution involves more globalism. "Every major country has attempted to solve its immediate problems essentially on its own and to defer common action to a later, less crisis-driven point," Kissinger wrote. "So-called rescue packages have emerged on a piecemeal national basis, generally by substituting unlimited governmental credit for the domestic credit that produced the debacle in the first place—so far without more than stemming incipient panic."

Kissinger strongly objected to nation-states acting as such to protect their domestic economies. "In the end, the political and economic systems can be harmonized in only one of two ways: by creating an international political regulatory system with the same reach as that of the economic world," he suggested, "or by shrinking the economic units to a size manageable by existing political structures, which is likely to lead to a new mercantilism, perhaps of regional units." He clearly preferred creating global political institutions to manage the global economy, as he positioned his second alternative of "mercantilism" to be reminiscent of some fourteenth-century Venetian economic structure, as objectionable as the "protectionalism" globalists typically rail against.

Kissinger also chided America for being overbearing, suggesting that "righteousness" has "characterized too many American attitudes, especially since the collapse of the Soviet Union." He charged that American righteousness has resulted in "a certain inherent unilateralism—the standard of European critics—or else an insistent kind of consultation by which nations were invited to prove their fitness to enter the international system by conforming to American prescriptions."

Not since John F. Kennedy has a president like Obama come on the scene, and "with such a reservoir of expectations," Kissinger argued.

Kissinger articulated his view that our partnerships with the European Union and China are the keystones to developing his perception of the new world order. He acknowledged that "the global financial collapse has devastated Chinese exports," threatening to lower Chinese growth to below the 7.5 percent rate "that Chinese experts have always defined as the line that challenges political stability." Yet he warned that "if protectionism grows in America or if China comes to be seen as a long-term adversary, a self-fulfilling prophecy may blight the prospects of global order."

Kissinger wants his vision of the new world order to be built upon a transatlantic reality in which the United States combines economically and politically with the European Union, and a transpacific reality in which the United States combines with China. "An international order can be permanent only if its participants have a share not only in building but also securing it," he concluded. "In this manner, America and its potential partners have a unique opportunity to transform a moment of crisis into a vision of hope."

Reading Kissinger, we are reminded of Jean Monnet, a key architect of the European Union. In his *Memoirs,* Monnet recalls that in his Luxembourg office he kept on his desk a photograph of the *Kon-Tiki*, the raft Norwegian explorer Thor Heyerdahl used in his 1947 expedition from South America to the Polynesian islands across the Pacific. When asked about the photograph, Monnet explained that he admired the young men who sailed the *Kon-Tiki* because once they chose a course, they knew they could not turn back. "We too are headed for our objective, the United States of Europe," Monnet openly proclaimed, "and for us too there is no turning back." [6]

3. WHAT CRITICS MISSED ABOUT OBAMA'S TREASURY CHIEF—GEITHNER PRESIDED OVER WALL STREET COLLAPSE AS REGIONAL FED PRESIDENT

While the nomination of Treasury Secretary Timothy Geithner generated plenty of heat because of his failure to pay income taxes for five years, almost unnoticed amid the controversy was the fact that he presided over the failure of some of the largest banking institutions in the world—institutions that he was specifically charged with overseeing and regulating as head of the New York region of the Federal Reserve Bank.

On November 17, 2003, Geithner became the ninth president and chief executive officer of the Federal Reserve Bank, a position he held until being nominated to be U.S. Treasury secretary under President Obama.

The Federal Reserve's charter calls for the bank to be responsible for the strength of the financial institutions operating in each of the Fed's twelve regional districts; the Federal Reserve Bank of New York presides over Wall Street–based financial institutions.

In the current financial crisis, the Federal Reserve has played a major role working out the continuing meltdown of banks and investment firms, including some of the nation's largest. During Geithner's tenure as CEO of the New York Fed, he presided over the following major economic failures:

- March 2008: Bear Stearns collapses from losses in subprime mortgage obligations and derivatives transactions; JPMorgan Chase buys Bear Stearns in a deal arranged by the Federal Reserve for the dramatically reduced value of two dollars a share, with the Federal

Reserve guaranteeing JPMorgan against $30 billion in Bear Stearns asset losses.

- September 2008: Wall Street investment bank Lehman Brothers closes its doors in bankruptcy after the U.S. Treasury and Federal Reserve refuse to arrange a merger plan, bailout, or a guarantee program to save the Wall Street giant.

- September 2008: Bank of America buys Wall Street investment bank Merrill Lynch in a $50 billion deal that saves Merrill Lynch from having to declare bankruptcy.

- September 2008: The Federal Reserve extends to insurance giant American International Group, or AIG, an $85 billion loan that saves AIG from going bankrupt from derivatives losses in AIG's massive $441 billion exposure to credit-default swaps.

- November 2008: Citibank receives an injection of $45 billion in TARP funds, plus Treasury Department, Federal Reserve, and FDIC guarantees on $306 billion in troubled assets held by the bank.

- January 2009: Morgan Stanley takes over Citibank's Smith Barney investment unit, as Citibank unravels the "financial supermarket" conglomerate accumulated when Sandy Weill combined Travelers Insurance, investment bank Smith Barney, and Citibank to form Citigroup in the 1990s.

The Obama administration has touted Geithner as one of the only financial wizards in the country who can preside over the U.S. Treasury during this period of economic crisis, despite the obvious failure of the New York Federal Reserve Bank to sustain the solvency of New York financial institutions during the period of Geithner's tenure.

Perhaps what decided Geithner's future was that globalists liked Geithner's credentials. Before joining the U.S. Treasury, Geithner worked for Kissinger Associates for three years in Washington, D.C. Then, from 1998 to 2001, Geithner served as undersecretary of the Treasury for international affairs under Clinton administration Treasury secretaries Robert Rubin and Lawrence Summers. He is also an active member of the Council on Foreign Relations.

Then, too, Geithner has deep ties to Obama. At the Ford Foundation in the early 1980s, Geithner oversaw its microfinance programs in Indonesia, during which time he supposedly met in person with Obama's mother, Ann Dunham-Obama-Soetoro, who also allegedly spent part of her career working in Indonesian microfinance after she received her Ph.D. in anthropology.

Looking at Geithner's career objectively, one sees that his credentials at the New York Fed should have made suspect his ability to manage financial crises successfully. Yet apparently more important to the Obama administration were his globalist credentials and his loyalty to Obama, both suggesting Geithner would implement Obama administration policies aimed at the federal government getting more control over financial institutions as a result of the economic crisis.

On February 4, 2009, Geithner and Obama announced at a White House press conference that executive compensation would be capped at $500,000 for those financial institutions that accepted TARP bailouts. "We don't disparage wealth. We don't begrudge anybody for achieving success. And we believe that success should be rewarded," Obama said at the press conference. "But what gets people upset—and rightfully so—are executives being rewarded for failure, especially when those rewards are subsidized by U.S. taxpayers."[7]

With the announcement, the Obama administration was letting financial institutions know that along with TARP funds they could expect to receive government intrusion into the management of their companies, with bureaucrats making decisions that typically were reserved for senior executives and boards of directors. Within days, Bank of America's chief executive officer, Ken Lewis, shot back during a CNBC television interview that rumors his company were in danger of being nationalized were "absurd." Still, with the possibility of a good bank/bad bank solution looming, Lewis's assertion of independence appeared anything but certain. The axiom "with government money comes government control" is hard to refute, even for bankers struggling to keep their companies afloat. Before TARP was created, placing caps on executive compensation at U.S. banks was unthinkable.

Now, in a post-TARP world, it is not altogether clear where government control will reach a limit.

INTRODUCTION

The New World Order

> We have before us the opportunity to forge for ourselves and for future generations a new world order—a world where the rule of law, not the law of the jungle, governs the conduct of nations.
>
> President George H. W. Bush, January 16, 1991 [1]

This book begins where my 2007 book, *The Late Great USA: The Coming Merger with the United States and Canada,*[2] ended.

I argued that economic "free trade" agreements such as the North American Free Trade Agreement, or NAFTA, and the Central American Free Trade Agreement, or CAFTA, were advanced by globalists calculating that regional and global political structures would necessarily follow regional and global trade agreements. The architects of North American integration saw the economics of free trade as the path of least resistance to force into creation regional governments that would supersede nation-states in North America, just as the creation of the European Common Market made the creation of the European Union inevitable. The plan was to create a North American Union as the successor to the nation-states of the United States, Mexico, and Canada.

As I write this book, the Economic Panic of 2009 is being manipulated by globalists to advance the North American integration agenda, a step on the path to global political integration. Americans would never abandon the dollar for a regional currency unless the dollar had collapsed. Similarly, Americans would never stand by and watch a wide range of U.S. assets, from financial services firms to public infrastructure, being sold to the government and foreign investors unless doing so was the only way to avoid complete economic collapse in the United States.

That is the core thesis of *America for Sale*: U.S. assets—from major U.S. corporations including banks and brokerage firms, to public infrastructure including highways—are being sold to the U.S. government and to foreign investors as we stand by and watch, as if we could do nothing to stop it.

Several recent economic developments have made the selling of America inevitable:

- The United States has experienced a large negative balance of trade under free-trade agreements, in the range of $700 billion a year.[3] As a result of exporting dramatically more to the United States than it imports, China has amassed an unprecedented almost $2 trillion in foreign-exchange reserves, some 80 percent of which is held in dollar assets, enough to have surpassed Japan in September 2008 as the largest buyer of U.S. Treasury debt.

- U.S. dependence on foreign oil is growing, such that we now import more than 60 percent of the nearly 21 million barrels of oil we consume per day.[4] As a consequence, foreign oil-producing states also enjoy a mass infusion of dollars in their foreign-reserve holdings. With oil prices ranging from recent lows of approximately $40 per barrel and an all-time high of $147 per barrel in July 2008, Middle Eastern petrodollar states such as the United Arab Emirates and Saudi Arabia have amassed trillions of dollars in sovereign wealth funds.

- The dramatic fall of the U.S. dollar, which reached all-time lows of approximately $1.50 against the euro in the summer of 2008, has made holding dollar reserves a losing proposition for nations with strong dollar holdings in their foreign-exchange reserves.

As I will demonstrate in the first section of this book, the bursting of the housing bubble in 2007 threw the U.S. economy into a deep recession that quickly reached global proportions. Banks and investment firms holding mortgage-backed securities in their asset portfolios have sought unprecedented "bailouts" from the federal Treasury. As a result, we are entering a mixed economy where the U.S. government has begun holding equity stakes in major banks and brokerage firms as the industry has consolidated. Those banks and brokerage firms unlucky enough not to get federal bailout funds have simply closed. The once unthinkable is now reality as prestigious firms including Bear Stearns and Lehman Brothers, with reputations that survived the Great Depression of the 1930s, have simply ceased to exist.

Economists define a recession as requiring two successive quarters of negative growth in the nation's gross domestic product. On March 26, 2009, the Bureau of Economic Analysis of the U.S. Commerce Department made it official that the U.S. economy had been in a recession since December 2008. According to the bureau's press release, the total output of goods and services produced by labor and property in the United States had declined at an annual rate of −6.3 percent in the fourth quarter of 2008, following a decline of −0.5 percent in the third quarter of 2008.[5]

The U.S. recession that officially began in December 2008 will not be resolved until foreign investment capital returns to the United States to buy up key U.S. assets, including banks and brokerage firms, and U.S. infrastructure. A precondition of this foreign capital infusion will be for the U.S. government to stabilize the tailspin of the Dow Jones Industrial Average and other major stock indices, and very possibly for the federal government to provide foreign investors with what will amount to guarantees. Foreign investors will want assurance from the U.S. government that their capital investments in the American economy will not be eroded by continued deterioration of stock prices. Unfortunately, foreign governments purchasing the trillions of dollars in U.S. Treasury debt needed to finance our massive and growing federal budget deficits will also want guarantees reaching beyond the "full faith and credit" of the U.S. government.

The recession is a capital crisis, not simply a credit crisis in which financial institutions are unwilling to lend. U.S. banks and brokerage firms may end up losing as much as $10 trillion in bad assets, once securitized portfolios of home loans, consumer loans, commercial loans, and municipal loans are fully marked to their diminished market value. This amount of unprecedented capital drain can be replaced only by foreign investment. Federal budget deficits aimed at bailing out failed banks and other corporations create only debt, not capital, with the result that the U.S. Treasury is forced to sell trillions of dollars of U.S. government-backed debt instruments to foreign nations, including China, Japan, and

Middle Eastern oil-producing states. The economic crisis of the United States will force foreign dollars to return to our shores, both to buy our debt as well as to invest in our corporations.

The result is that U.S. sovereignty will be compromised, and globalists will force the United States toward a regional currency and a regional North American set of political institutions, on the way to a one-world currency and a one-world government.

The United States of America is unlikely to emerge from the Economic Panic of 2009 as the same sovereign or independent and self-governing nation that it was as recently as the administrations of President Truman or Eisenhower at the end of and after World War II.

The last barrier globalists face is the possibility that American patriots may simply say no in our desire to preserve, protect, and defend U.S. sovereignty, even at this late hour.

THE LATE GREAT U.S.A.

The globalist model being used to attack U.S. sovereignty was first tested and proven in the creation of the European Union. Over a fifty-year period, Europe transformed from a group of sovereign nations into a full-fledged regional European Union government, complete with a European Union central bank and a regional currency, the euro, which replaced the national currencies of the participating nations. The transformation was accomplished by advancing economic agreements that were advocated solely as job-creating inventions, not nation-destroying agendas.

Architects of the European Union such as Jean Monnet used deception to advance their regional goals, proclaiming that their only interest was to obtain economic efficiency and increased productivity through a cooperating group of regional nations, while the real goal was to erode over time the very sovereignty of the participating states. By constantly denying that their goal was to create a regional government on the way to a one-world government, Monnet and his allies encouraged the participating nations to allow their citizens to migrate freely across opening borders. Economic integration was accomplished step-by-step, as the European Coal and Steel Agreement gave way to a European Economic Community, followed by a European Atomic Energy Commission and ultimately a European Free Trade Association.

In the last two sentences of his memoirs, Monnet admitted that his goal from the beginning was a globalist one, such that he saw even the creation of the European Community as only a transitional step on the way to world government. "The sovereign nations of the past can no longer solve the problems of the present; they cannot ensure their own progress or control their own future," Monnet wrote. "And the [European] Community itself is only a stage on the way to the organized world of tomorrow." [6] Walter Hallstein, the first executive director of the European Economic Community, agreed with Monnet. "Integration in the economic field is not merely a step on the way to political integration: it is already itself political," [7] Hallstein openly admitted in his book *Europe in the Making*, in 1972.

By the time the Treaty of Maastricht was signed in 1992, Europeans were ready to accept as their own the European Union flag first introduced in 1985, consisting of twelve yellow stars in a circle, representing the European nation-states, against a blue background, representing Europe. The European Union passport supplemented and then supplanted the national passports of the various participating countries. When the euro was introduced on January 1, 2002, the participating nations were willing to abandon their national currencies. Citizens who went to ATMs could get only euros, instead of their traditional currencies. Gone were the French franc, the Italian lira, and the German mark as the European Union countries submitted to the supranational authority of the European Central Bank. Countless European Union bureaucrats in Luxembourg and Brussels took upon themselves the job of writing the new European Union legislation that henceforth the various national legislatures of the participating EU nations would be required to ratify.

THE FREE-TRADE AREA OF THE AMERICAS

The administration of President George W. Bush tried to extend the NAFTA free-trade area, composed of the United States, Mexico, and Canada, and CAFTA, extending through Latin America, to the entire Western Hemisphere, from Canada's arctic regions to the subarctic limits of the tip of Argentina, by pushing the FTAA, or Free Trade Area of the Americas. Ironically, the Bush administration most likely would have succeeded with the FTAA had it not been for the outspoken opposition of Venezuela's socialist president Hugo Chavez at the IV Summit of the Americas held in Mar del Plata, Argentina, in November 2005. This was acknowledged by Mexico's former president Vicente Fox in

2007. Promoting his new book on CNN's *Larry King Live*, Fox told King that he and President Bush had a plan to extend NAFTA long-term to include all of the Americas, through a series of incremental steps that would ultimately involve creating a new currency.

"What we proposed together, President Bush and myself, it's ALCA, which is a trade union for all the Americas," Fox told King.[8] ALCA is the acronym in Spanish for the Área Libre Comercio de las Américas, the Spanish name of the FTAA. Fox further admitted that "long-term" the plan he and Bush shared was to evolve the trade agreements into a regional currency "like the euro dollar" for the Americas. "Everything was running fluently until Hugo Chavez came," Fox admitted. "He [Chavez] decided to combat the idea and destroy the idea." Although the interview received almost no attention from the mainstream media at the time, Fox's meaning could not have been clearer.

But then, this was nothing new. Fox had been proclaiming the wisdom of North American integration since he first took office in Mexico. On July 4, 2000, two days after winning election as president of Mexico, Vicente Fox called for a twenty-year timetable for the creation of a North American common market. Termed his "20/20 vision," which Fox hoped would be realized by 2020, his plan for North American integration was ambitious. The North American Forum on Integration's website defined Fox's 20/20 vision as including the following elements: a customs union, a common external tariff, greater coordination of policies, common monetary policies, free flow of labor, and fiscal transfers for the development of poor Mexican regions.[9] Utilizing the model of the European Fund, Fox suggested the United States might need to invest $10–30 billion in NAFTA to support undeveloped regions through an international financial institution such as the Inter-American Development Bank.

Globalists seeking to create a "one-world economy" and, as a consequence, a "one-world government" intend to proceed incrementally, one step at a time, relying on deception and misdirection to keep the U.S. public from fully appreciating their intentions. In *The Late Great USA*, I predicted both a dollar collapse and a severe economic recession that would result from the bursting of the subprime real estate bubble that reached its peak in 2006. I also predicted that the U.S. economy would enter a severe recession that would spread worldwide. My key argument was that globalists would use the economic crises not as an opportunity to shore up the fundamentals of the U.S. economy, but instead to push their global agenda as the only viable solution to the collapse of the U.S. economy and the dollar.

America for Sale presents a constructive alternative to globalist ambitions: the United States can be a major player in a world economy without having to sacrifice our sovereignty, the strength of our national domestic economy, or the dollar. A strong U.S. domestic economy can and should be promoted as a precondition of our entering a world economy. The globalists who plan to level the United States economically as an inevitable consequence of the U.S. entering the world economy do so perhaps out of resentment of America's disproportionate use of world resources or the relatively high standard of living Americans typically enjoy.

To appreciate the globalist assault on the U.S. economy, consider the following three points:

- If the principle of globalism is for multinational companies to assert to U.S. workers that "we can find a slave or near-slave somewhere in the world that will do your job cheaper than you will," then U.S. workers inevitably lose.

- With 300 million people in the United States and more than 6 billion people globally, the push by multinational corporations to bottom-fish for labor works inevitably to the disadvantage of the U.S. worker.

- A homeowner cannot send his lawn to China to be mowed. We can, however, allow an underclass to cross our border with Mexico to compete for low-skilled jobs by their willingness to work for lower pay and fewer benefits than most U.S. workers would find acceptable.

But there is an alternative principle to globalism: the United States can participate in a global economy as a sovereign nation, as long as we are resolved to maintain a strong U.S. economy, in which U.S. workers earn economically viable wages and benefits, with a strong middle class that can serve as the consumer engine needed to fuel a global economy.

THE LITTLE GREEN FROG PRINCIPLE

The Little Green Frog analogy is the first of two principles that are important to understanding how the U.S. economy and government are being morphed by economic crisis from a sovereign configuration to a worldwide economy and a global governance system.

The analogy begins with imagining that a person drops a little green frog into a pot of cold water on the top of a stove and turns on the heat. The frog initially swims comfortably in the water, not aware of the ultimate danger the gradually increasing temperature of the water represents. Ultimately, as the water comes to a boil, the frog cooks to death, having been lulled to sleep or otherwise rendered unconscious by what has become fatally dangerous warm water.

Yet, if you took the same little green frog and simply dropped it into a pot of boiling water on the stove, the frog would immediately perceive the danger and try to jump out of the water to safety. The frog might get uncomfortably warm, but it would still live.

The point of the analogy is to emphasize that we human beings often find incremental change hard to perceive, even if the end result of the gradually occurring change is a fundamentally different environment dangerous to our health or well-being.

THE TRANSFORMATION FROM FREE TRADE
TO REGIONAL GOVERNMENT

Globalists typically work by inducing gradual change, constantly denying that their goal is to create regional or global government. Thus globalists sell "free trade" to a gullible public on the premise that removing trade barriers between countries will encourage more exports and produce more jobs. Regardless of whether we gain or lose domestic jobs, globalists know that "free trade" necessitates regional and ultimately global governance. This is why Walter Hallstein insisted economic integration is inherently political integration. Disagreements are inevitable under free-trade agreements and the disagreements can be resolved only through regional or otherwise transnational rules and regulations.

For example, in *The Late Great USA*, I argued that the Trans-Texas Corridor, a car, truck, train, and pipeline toll road four football fields wide parallel to Interstate 35, had been planned by the Texas Department of Transportation, or TxDOT, with the financing to come from a foreign corporation, Cintra Concessiones de Infrastructures de Transporte, a capital group in Spain. I also argued that the toll road was designed to connect ultimately with the deep-water ports of Lázaro Cárdenas and Manzanillo in Mexico on the Pacific Ocean, south of Texas. The goal of this plan, I argued, is to transport into North America containers of cheaply made goods produced in China, utilizing Mexican trucks and Mexican trains. The U.S. Department of Transportation in the second term of the Bush administration pushed to implement a Mexican truck-demonstration project in which up to a hundred Mexican trucking companies were given unlimited access to U.S. roads to haul international cargo as part of a pilot program.[10] The goods in the Chinese containers are taken to U.S. companies that have purchased the goods, typically for retail sale in mass-marketing retail outlets in the United States.

If a Mexican truck gets into an accident while driving along the completed TTC-35 toll road, which country's law will apply to resolve the dispute? Spanish law might apply, since Cintra will be operating the toll road under a public-private partnership contract with TxDOT. Mexican law might apply because the truck involved in the accident is Mexican and the driver is presumably the holder of a valid Mexican commercial driver's license. The container and goods are the property of a Chinese company, until they are delivered to the U.S. purchaser.

Even though the accident happens in Texas, we cannot be assured that Texas law will be the only applicable law in resolving the dispute. Certainly, lawyers for one of the various parties involved in the dispute could well seek reference to the rules and regulations specified under NAFTA or the World Trade Organization (WTO). Lawyers might also inquire into the new memoranda of understanding or other agreements signed by the bureaucrats of the United States, Mexico, and Canada in the Security and Prosperity Partnership of North America, or SPP, organized as "working groups" under the authority of the trilateral SPP declaration issued at Waco, Texas, by the three North American leaders on March 23, 2005.

The point is that free-trade agreements necessarily result in international governance, simply because international rules and regulations are required to resolve free-trade disputes that are international in nature.

Most Americans are completely unaware that under NAFTA we have constituted with Mexico and Canada what are known as Chapter 11 Tribunals, which function as administrative courts with authority to supersede the sovereign laws of the United States, Mexico, and Canada if a tribunal determines the legitimate economic rights of a NAFTA investor or corporation have been violated under the terms of NAFTA itself. Put simply, NAFTA Chapter 11 Tribunals trump the U.S. Supreme Court in NAFTA trade disputes. U.S. law could have applied as the final arbiter of the dispute only if U.S. negotiators had taken the care to specify, when negotiating NAFTA, that trade disputes occurring in the United States under the agreement would be resolved solely by reference to U.S. state and federal laws and regulations. NAFTA was not so negotiated.

In April 1974, U.S. ambassador Richard N. Gardner wrote a pivotal essay, published in the Council on Foreign Relations magazine *Foreign Affairs*, titled "The Hard Road to World Order." There Gardner gave a concise statement of the incremental method applied to creating a one-world government, writing, "In short, the case-by-case approach can produce some remarkable concessions of 'sovereignty' that could not be achieved on an across-the-board basis." [11] Gardner understood the Little Green Frog Principle that the peoples of no sovereign nation would easily or readily abandon their generations-revered nation-states unless a series of almost imperceptible changes were coordinated to lead the people almost unconsciously in that direction. Yet moving from the United States of America to a North American Union (NAU) could be made to seem inevitable, especially if an economic crisis or a weakened dollar made the regional expansion of NAFTA free trade into the regional governmental structures appear a natural progression to enhance the economic competitiveness of North America. Then, should a North American Union be formed, progression to unite the NAU with the other regional compacts—including the EU and the emerging African and Asian unions—could be more easily accomplished.

WHY SIZE MATTERS

The second principle important to this book derives from mathematics. The principle is that a difference in size is a difference in phenomenon.

We can understand the concept if we contemplate a bumblebee. A bumblebee is able to fly, given the size of the bumblebee as well as the size and dynamic construction of its wings. Yet if a bumblebee is made to be ten times or a hundred times its normal size, the bumblebee can no longer fly, even if its wings are increased proportionately, such that the dynamic construction of its wings is maintained. A bigger bumblebee is not the same critter made larger. A larger bumblebee is a different order of critter that requires different mathematical principles if the critter is to fly in its larger form. In other words, larger is not the same thing just made bigger. A difference in size typically involves a difference in phenomenon, such that the laws and principles that operate at the smaller size may no longer function or apply at the larger size.

Another example of the principle is the *Spruce Goose* that aviator Howard Hughes constructed in the 1940s. The airplane, registered as the Hughes H-4 Hercules, was a prototype heavy transport airplane made largely of wood. The *Spruce Goose* flying boat flew just once, on November 2, 1947. What Hughes had failed to realize was that a larger transport plane was not just a bigger version of a propeller-driven transport aircraft that flew on a smaller scale. The H-4 Hercules, conceptualized as a redesign of the C-47, was bound to have trouble flying. Today we have passenger and transport aircraft built successfully on a scale that dwarfs the *Spruce Goose*. The point is that today's larger aircraft are typically jet aircraft designed with an entirely different aerodynamic design than that of the propeller-driven *Spruce Goose*.

We cannot imagine that a regional or global economy will function exactly as a national economy or a national government, just on a larger scale. This concept violates the principle that a regional or global economy must be expected to function on economic principles derived for the regional or global environment itself, not for the national environment. A difference in size involves a difference in phenomenon. The same applies when we get to governments. A regional or one-world government is not simply a national government made larger.

The nations of the European Union are beginning to realize this. National governments, for instance, have given up much national control of their domestic economies because they have relinquished their national central banks and given up their national currencies as a necessary condition of creating the European Central Bank and the euro. Losing sovereignty over monetary policy leaves national governments in the EU with only fiscal policy tools involving government spending and taxation policies with which to control the strength of their domestic economies. This new condition represents a fundamental change for European leaders whom domestic voters still hold responsible for promoting economic growth.

In an essay titled "On Being the Right Size,"[12] first published in the 1930s, scientist and geneticist J. B. S. Haldane speculated that "extreme socialists desire to run every nation as a single business concern." He then observed that Henry Ford would have difficulty running Andorra or Luxembourg on a socialistic basis, even though Ford probably had more people on his payroll than the population of other countries. Haldane doubted a syndicate of Fords could make Belgium Ltd. or Denmark Ltd. a paying concern. He observed, "I find it no easier to picture a completely socialized British Empire or United States than an elephant turning somersaults or a hippopotamus jumping a hedge." Haldane's point was that while Ford might run a business in which his corporation provided workers a living wage plus reasonable benefits, we should not assume a nation can do the same without running huge deficits. Unfortunately, Haldane did not live to see Great Britain or the United States under the administrations of George W. Bush or Barack Obama, where even trillion-dollar deficits to maintain social-welfare programs are being considered normal.

That Haldane was also a self-professed Marxist should give even more weight to his skepticism about whether principles of corporate responsibility could ever be transferred in a one-to-one relationship onto a socialist state.

THE NEW WORLD ORDER

Globalists from both the political Left and the political Right aim to create a "new world order" in which regional governments are created to supplant the sovereignty of individual nation-states. Consider the following:

- From the Left, the importation into the United States of an underclass workforce is seen as generating future generations of Democratic Party voters, dependent upon electing Democrats to political office in order to continue generous social-welfare benefits that permit the underclass work force to compete with U.S. labor by working for lower wages and fewer benefits.

- From the Right, what has been known as "the Rockefeller wing" of the Republican Party views underclass labor worldwide, whether imported from south of the border with Mexico or found in foreign countries including China, as important to increasing multinational corporate profits so that U.S. companies remain competitive in a global economy.

The ultimate goal from both the Left and the Right is to create a global reality for the future of the United States, in which a one-world government with a one-world currency will be created to supersede the sovereignty of the United States of America. From the political Left, a worldwide proletariat has been seen as a powerful force for progressive social change since communists first proclaimed slogans such as "Workers of the World Unite!" From the political Right, David Rockefeller and the Council on Foreign Relations would argue that multinational corporations transcend national borders by their very operations, with U.S. regulations and currency thus adding risks and operating as "speed bumps" on the road to maximum corporate profits.

An underlying assumption of the "new world order" thinking is that a one-world government born of one-world economics would work much like a nation-state, only on a larger scale. The regional structures, and ultimately the one-world economic and governmental structures, would work according to the principle of subordination. It is this principle through which the U.S. government, as a superior authority comprising all state governments, supersedes state-government authority. Under a regional government structure, nation-states are subordinated to regional governments that supersede the sovereignty of the nation-states composing the region. A one-world government would in turn supersede the regional compacts.

Still, regional and one-world structures must obey the principle that a difference in scale is a difference in phenomenon. Put more directly, nation-states continue to be relevant even after the creation of entities such as the EU, or the NAU should a North American Union ever truly come to be.

In other words, U.S. workers will not easily be unemployed, especially not in large numbers, simply because workers in China are dramatically cheaper under the auspices of the World Trade Organization. Nor will the nations of Europe sit by idly as the European Central Bank raises interest rates in favor of the EU as a whole to the detriment of struggling countries such as Italy, Ireland, or Spain. The EU countries may be fine without central banking authorities of their own, but only so long as the economics remain favorable and their national economies are experiencing growth. In deep economic recessions, all political questions quickly become personal and local. In economic crises, even with regional or one-world government structures in place, national policies designed to employ national workers and stimulate national economies once again become relevant, as we have seen in the Economic Panic of 2009.

AN ARGUMENT FOR TAKING AMERICA BACK

America is for sale, from a political Left that sees socialism as the answer, as well as from a political Right that sees unbridled free trade as the answer. If globalism and unbridled free trade are the problem, maintaining the sovereignty of the United States is the solution.

U.S. sovereignty is under attack by international organizations embraced variously by the Left and the Right, including the International Monetary Fund and the World Bank, the North American Free Trade Agreement, and the World Trade Organization, as well as by the United Nations itself.

As I wrote in my latest book, *The Obama Nation,* Barack Obama's radical leftist politics are leading the United States in a costly and self-destructive direction, both at home and abroad.[13] In the final analysis, President Barack Obama is turning out to be a globalist every bit as much as President George W. Bush was. Both presidents have put America up for sale by pursuing an increasingly reckless policy of running huge and growing budget deficits that cannot long be papered over by selling trillions of dollars of U.S. government debt to foreigners.

To prevent America from being put up for sale before it is too late, we must recapture the social and economic argument from the political Left. We must challenge Barack Obama's claim that by winning the presidential election of 2008 the Democratic Party has achieved a mandate for an unprecedented growth of government and a massive redistribution of wealth and income in the United States that will make the Obama administration look like a New Deal on steroids.

Equally, we must recapture the argument from the political Right. We must challenge the "free trade" prosperity myth that the United States can engage in unbridled world trade that allows U.S. domestic businesses to import an underclass of cheap immigrant labor and multinational corporations to outsource to cheap foreign labor overseas. Instead, we must work to preserve U.S. jobs and protect the dollar.

We must fight back as a nation if we are to avoid being pushed into a European Union–type North American common market and North American monetary union, on the way to a one-world government dominated by one-world globalism. Today the United States is at risk of losing within the next generation the greatest middle class ever created in the history of the world. We will have to take America back to the fundamental freedoms and principles of limited government that our Founding Fathers fought and died to establish. Otherwise, we will not see a sovereign and independent United States of America emerge through the twenty-first century as an economically and militarily strong nation-state. The rest of the world can develop economically, not by reducing the economic power and military strength of the United States, but rather by applying the example of American free enterprise to their own social, economic, and political development.

The Republican Party, if it is to return from the electoral defeats that have caused it to lose both houses of Congress and the White House, must return to its political base. Millions of Americans who want to see the politics of Ronald Reagan embraced once again long to return America to the decades of economic and military success the nation enjoyed since the end of World War II.

America for Sale is a clarion call to take America back before it is too late. *America for Sale* is a clarion call to prevent the globalists from outsourcing U.S. jobs that will never return to our shores, and from erasing our borders and destroying the dollar.

American patriots do not want to live in Barack Obama's internationalist social-welfare state any more than we should want to live in George H. W. Bush's internationalist "new world order."

Part I

THE GLOBAL ECONOMIC PANIC OF 2009

In the economic history of the United States, economic panics unfortunately are not rare. Even more disturbing, they often precede prolonged depressions, involving many years of painful economic readjustment in which incomes decline or disappear as jobs and homes are lost.

The Economic Panic of 2009 had global reach after the bursting of the subprime-mortgage bubble in the United States sent shock waves around the world.

In July 2007, when the Dow Jones Industrial Average topped 14,000, many economists and investors believed the stock market was in robust shape, capable of hitting even new highs. In March 2008, the Dow had dropped almost two thousand points, to 12,300, when *Barron's* magazine published an article predicting the Dow would "rocket" to new heights around 18,000 to 20,000 by March 2009.[1] *Barron's* published no retraction in March 2009, when the DJIA instead of "rocketing" ended up torpedoing, to end up trading in the range of 7,000, having lost approximately half its value and trillions of dollars of market capitalization.

The *Economic Report of the President for 2007*, prepared by the Council of Economic Advisers, was strongly optimistic, proclaiming, "Economic growth in the United States has been above the historic average and faster than any other major industrialized economy in the world." At that time, no end to economic growth was foreseen: "January was the 41st month of uninterrupted job growth produced by this economy, in an expansion that has thus far added more than 7.4 million new jobs. Unemployment is low, inflation is moderate, and real wages are rising." President George W. Bush signed off on the declaration that "our economy is on the move and we can keep it that way by continuing to pursue sound economic policy based on free-market principles."

In February 2007, when that economic report was signed by President Bush and sent to Congress,[2] few could have anticipated that less than two years later, by the end of 2008, U.S. households would suffer an 18 percent decline in wealth, with a loss of $11.2 trillion in household net worth[3]—a loss almost equal to the nation's 2008 gross domestic product of approximately $14 trillion.[4]

In 2008, the mortgage bubble burst and the U.S. economy went into a tailspin. By the beginning of 2009, U.S. federal budget deficits began reaching into trillions of dollars as the Federal Reserve prepared to enter the bond market as a purchaser of last resort for U.S. Treasury debt.

The global Economic Panic of 2009 was particularly unexpected after international economists had promised for decades that the formation of a global economy would ensure sufficient economic activity in other countries, such that even a serious economic downturn in the United States would not cause the world economy to collapse.

How and why did the U.S. economy crash, causing in turn the global economy to crash, resulting in the global Economic Panic of 2009? The culprits begin with a Federal Reserve policy determined to keep interest rates at a historically low 1 percent rate in 2003 and 2004. Then U.S. government policies caused a continuing adverse impact on the U.S. dollar because of U.S. dependence on foreign oil and a growing U.S. negative balance of trade, especially with China. As a result, the dollar weakened and U.S. economic dependence on foreign nations increased.

The economic future of the United States in a global economy was jeopardized by government policies that allowed U.S.-based multinational corporations to outsource high-paying manufacturing jobs overseas. At the same time, government policies allowed an underclass from south of the border to immigrate into the United States to compete for the lower-paying, unskilled jobs that could not be outsourced.

Meanwhile, urban poverty persisted in the U.S. global village, largely because unemployment for millions of Americans became persistent, such that millions of workers abandoned altogether the search for employment. If money alone were sufficient to eliminate poverty, the trillions of dollars spent by the federal government on social-welfare programs would have alleviated the problem in the decades since the New Deal. Instead, we have created welfare dependency at a time when the educational and training demands for employment in the global economy have raised the bar for everyone.

If anything, the global Economic Panic of 2009 should refute globalism once and for all.

Globalism, instead of creating an era of flourishing U.S. employment, has left millions of U.S. workers behind, such that no amount of education and training will enable them to compete with a world population ready and willing to work for a fraction of what U.S. workers demand in terms of wages and benefits.

The global Economic Panic of 2009 is a direct result of decades during which Republican and Democratic administrations alike have pursued international free trade as a panacea to U.S. and world economic concerns. Yet instead of producing a recession-proof world, the global economy merely created the conditions by which a recession in the United States translated into a global recession, almost as instantaneously as information travels the globe.

In the final analysis, America is for sale precisely because globalism failed, precisely because a "free trade" international economy failed to fulfill the promises the globalists made.

ONE

The U.S.A. Bankrupt

Debt cannot go on compounding faster than output forever.

—James Dale Davidson and
Lord William Rees-Mogg,
The Great Reckoning, 1991[1]

In February 2009, as the Obama administration pushed a $787 billion deficit-spending economic stimulus plan through Congress, the American public was largely unaware that the true deficit of the federal government was already measured in trillions of dollars.

Moreover, total U.S. obligations, including Social Security and Medicare benefits to be paid in the future, have effectively placed the U.S. government in bankruptcy, even before we take into consideration the future and continuing social-welfare obligations embedded within the Obama administration's massive new spending plan. According to the U.S. Treasury, the total obligations of the United States in 2007 exceeded a negative $59 trillion, a sum that was more than the 2007 gross domestic product, or GDP, of the world, which the World Bank estimated to be $54 trillion.[2] By 2008, the total obligations of the U.S. had grown to over $65 trillion, with no end in sight.

There is no way the federal government could ever meet the future obligations of the massive social-welfare state we have created since Franklin Roosevelt signed the Social Security Act, even if we confiscated all salaries and corporate earnings of individuals and corporations in the United States as an emergency form of taxation. The United States today is bankrupt, whether or not the government wants to admit it, and whether or not the public is aware of how extreme the situation has become.

Understanding that the United States is bankrupt is fundamental to understanding the true dimensions of the Economic Panic of 2009. Had the United States been running federal budget surpluses on a cash basis, the nation would still be bankrupt. Why? The answer is that future liabilities in federal social-welfare-entitlement programs have grown beyond the ability of the federal government to raise by taxes enough money to pay what is already due to the baby boomers as they retire.

This reality severely limits the ability of the federal government to manage a financial crisis like what we have faced since the mortgage bubble burst. It is necessary to appreciate fully just how bankrupt the federal government truly is: Mortgage losses as well as losses in a variety of consumer credits plus losses in commercial loans and commercial real estate already total trillions of dollars. We are certain to have more losses in complicated investments including hedge funds and derivatives, regardless of how smart the federal government officials at the U.S. Treasury and the Federal Reserve appear to be or how clever Wall Street experts seem. Ultimately, financial bubbles have no alternative but to burst.

DOESN'T $65 TRILLION TERRIFY *ANYONE?*

The real 2008 federal budget deficit was $5.1 trillion, not the $455 billion previously reported by the Congressional Budget Office,[3] according to the *2008 Financial Report of the United States Government* released by the U.S. Department of the Treasury.[4]

The difference between the $455 billion "official" budget deficit number and the $5.1 trillion deficit based on data reported in the 2008 report is due to the fact that the official budget deficit is calculated on a cash basis, where all tax receipts, including Social Security tax receipts, are used to pay government liabilities as they occur. The calculations in the 2008 report are calculated on a GAAP basis ("Generally Accepted Accounting Principles"), which includes year-for-year changes in the net present value of unfunded liabilities in social-insurance programs such as Social Security and Medicare. Under cash accounting, money is spent as it comes in, while the government makes no provision for future Social Security and Medicare benefits in the year in which those benefits accrue.

"As bad as 2008 was, the $455 billion budget deficit on a cash basis and the $5.1 trillion federal budget deficit on a GAAP accounting basis does not reflect any significant money from the financial bailout or Troubled Asset Relief Program, or TARP, which was approved after the close of the fiscal year," John Williams, an economist who publishes the website Shadow Government Statistics,[5] told World Net Daily.[6]

"For 2009, the Congressional Budget Office estimated the fiscal year 2009 budget deficit as being $1.2 trillion on a cash basis and that was before taking into consideration the full costs of the war in Iraq and Afghanistan, before the cost of the Obama $787 billion economic stimulus plan, or the cost of the second $350 billion tranche in TARP funds, as well as all current bailouts being contemplated by the U.S. Treasury and Federal Reserve," he stressed.

"The federal government's deficit is hemorrhaging at a pace which threatens the viability of the financial system," Williams added. "The popularly reported 2009 budget deficit will clearly exceed $2 trillion on a cash basis and that full amount has to be funded by Treasury borrowing. It's not likely this will happen without the Federal Reserve acting as lender of last resort for the Treasury by buying Treasury debt and monetizing the debt."

"Monetizing the debt" is a term used to signify that the U.S. Treasury will ultimately be required simply to issue huge amounts of new debt to meet current Treasury debt obligations. We have monetized the debt when we are forced to issue debt both to cover current budget deficits and to pay interest on outstanding federal debt. So far, the Treasury has been largely dependent upon foreign buyers, principally China and Japan and other major holders of U.S.-dollar foreign-exchange reserves, including Middle Eastern oil-producing nations purchasing U.S. debt through their financial agents in London. "The appetite of foreign buyers to purchase continued trillions of U.S. debt has become more questionable as the world has witnessed the rapid deterioration of the U.S. fiscal condition in the current financial crisis," Williams noted.

The sad reality is that the U.S. Treasury has not reserved any funds to cover the future Social Security and Medicare obligations we are incurring today. "Truthfully," Williams pointed out, "there is no Social Security 'lock-box.' There are no funds held in reserve today for Social Security and Medicare obligations that are earned each year. It's only a matter of time until the public realizes that the government is truly bankrupt. No taxes are being held in reserve to pay in the future the Social Security and Medicare benefits taxpayers are earning today."

If President Obama manages to add universal health care to the list of entitlement payments the federal government is obligated to pay, the negative net worth of the United States government can only get worse.

Calculations from the *2008 Financial Report of the United States Government,* as displayed in the chart below, show that the GAAP negative net worth of the federal government has increased to $59.3 trillion while the total federal obligations under GAAP accounting now total $65.5 trillion.

U.S. FEDERAL BUDGET DEFICITS, GAAP ACCOUNTING

Fiscal Year	Formal Cash-Based Deficit (billions)	GAAP Deficit w/o Social Security or Medicare (billions)	GAAP Deficit with Social Security and Medicare (trillions)	GAAP Federal Negative Net Worth (trillions)	Gross Federal Debt (trillions)	Total Federal Obligations— GAAP (trillions)
2008	$454.8	$1,009.1	$5.1	$59.3	$10.0	$65.5
2007	162.8	275.5	1.2	54.3	9.0	59.8
2006	248.2	449.5	4.6	53.1	8.5	58.2
2005	318.5	760.0	3.5	48.5	7.9	53.3
2004	412.3	615.6	11.0	45.0	7.4	49.5
2003	374.8	667.6	3.0	34.0	6.8	39.1
2002	157.8	364.5	1.5	31.0	6.2	35.4

Source: John Williams, Shadow Government Statistics, ShadowStats.com, relying upon U.S. Treasury, *Financial Report of the United States, 2002–2008.*

"Put simply, there is no way the government can possibly pay for the level of social welfare benefits the federal government has promised unless the government simply prints cash and debases the currency, which the government will increasingly be doing this year," Williams said, explaining in more detail why he feels the government is now in the process of monetizing the federal debt.

"Social Security and Medicare must be shown as liabilities on the federal balance sheet in the year they accrue according to GAAP accounting," he argued. "To do otherwise is irresponsible, nothing more than an attempt to hide the painful truth from the American public. The public has a right to know just how bad off the federal government budget deficit situation really is, especially since the situation is rapidly spinning out of control."

Williams makes a compelling case that in a post-Enron world, if the federal government were a private corporation, "the president and senior Treasury officers would be at risk of being thrown into a federal penitentiary."

ARE MASSIVE FEDERAL DEFICITS SUSTAINABLE?

On March 12, 2008, David M. Walker resigned as comptroller general of the United States and head of the Government Accountability Office, or GAO, out of concern that as head of the GAO, he could no longer certify the financial soundness of the U.S. government under the GAAP accounting analysis of the federal budget conducted annually by the U.S. Treasury. As the CBS television show *60 Minutes* noted, even before he resigned Walker had begun "traveling the country like an Old Testament prophet, urging people to wake up before it is too late." Walker was highly regarded as a respected public official while head of the GAO, charged with managing its more than three thousand employees. The GAO serves as auditor of the government's books, as an investigative office of the U.S. Congress.

"I would argue that the most serious threat to the United States is not someone hiding in a cave in Afghanistan or Pakistan, but our own fiscal irresponsibility," Walker, once the nation's top accountant, told *60 Minutes,* in an obvious reference to Al Qaeda terrorist leader Osama bin Laden.[7]

"We are spending more money than we make," Walker told a group on his "Wake-Up Tour" throughout America. "We are charging it to a credit card," he said, warning that by 2040, U.S. tax dollars would not be able to keep up even with just the interest payments on our national debt. No federal funds would be left for any other programs, including national defense or homeland security. "We suffer from a fiscal cancer that is growing within us and if we do not treat it, the cancer will have massive consequences for our country," he said.

Walker's concern is that the massive entitlement programs the federal government has created over the past few decades will go bankrupt as the baby boom generation retires. "The first baby boomer will reach 62 and be eligible for benefits under Social Security on January 1, 2008," Walker pointed out. "They will be eligible for Medicare just three years later. When those boomers start retiring en masse, we will face a tsunami of spending that could swamp our ship of state if we don't get serious." Walker warned that the real coming problem was the health-care problem, which he viewed as five times more serious than the problem with Social Security, largely because modern medicine allows people to live longer and the cost of medical treatments continues to escalate.[8]

In testimony before Congress in 2007, Federal Reserve Chairman Ben Bernanke specifically endorsed the warnings that Walker was then issuing from the GAO. "Unfortunately, economic growth alone is unlikely to solve the nation's impending fiscal problems," Bernanke testified, rejecting the proposition that future rates of U.S. economic growth would be sufficient to provide adequate tax revenue to handle federal debt comfortably. Bernanke envisioned a scenario where U.S. debt could approach 100 percent of gross domestic product, the ratio the United States experienced in World War II. Alan Greenspan dismissed the World War II comparison, noting that people "at that time understood the situation to be temporary and expected deficits and the debt-to-GDP ratio to fall rapidly after the war, as in fact they did." Today is different, Greenspan argued. In 2007, before the economic downturn and the new trillions in then-unanticipated deficit spending caused by the TARP and Obama economic stimulus programs, Bernanke projected the debt-to-GDP ratio could reach 100 percent by 2030. "Ultimately, this expansion of debt would spark a fiscal crisis, which could be addressed only by very sharp spending cuts or tax increases, or both," Bernanke warned Congress.[9]

Bernanke saw the crisis as one that would continue beyond the retirement of the baby boomers. "Rather, if the U.S. fertility rate remains close to current levels and life expectancies continue to rise, as demographers generally expect, the U.S. population will continue to grow older, even after the baby-boom generation has passed from the scene," he told Congress in 2007. "If current law is maintained, that aging of the U.S. population will lead to sustained increases in federal entitlement spending on programs that benefit older Americans, such as Social Security and Medicare."[10] Bernanke agreed with Walker. Both saw the United States headed toward a crisis of irreversible budget deficits and future obligations under federal entitlement programs that would create a level of federal debt that anticipated U.S. economic growth would not be able to sustain.

TREASURY TO BORROW TRILLIONS, NOT BILLIONS

Almost certainly, 2009 will be the largest cash-basis federal deficit ever reported in the history of the United States. According to the minutes of the U.S. Treasury's Borrowing Advisory Committee, or TBAC, a key advisory committee to the Treasury Department, Acting Assistant Secretary of the Treasury for Financial Markets Karthik Ramanathan affirmed estimates for Treasury borrowing needs range as high as $2.5 trillion for fiscal year 2009.[11] The TBAC's formal report warned that federal borrowing in fiscal year 2010 could reach levels as high as $4 trillion.

While conservatives faulted the Bush administration for running large deficits and increasing the national debt, the magnitude of the national deficit problems under the Bush administration was small compared to the Obama administration. The Bush administration added more than $4 trillion to the national debt, increasing the national debt more than 70 percent from the time George W. Bush took office on January 20, 2001.[12] With federal budget deficits projected to run into the trillions of dollars, the Obama administration appears willing to increase the current $10 trillion U.S. national debt by 65 percent in just two years. If the Obama administration increases the national debt by 65 percent every two years, our national debt will be $16.5 trillion in 2010 and $27.225 trillion by 2012, the year of the next presidential election.

The U.S. national debt, which was at approximately 40 percent of U.S. gross domestic product at the end of 2008, is now expected to be at 60 percent by 2010 as a result of the economic slowdown, the TARP, other bailout programs, the $787 billion deficit-funded Obama administration economic stimulus program, and the proposed Obama administration $3.6 trillion federal budget for 2009.[13] If the national debt does grow this fast, the national debt could exceed 100 percent of U.S. gross domestic product sometime before 2012, an uncomfortable phenomenon that has not happened since the World War II era, when the national debt reached 122 percent of GDP in 1946.

JUST HOW BIG IS A TRILLION?

To answer the question of how big a problem borrowing $6.5 trillion will be over the next two years, we need to examine just how large a trillion actually is.[14]

One trillion is the number 1 followed by twelve zeroes, as in: 1,000,000,000,000.

- If you had gone into business on the day Jesus was born, and your business lost a million dollars a day, day in and day out, 365 days a year, it would take you until October 2737 to lose $1 trillion.

- If you spent $1 million a day, every day since Jesus was born, you would still be only slightly more than three-quarters of the way to spending $1 trillion.

- One trillion dollars divided by 300 million Americans comes out to $3,333 per person.

- One trillion one-dollar bills stacked one on top of the other would reach nearly 68,000 miles into the sky, about a third of the way from the earth to the moon.

- Earth's home galaxy, the Milky Way, is estimated to contain about 200 billion stars; so, if each star cost one dollar, $1 trillion would buy five Milky Way galaxies full of stars.

- One trillion seconds of ordinary clock time equals 31,546 years. So, spending money at the rate of one dollar every second, or $86,400 every day, a spending spree would still take nearly 32,000 years to reach $1 trillion.

- If someone were to build city blocks that contained ten homes valued at $100,000 per home, you would end up with ten houses to a block, ten blocks to a mile, and a hundred blocks per square mile. It would take 10,000 square miles to reach $1 trillion in value. This would be more than six of our states: Vermont, 9,615 square miles; New Hampshire, 9,351 square miles; New Jersey, 8,722 square miles; Connecticut, 5,544 square miles; Delaware, 1,954 square miles; and Rhode Island, 1,545 square miles.

With the estimated 2009 population of the United States at 305,556,415 people, each citizen's share of the national debt is

$34,769.40. Craig Smith, founder and CEO of Swiss America Trading Corporation, has estimated it would take approximately four generations of Americans to pay off the interest of the U.S. Treasury bonds sold as debt to create $1 trillion, factoring in a 3 percent growth rate in the economy.

As noted above, the U.S. national debt now exceeds $10 trillion and was estimated at $10,624,012,813,982.43, on January 30, 2009, at 6:44:38 P.M., according to the U.S. National Debt Clock, at Times Square in New York City.[15] In September 2008, the digital display on the Times Square debt clock was modified to eliminate the dollar sign, so the national debt in tens of trillions of dollars could be displayed. The clock, which was created in 1989 by Manhattan real estate developer Seymour Durst, is now being redesigned so the new clock can display the national debt in numbers measured in the hundreds of trillions, with a dollar sign that could be eliminated should the national debt ever reach $1 quadrillion.

As pointed out previously, a difference of scale is a difference of phenomenon. The U.S. Treasury has never had to finance a U.S. debt that exceeded $1 trillion on a cash basis. Treasury debts measured in the hundreds of billions have proved manageable up until now. Will financing trillions of dollars in debt be the same phenomenon? Most likely, the answer is no.

In the Economic Panic of 2009, we have raced past the point where U.S. Treasury debt financing can be considered "business as usual." If the Treasury is projecting a need to raise $4 trillion in debt financing to sustain the federal deficit on a cash basis in 2010, will a debt of that magnitude be sustainable, or will the dollar simply collapse? If the federal deficit on a cash basis in 2010 is $4 trillion, the GAAP-accounted federal deficit will jump even more tens of trillions of dollars. Deficits of this magnitude have never been managed by any government on earth in human history.

IN DEBT TO CHINA

Selling a trillion dollars in debt is not like selling hundreds of billions of dollars in debt, just more. Psychologically, a threshold is crossed when the Treasury goes into the world market to sell $1 trillion in debt. Foreign governments suddenly begin to ask if the United States is bankrupt. This translates into a concern that the unthinkable might become think-

able, possibly even today. If U.S. federal budget deficits continue to spiral out of control, is it possible the U.S. government might default not
only on future Medicare, Medicaid, and Social Security obligations,
but also on trillions of dollars of debt sold by the U.S. Treasury? Or, will
the U.S. government continue to meet debt obligations but only with seriously devalued dollars?

Yu Yongding, a former adviser to the Chinese central bank, the
People's Bank of China, expressed concerns to journalists in September
2008 that China was growing increasingly cautious about purchasing
more U.S. Treasury debt.[16] In March 2009, Chinese premier Wen Jiabao
lent his voice to warning the United States that China's appetite to buy
Treasury debt was not unlimited. "We have lent a huge amount of money
to the U.S., so of course we are concerned about the safety of our assets," Wen Jiabao said at a press conference in Beijing. "Frankly speaking, I do have some worries."[17] The Chinese premier called on the United
States to honor its words, remain a credible nation, and ensure the safety
of Chinese assets.[18]

By the end of 2008, China had amassed nearly $2 trillion in foreign-
exchange reserves, the largest amount held by any nation, largely because of its strong exports to the United States and the resulting negative
balance of trade, which the United States has allowed to grow to unprecedented levels with China. Approximately 80 percent of Chinese
foreign-exchange reserves have been held in U.S. assets, including Treasury bills and other U.S. debt obligations, such as bonds issued by U.S.
mortgage giants Freddie Mac and Fannie Mae. At the end of 2008,
China held $696 billion of U.S. government securities, having surpassed
Japan as the largest purchaser of U.S. Treasury debt.[19]

In 2009 and 2010, the Obama administration will need to almost
double the amount of Treasury bills held in Asia. Should concerns about
the solvency of the United States continue to mount, will holders of U.S.
Treasury bills begin dumping them on the open market? "We are in the
same boat, we must cooperate," Yu told Bloomberg. "If there's no selling in a panicked way, then China willingly can continue to provide our
financial support by continuing to hold U.S. assets."[20] Clearly, China
was giving warning signs, suggesting a likelihood China would begin
diversifying its foreign-exchange reserve assets away from U.S. government debt.

U.S. bondholders face the risk that the value of their bonds on the
current market could easily deteriorate, causing the foreign holders of
U.S. debt to lose money on their U.S. debt portfolio. For example, the

Telegraph in London pointed out that if China's holdings match the U.S. Treasury's average forty-eight-month duration, then a 5 percent rise in yields, from 1.72 percent on the five-year note to 6.72 percent, would cost China 17.5 percent of its holdings' value, or $119 billion.[21] Foreign buyers have typically absorbed only about $200 billion of Treasury debt annually, little help when the Treasury is planning to issue as much as $2.5 trillion of new debt in 2009 and $4 trillion in 2010.

In February 2009, Yu Yongding demanded U.S. government guarantees on various U.S. Treasury debt securities, including Treasury bills. On its face, Yu's request appears to ask for a redundant guarantee, since U.S. Treasury bills are by design backed by the full weight and force of the U.S. government. The request for an additional specific U.S. government guarantee only underscored China's increasing uneasiness with continuing to buy burgeoning levels of U.S. federal debt. China's concerns came as China was struggling to finance its own $600 billion bailout for Chinese financial institutions and corporations fighting for survival in the global economic downturn.[22] In January 2009, China's exports dropped 17.5 percent, while imports collapsed 43.1 percent.[23] China's economy, heavily dependent on making cheap goods for the U.S. market, was cast into its own deep recession by the U.S. economic downturn.

In February 2009, Luo Ping, a director-general at the China Banking Regulatory Commission, told reporters after a speech in New York that China would continue to buy U.S. Treasuries in spite of its concerns about U.S. finances. Speaking at the Global Association of Risk Professionals 10th Annual Risk Management Convention, he asked, "Except for U.S. Treasuries, what can you hold?" He answered his own question, suggesting gold may be the only alternative. "Gold?" he asked rhetorically. "You don't hold Japanese government bonds or U.K. bonds. U.S. Treasuries are the safe haven. For everyone, including China, it is the only option." Still, Luo was not enthusiastic. "We hate you guys," he added. "Once you start issuing $1 trillion—$2 trillion . . . we know the dollar is going to depreciate, so we hate you guys. But there is nothing much we can do."[24]

If the dollar depreciates in value as a consequence of massive borrowing in 2009 and 2010, all holders of U.S. Treasury securities, including China, will take a loss in the value of their asset holdings. Dollar devaluation, whether officially declared or not, affects the buying power not only of U.S. citizens but of all foreign nations that hold U.S. debt securities. China has been steadily reducing the percentage of its foreign-exchange currency assets held in dollars, down from a 2003 high, when it was 83 percent. Should China decide to reduce those holdings to 65 percent or lower, the U.S. Treasury would have a much more difficult time subsidizing massive U.S. budget deficits.

Unwittingly, we have empowered China to inflict massive damage on the United States without firing a shot. All China would have to do is sell U.S. Treasury bonds on foreign exchanges at a deep discount. While China might lose billions of dollars in the process, the cost could be seen as cheap, especially if the result were to inflict permanent economic damage on an archrival that was once the world's sole superpower. Truly, China would be making wiser investments to stop buying U.S. Treasuries altogether, resolving instead to use its $2 trillion in foreign-exchange reserves to buy gold, land in the United States, and oil and natural gas reserves around the world.

BUYING OUR OWN DEBT

Early in 2008, Bernard Connolly, a global strategist at Banque AIG in London, became concerned that the failures in the U.S. banking sector could set off another great depression. As a step to prevent this from happening, he recommended the U.S. government and Federal Reserve take the unprecedented step of buying a wide range of assets, including stocks and Treasury securities.[25] Changes in federal law would be required to allow the Federal Reserve to purchase stocks, say on the New York Stock Exchange or NASDAQ, but currently the Fed is authorized to purchase Treasury securities and debt issued by U.S. agencies, including the Government-Sponsored Enterprises, or GSEs, Freddie Mac and Fannie Mae. By purchasing U.S. debt securities, the Fed would be hoping to create enough U.S. government demand for U.S. government debt that the yield, the price the government has to pay to get purchasers to buy the bonds, would actually go down, making the debt cheaper for the U.S. Treasury to finance.

By the end of 2008, Federal Reserve Chairman Bernanke and the Federal Reserve were taking the idea seriously. In a speech to the Chamber of Commerce in Austin, Texas, on December 1, 2008, Bernanke noted the Fed could purchase longer-term Treasury or U.S. agency securities on the open market in substantial quantities. "This approach might influence the yields on these securities, thus helping to spur aggregate demand," Bernanke said. "Indeed, last week the Fed announced plans to purchase up to $100 billion in GSE debt and up to $500 billion in GSE mortgage-backed securities over the next few quarters. It is encouraging that the announcement of that action was met by a fall in mortgage interest rates." [26]

Yet the idea that the U.S. government would become a major buyer of U.S. debt was risky, especially at a time when the federal debt was increasing so dramatically. After all, if yields on Treasuries go up because the U.S. Treasury is entering the market to borrow trillions of dollars of debt, the Fed could take substantial losses on Treasury securities previously purchased. Also, if the Fed bought mortgage-backed securities (MBSs) at or near the original offering price, the Fed could take substantial losses when the MBSs which contained losses were marked to market. The resale value of Fed-purchased MBSs would likely reflect a lower current market value, especially if the Fed were motivated to buy the MBSs from the balance sheets of financial institutions to relieve them of their toxic assets. Marked to market, most MBS securities today would have to have prices lower than their initial-issue prices, reflecting the subprime or other mortgage losses experienced since the mortgages were bundled together to create the MBS issues in the first place.

TWO MORE BUBBLES TO BURST

Federal budget deficits counted in trillions of dollars are staggering, until we realize that a nearly $1 quadrillion bubble is still building in derivatives.

The Bank of International Settlements (BIS), in Basel, Switzerland, now estimates that derivatives, the complex bets financial institutions and sophisticated institutional investors make with one another on everything from commodities options to credit swaps, now top $680 trillion worldwide—that's $0.68 quadrillion. [27]

- A quadrillion is the number 1 followed by 15 zeroes, as in: 1,000,000,000,000,000.

- To visualize a quadrillion, you need to multiply one trillion by one thousand.

The hedge-fund and derivatives markets are so highly complex and technical that they are little understood, even by many top economists and investment-banking professionals. Moreover, both markets are almost totally unregulated, either by the U.S. government or by any other government worldwide.

While the hedge-fund market is small in comparison to derivatives, hedge funds in the United States are still a $1.5 trillion industry. Hedge funds and derivatives share a common characteristic in that both were initially set up by professional investment advisers to assist them in managing the risk contained in institutional investment portfolios, including mutual-fund assets or pension funds that typically involved hundreds of millions of dollars.

Hedge funds were set up originally to assist professional money managers of corporate portfolios, including bank and investment-company assets, and mutual funds in increasing their yield, by making esoteric investments in various interest-rate or other instruments that would theoretically increase in value even when stock prices went down. A popular hedge-fund concept is the "fund of funds," in which an investor's cash is used to buy fractional shares in a pool that owns many mutual funds. The original idea of a hedge fund was to diversify a large, typically institutional investment to reduce risk. The concept of diversifying an investment generally works, unless, as today, the entire market is down. In down markets there are too few up-value stocks or funds in any "fund of funds" to balance out the losses that must inevitably be taken.

One of the original ideas behind derivatives was the realization that professional money managers, including those in banks, investment companies, and hedge funds, needed to make bets to offset the possibility of taking losses. To make this clearer, let's consider an investment manager of a multimillion-dollar bond fund who is worried about how interest-rate changes will affect the value of the bonds in the portfolio. A popular form of derivative contract was developed to permit one money manager to "swap" a stream of variable-interest payments with another money manager for a stream of fixed-interest payments. The idea was to use derivative bets on interest rates to "hedge" or balance off the risks taken on interest-rate investments owned in the underlying portfolio. In other words, let's say an institutional investment manager held $100 million in fixed-rate bonds. To hedge the risk, should interest rates rise or fall in a manner different than the institutional investment manager had projected, a purchase of a $100 million variable-interest-rate derivative could be constructed to cover the risk. Whichever way interest rates went, one side to the swap might win and the other might lose. The money manager losing the bet could expect to get paid on the derivative to compensate for some or all of the losses.

Another dangerous form of derivatives involved credit-default swaps, or CDSs. Here Bank A, the swap seller, purchased protection on a portfolio of loans or bonds, insuring the loans or bonds in case of default. The swap seller, Bank B, acted much like an insurance company selling protection, in effect agreeing to take a premium amount for promising to make good the loan or bond principal should the loans or bonds default. Bank A had limited risk, in that the premium paid to Bank B would be lost if the loans or bonds did not default. Bank B, however, had a much higher potential for loss, should the loans or bonds default and Bank B were required to make good the principal amount of loans or bonds that defaulted.

That Bank A could buy a CDS derivative encouraged Bank A to be more aggressive in making loans or buying bond portfolios. Bank B had a good business, collecting premiums to insure against loss, as long as the loans or bonds that were being insured continued to perform as expected. In a down economy, Bank B might be wiped out, should the derivative losses exceed Bank B's capital. Billions of dollars in credit-default-swap losses were a major factor in the losses that caused insurance giant AIG to fail, as loans and bond portfolios that AIG ended up insuring went into default as the mortgage bubble burst and the credit crisis deepened in late 2008. As the mortgage bubble burst, trillions of dollars in mortgage-related CDS derivatives also defaulted.

In the strong stock and mortgage markets we experienced beginning in the historically low 1 percent interest-rate environments of 2003 through 2004, the number of hedge funds soared, just as the volume of derivative contracts soared from a mere $300 trillion in 2005 to the nearly $700 trillion of derivatives floating around the world today. Bloomberg reported that the number of hedge funds tripled in the last decade to a record of 10,233 at the end of June 2008, according to the Chicago-based Hedge Fund Research, Inc. Even more frightening, Bloomberg reported that up to one-third of these hedge funds could be "wiped out" in the economic downturn that began in December 2008.[28] The BIS makes no estimate how much of the $684 trillion in outstanding derivative contracts are today vulnerable to collapse.

Deepcaster.com, a financial newsletter that tracks derivatives, explains there are many types of derivatives, but the most common involve stock options, commodities, and financial futures options.[29] In a commodity option, for instance, the value of the future contract is dependent on, or derived from, the underlying price of the commodity in question. The value of a corn-futures contract depends on the current price of corn, just as the value of a silver-futures contract depends on the current price of silver. The problem internationally derives from the more complex kinds of derivatives we have just examined.

Most derivatives are traded over the counter in largely unregulated markets outside the stock exchanges and clearinghouses. Financial professionals consider derivatives to be "dark liquidity," with billions of dollars changing hands privately, largely between financial institutions, without any public record in regulated entities such as stock exchanges, where transactions are subject to public and regulatory scrutiny.

If you still don't fully understand derivatives, you're not alone. As noted at the start of this discussion, very few financial professionals have a clear understanding of how derivatives work or the trillions of dollars in risk the contracts contain. The problem is that as the mortgage bubble grew in the United States, the derivatives bubble has grown dramatically worldwide.

WHY SHOULD WE WORRY ABOUT DERIVATIVES?

Most banks and brokerage firms in the United States and abroad have invested heavily in derivatives. With the current turmoil in global financial markets, trillions in derivative losses are being realized by financial institutions that are doing everything possible to keep the losses hidden from the public. A good example is Merrill Lynch, a major U.S. investment and brokerage firm that has had to admit massive losses in both derivatives and collateralized mortgage securities, even though it has done everything possible to avoid specifying the quantity and nature of the losses. According to *Forbes* magazine, in July 2008, Merrill Lynch realized $9.4 billion in losses, largely from write-downs in mortgage-backed securities and derivatives.[30]

In September 2008, the U.S. Treasury and Federal Reserve talked Bank of America, or BofA, into absorbing Merrill Lynch in a $50 billion transaction that was engineered by the government to keep Merrill Lynch from collapsing.[31] Mortgage-backed securities and credit-swap derivative losses measured in the billions were the reason Merrill Lynch technically went bankrupt. Even after Bank of America absorbed Merrill, additional losses at Merrill from mortgage-backed securities and credit-swap derivatives losses forced BofA to return to the government in January 2009 for another $20 billion in bailout funds, with an additional federal guarantee of $118 billion to cover yet more anticipated losses from mortgage-backed securities and credit-swap derivatives that still remained on Merrill Lynch's balance sheet.[32]

The lesson here is that Merrill Lynch, even with a $1 trillion balance sheet, was unable to absorb these huge losses without triggering insolvency. Yet even as Merrill collapsed, Merrill and the Bank of America remained unwilling to report exactly the amount of losses attributed to derivatives, choosing instead to lump derivative losses into "other revenue" categories on financial reporting forms required by regulators.

Many hedge-fund and derivative-contract bets that were good when the Dow topped 14,000, as it did in July 2007, no longer worked when the Dow started trading under 7,000, as it did in March 2009. Should the bubble in hedge funds and derivatives burst, financial institutions around the world could be faced with having to absorb hundreds of billions of dollars and possibly even trillions of dollars in losses, an amount of money almost inconceivable in any other era of global financial history. If those bubbles burst, the world financial system will melt down quickly, with no government in the world able to provide a solution, except to print the hundreds of billions or trillions of dollars in near-worthless fiat currency needed to nationalize the bankrupt banks and investment companies involved in the collapse.

STIMULUS PLAN OR WEALTH REDISTRIBUTION?

As the administration pushed the $787 billion economic stimulus package through Congress in February 2009, President Obama warned that the financial crisis could turn into a "catastrophe" if the measure was not passed by Congress immediately. "No plan is perfect," Obama told conservative critics who charged that the bill was the largest welfare bill ever passed in the United States and that it depended entirely upon deficit spending.[33]

Since the Great Depression of the 1930s, the economics of John Maynard Keynes has influenced Republican as well as Democratic presidential administrations. The key Keynesian theory that has become dogma is that government fiscal policy can and should sustain federal budget deficits to stimulate economic growth.[34]

Whether a 2009 federal deficit in the range of $2 trillion would solve the problem of reduced U.S. consumer demand or deepen the economic recession that began in December 2008 remained to be seen. What was clear was that President Obama and the Democrats in Congress had decided to roll the dice, betting that massive government spending would stimulate the economy and create more jobs than widespread tax cuts would. Republicans countered that the Democrats were trying to outdo Franklin D. Roosevelt in using deficit spending to create a new generation of Democratic voters dependent upon government-entitlement programs.

Either way, with the passage of the $787 billion economic stimulus plan in February 2009, Obama and the Democrats were beginning to own the economic problem the administration inherited from President Bush. The Obama administration was prepared to argue that the bill would be successful if it prevented job losses that would have occurred had the bill not been passed. Yet that argument appeared a hedge, designed principally to lower expectations. After all, the bill had been sold as an economic stimulus plan, not as an economic stabilization plan.

Was deficit spending and an expansion of government-funded programs the way to end the Economic Panic of 2009? Or would they end up pushing the U.S. national debt to the breaking point? Once the bill was signed into law, President Obama owned the results. The success of the plan would ultimately depend on whether the massive deficit-spending proposed in the bill did what it was supposed to do—namely, stimulate the economy and create the millions of jobs needed to end the recession. Saving jobs would not only be hard to prove, it would be hard to sell, unless enough new jobs were created to reverse growing unemployment and get the nation back to work.

An Obama plan to redistribute wealth through massive social-welfare programs with the result of dramatically increasing the federal debt could never be sold directly. Yet utilizing the economic crisis as an excuse and selling an income-redistribution agenda as an economic stimulus plan are risky: if more financial institutions continue to fail and more Americans continue to be unemployed, the Obama administration will be vulnerable to a charge that the stimulus package only made the economic problem worse. Moreover, since the nation never committed directly to a massive expansion of the government and the welfare state as such, a backlash against the welfare state will be inevitable if the Obama plan fails to stimulate the economy.

The modern social-welfare state, despite all the humanitarian arguments that can be made to support it, may in the final analysis end up being too expensive for either Europe or the United States to afford, especially during periods of economic downturn. That massive government deficit spending is the solution to stimulating the economy enough to create the jobs needed to make the modern welfare state affordable may well turn out to be an exercise in wishful thinking.

OBAMA'S OPTIMISM

A "highly optimistic" President Obama, speaking to top executives of the Business Roundtable in Washington, D.C., on March 12, 2009, gave an upbeat view of the economic downturn, saying that the national crisis is "not as bad as we think" and trying to reassure the audience that his economic stimulus plans would speed recovery.[35]

Yet some bad news may be too big to ignore. Estimates of the losses experienced in the global economic recession are staggering.

Stephen Schwarzman, chief executive officer of private-equity company Blackstone Group, told Reuters that between 40 and 45 percent of the world's wealth had been destroyed in the past year and a half. "This is absolutely unprecedented in our lifetimes," he said.[36]

In 2008, U.S. households suffered a record 18 percent drop in wealth, or $11.2 trillion, to end the year at total U.S. household net worth of $51 trillion. Since a second-quarter 2007 peak of $64.4 trillion, U.S. household wealth has dropped by more than 20 percent.[37] The *Wall Street Journal* noted that the single-year decline of $11.2 trillion equaled the combined annual output of Germany, Japan, and the United Kingdom. The *Journal* commented that the data signaled the "end of an epoch defined by first and second homes, rising retirement funds and ever-fatter portfolios."[38] The decline was especially disturbing given that household wealth had increased by nearly 50 percent in 2006, reflecting the bubble-like increase in housing prices at the peak of the housing boom.

Also, consider the following, reported by Reuters:[39]

- The Asian Development bank estimated that financial assets lost around the world may exceed $50 trillion, a collapse of wealth equivalent to a year's worth of world economic output.

- The World Bank concluded that the volume of world trade in 2009 will fall for the first time since 1982, suffering the biggest decline in eighty years.

- The World Bank also predicted that world gross domestic product, or GDP, will decline in 2009 for the first time since World War II.

- China, the largest exporter among emerging economies, has seen 20 million jobs disappear, while India reports 3 million jobs were lost because of shrinking exports.

- The Institute of International Finance, a Washington, D.C., think tank, reported that net private flows to emerging markets declined 50 percent in 2008, to less than $500 billion; net private-capital flows to emerging markets in 2009 are expected to decline even further, to $165 billion.

- The World Bank anticipates that ninety-eight developing countries will face a cumulative financing gap of between $270 billion and $700 billion in 2009.

On September 29, 2008, when the market dropped 778 points for its biggest single-day point loss ever, approximately $1.2 trillion was wiped out in market capitalization. It was the first $1 trillion daily loss in Wall Street history.[40] The MSCI World Index, a Morgan Stanley–maintained index of world stocks, calculated world stock losses at $21 trillion from a market peak in October 2007 to the trough of November 2008. That is $21,000 for every individual in the developed world.[41]

So, regardless of President Obama's optimism, the recession that officially began in the United States in December 2008 quickly became the worst economic decline the world has seen since the end of the Great Depression of the 1930s.

A BANKRUPT U.S.A.

Should the Obama administration manage to double the national debt within its four years in office and should the Federal Reserve begin buying the debt issued by the Treasury, the risk of "hyperinflation" could become very real. Even the mention of hyperinflation immediately brings to mind the frightening images of the Weimar Republic in Germany at the end of World War I, when hundreds or thousands of German marks were required simply to buy a loaf of bread or mail a letter through the government post office. The unfortunate reality is that during the Obama administration, the U.S. economy could experience a severe recession and hyperinflation at the same time. The last incident of U.S. stagflation occurred in President Jimmy Carter's term of office in the 1970s; we suffered both a slowdown in economic growth and double-digit interest rates, a situation made even more unbearable by unemployment, then as high as 7 percent, and a spike in oil prices after the Arab oil embargo in 1973.

In the final analysis, the idea that the U.S. government would be reduced to being the final buyer of U.S. debt is bizarre. Has money become so meaningless that we are free to print whatever we need? If so, why stop at a federal deficit of $2.5 trillion in 2009 or $4 trillion in 2010? As we will see in the next chapter, the mortgage bubble's bursting may have left financial institutions around the world holding $10 trillion or more in unmarketable mortgage-backed securities. Why shouldn't the federal government simply print enough money to buy all those troubled assets off the balance sheets of the troubled financial institutions, so banks and brokerage firms might lend again freely, without the burden? Why not simply print enough money to buy every mortgage in America? Why not simply buy unoccupied homes and give them to the poor?

Unfortunately, even for the federal government, at some point deficits have a limit, even if the nation went along step-by-step to accept what only a few years ago would have been federal budget deficits of unimaginable magnitudes. This is the impact of the Little Green Frog analogy. The U.S. taxpayer is in the pot on the stove and the heat is turned on.

When no other foreign government will purchase U.S. debt, the U.S. government may have no choice but to consider seriously declaring bankruptcy and reorganizing. Incrementally, the United States has allowed a negative net worth to grow to a magnitude where the phenomenon has changed, such that the very economic viability of the U.S. government itself is now in question.

That the government could default on the "full faith and credit" obligations of the U.S. Treasury is now imaginable, for the first time in U.S. history. And if the government is incapable of managing its finances responsibly, then the larger setting of a regional economy and a regional government may be offered as the only solution.

We must realize that the U.S. government is bankrupt if we are to understand why a one-world government and a one-world currency may end up being the only solution the globalists offer to the problem.

TWO

The Mortgage Bubble Bursts

The housing bubble was a major cause, if not *the* cause, of the
subprime crisis and of the broader economic crisis we now face.

—Robert J. Shiller, Professor of Economics,
Yale University, 2008[1]

The precipitating cause of the Economic Panic of 2009 was the bursting of the U.S. mortgage bubble.

The growth of the mortgage bubble can be traced back to interest-
rate policies set by the Federal Reserve under the direction of Chairman
Alan Greenspan after the 9/11 terrorist attacks against the World Trade
Center and the Pentagon.

Democrats as well as Republicans in Congress played key roles in
ending the regulations that had separated banking, insurance companies, and investment brokerages since the Great Depression of the 1930s.
Democrats as well as Republicans allowed Freddie Mac and Fannie Mae
to expand subprime lending, even after warning signals had been given
that abuses were occurring at both agencies.

Democrats have been drawn to support agencies such as Fannie and
Freddie as vehicles to extend the Great Society initiatives established by
President Lyndon Johnson in the 1960s after the assassination of President John F. Kennedy. Over many years, Senator Christopher Dodd, a
key Democrat on the Senate Banking Committee, and Democrat repre-

sentative Barney Frank of Massachusetts, a key member of the House
Financial Services Committee, did their best to deflect and defeat any
attempts that came before their committees to place Freddie and Fannie
under tighter government regulation, even though such steps might have
prevented the subprime-mortgage bubble from building to dangerous
proportions.

Granted, President George W. Bush and Senator John McCain gave
abundant warnings that Fannie Mae and Freddie Mac, the two federal
institutions at the core of the mortgage business, were out of control.
Still, Republicans generally shared the Democratic Party's enthusiasm
to expand homeownership among the poor. Moreover, concerns that
key Democratic administrators were bending the rules at Freddie and
Fannie were not enough for Republicans to force through legislation reforming the agencies, even when Republicans held control of Congress.
Typically, on the issue of expanding homeownership, the Bush administration sided with key Democrats, including Dodd and Frank. President
Bush frequently touted an "ownership society," code words for making
sure typically unqualified buyers could yet own homes.

The goal here is not to blame the subprime-mortgage meltdown on
Democrats or Republicans. Villains are pointed out to cast light on the
abuses the mortgage system encouraged as the bubble grew, not to de-
monize one political party or the other. In any economic collapse, the
"blame game" starts almost immediately. Yet, in analyzing the mortgage-
market meltdown that caused the recession that began in December
2008, there is clearly plenty of blame to go around, both for Democrats
who championed and exploited Freddie and Fannie and for Republicans
whose enthusiasm to create the "ownership society" led them to go along
with Fannie and Freddie despite the abuses. The objective here is to understand the dynamics of the mortgage bubble, especially in terms of
how it grew and why it burst. The mortgage bubble would never have
grown had the Federal Reserve not kept interest rates artificially low and
provided ample credit into a system that was encouraged to extend loans
irresponsibly.

The mortgage bubble was the second bubble that Federal Reserve
Chairman Alan Greenspan had allowed to grow and burst. The first
was the dot-com bubble, which burst in the final year of President Bill
Clinton's administration. In retrospect, Greenspan's reputation has been
tarnished by the argument that he was simply a "bubble master" whose
only accomplishment was to keep interest rates low enough to encourage "irrational exuberance" to predominate, whether that enthusiasm

was for dot-com stock evaluations that had no basis in reality, or home prices that in many markets doubled by the peak in 2006.[2]

FEDERAL-FUNDS RATE 2000–2008

The federal-funds rate is the rate at which depository institutions lend balances at the Federal Reserve to other depository institutions, typically overnight.[3] Federal-fund rates are set by the Federal Open Market Committee, or FOMC, which meets in eight regularly scheduled meetings each year and consists of the seven members of the Board of Governors of the Federal Reserve System, along with the president of the Federal Reserve Bank of New York, and four of the remaining eleven Federal Reserve Bank presidents, who serve one-year terms on a rotating basis.[4] There are no rules for how the FOMC must set federal-funds rates, but since February 2000 the FOMC has issued a statement shortly after each meeting, reporting on the committee's assessment of the risks of attaining the long-term goals of price stability and economic growth.

The fed-funds rate is the principal tool the Federal Reserve uses to implement monetary policy. The term "monetary policy" refers to the actions taken by a central bank, the Federal Reserve in the United States, to influence the availability and cost of money as well as credit. Many interest rates, including mortgage rates, key off the federal-funds rate, and so increases in the federal-funds rates typically lead to increases in mortgage rates, while decreases in the federal-funds rates lead to decreases in mortgage rates.

Chairman Greenspan, by keeping federal-funds rates as low as 1 percent in 2003 and under 2 percent until December 2004, created the interest-rate conditions needed for the mortgage market to bubble up. Lower interest rates stimulated not just the subprime housing market but the housing market as a whole. With mortgages more affordable, home prices across the nation began to rise.

By 2006, housing values in many parts of the country had nearly doubled; a home valued at $100,000 when George W. Bush took office on January 20, 2001, was suddenly a $200,000 home by sometime in 2005 or 2006. Similarly a $500,000 home bubbled to being a $1 million home and a $1 million home was suddenly valued at $2 million. This is what we mean by a "housing bubble"—in a short period of time homes in markets across the nation dramatically increased in value. The housing bubble occurred not only because home prices doubled over a short period of time but also because people were willing and ready to believe that the price increases of this magnitude were real and permanent.

INTEREST RATES AT 1 PERCENT

A necessary condition for the housing bubble to be created was historically low interest rates, which made home financing easier because homeowners could still afford monthly payments on larger-value houses as long as interest rates remained low.

Federal-funds rates had not been in the 1 percent range since Eisenhower was president in the 1950s. Low mortgage rates alone were not enough to create the housing bubble, but they did contribute to the perfect storm that became the housing bubble we experienced from 2001 through 2006.

The chart below helps illustrate how the mortgage bubble developed and burst, listing the monthly federal-funds rate from the beginning of President George W. Bush's administration, in January 2001, through the beginning of President Barack Obama's administration, in January 2009.[5]

Federal-Funds Rate 2000–2008

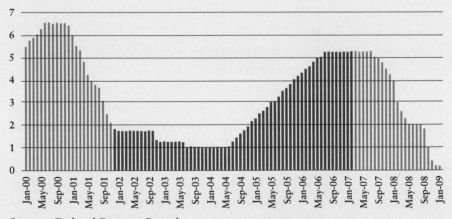

Source: Federal Reserve Board

The first months of the Bush presidency were focused on an economic slowdown that had started in the final year of the Clinton administration. A major initiative of Bush's first year in office was to get a $1.35

trillion tax cut signed into law on June 7, 2001. Federal-funds rates reached a peak at 6.54 percent the year before, in July 2000. Beginning in late summer 2000, while Clinton was yet in office, the Fed began cutting the rate. On September 11, 2001, the day of the terrorist attacks on the World Trade Center and the Pentagon, fed funds were at 2.09 percent, nearly 4.50 points below the July 2000 peak.

The stock market hit a 2001 peak on May 21, with the Dow closing at 11,337.92. Still, through that summer, the Dow dropped dramatically.

Then came the terrorist attacks on 9/11 and the economy shut down in shock. When the stock market reopened, on September 17, the Dow fell to 8,920.70, losing 684.81 points, a drop of approximately 7.13 percent in one day.

Alan Greenspan, who was Federal Reserve chairman at this time, is fairly direct in his 2007 autobiography, *The Age of Turbulence*, when he admits he was puzzled by the course the 2001 recession was taking. Gross domestic product, or GDP, defined as the measure of all goods and services produced by the economy, remained steady throughout what was shaping up to be a "shallow recession." Greenspan typically attributed the lowering of interest rates before 9/11 to "global forces."

Even before 9/11, Greenspan noted that the lower interest rates had "ignited a sharp rise in home prices in many parts of the world." He specifically commented that in the United States "homes had increased in value so much that households, feeling flush seemed more willing to spend."[6] Part of the willingness to spend came from banks aggressively marketing home-equity loans or refinancings in a way that encouraged homeowners to take cash out of their home-equity buildup, so the windfall in rapidly rising home-equity values could be spent now. Home-equity loans and cash taken out of homes in refinancing were often spent on typical consumer purchases, including family vacations, while others used the cash to pay bills, including credit-card bills. Still, consumer debt expanded overall in a lifestyle suddenly made affordable by the housing bubble.

After 9/11, Greenspan and the Federal Reserve began cutting interest rates aggressively in an effort to jump-start a badly shocked U.S. economy. "For a full year and a half after September 11, 2001, we were in limbo," Greenspan wrote. "The economy managed to expand, but its growth was uncertain and weak. Businesses and investors felt besieged."[7] Greenspan is open about his policy during this time. "The Fed's response to all this uncertainty was to maintain our program of aggresively lowering short-term interest rates," he wrote. Under Greenspan's direction the FOMC extended a series of seven cuts made in early 2001 to lower the fed-funds rates down to around 1.25 percent by the end of 2002, a figure Greenspan admits "most of us would have considered unfathomably low a decade before."

Greenspan admits that the Fed was aware that maintaining these low interest rates "might foster a bubble, an inflationary boom of some sort, which we would subsequently have to address." [8] Still, he claimed the Fed was worried that the economic slowdown after 9/11 might cause deflation, an international concern since the deflation that plagued the Great Depression of the 1930s. U.S. consumer spending, the engine of the world economy, revived in this low-interest-rate environment and the GDP continued to grow. Unfortunately, this was the beginning of the real estate bubble. "In many parts of the United States, residential real estate, energized by the fall in mortgage rates, began to see values surge," Greenspan admitted in his autobiography. "The market prices of existing homes rose 7.5 percent a year in 2000, 2001, and 2002, more than double the rate of just a few years before." He noted that not only did construction of new homes rise to "record levels," but also historic numbers of existing homes changed hands. "This boom provided a big lift in morale," he argued; "even if your house was not for sale, you could look down the block and see other people's homes going for what seemed like astonishing prices, which meant your home was worth more too." [9]

Greenspan was also keeping a sharp eye on the stock market. The Fed held fed-funds rates at or near 1 percent through June 2004, a historically unprecedented three-year stretch of rates this low. On October 9, 2002, the stock market hit a low at 7,286.27. Then, on October 15, 2002, the stock market closed once again above the 8,000 benchmark, at 8,255.68. From there, the Dow climbed steadily for the next five years, reaching an all-time high of 14,164.53 on October 9, 2007.

As 2007 came to a close, Greenspan was a hero on Wall Street. Investors who had made billions of dollars hailed Greenspan's low-interest-rate policy as the key to engineering an unprecedented surge of wealth on Wall Street. As 2007 progressed, those warning that the economy had peaked and the real estate bubble had already burst were being received as prophets of doom whose ill tidings risked spoiling the party. As 2008 began, many still-optimistic pundits were predicting the DJIA would climb past 15,000 without much difficulty. Unfortunately, such optimism was unfounded. In December 2008, few realized that month would later be identified as the official start of the most severe economic downturn in U.S. history since the Great Depression of the 1930s.

THE COMMUNITY REINVESTMENT ACT OF 1977 AND MORTGAGE-BACKED SECURITIES

The Community Reinvestment Act, or CRA, was signed into law by President Jimmy Carter in 1977, with the goal of forcing banks to provide credit to businesses and homeowners with poor credit. The CRA represented a social agenda in that the true purpose was to stop banks from "redlining" inner-city areas. Redlining was a practice in which banks refused to lend into low-income poverty areas because the risk of loan repayment was too high. Even though lending to those with poor credit is inherently risky, the Carter administration was intent on forcing banks to accept a social responsibility to provide credit to homeowners and businesses in low-income neighborhoods. The CRA became supercharged during the Clinton administration with a set of new rules that allowed subprime mortgages to be securitized. Federal Reserve Chairman Ben Bernanke, in a speech to the Community Affairs Research Conference in Washington, D.C., on March 30, 2007, noted that a 1992 law passed during the Clinton administration expanded the CRA market by requiring the government-sponsored enterprises Fannie Mae and Freddie Mac to securitize "affordable housing loans," a euphemism widely understood to mean low-income housing loans.[10]

Securitization involves a process in which Wall Street investment bankers buy mortgage pools from mortgage investors and repackage the mortgages into complex securities products known as mortgage-backed securities, or MBSs. In the securitization process, mortgage loans are typically sold to an investment banker who buys the mortgage to include it in a package of mortgages destined to become bundled into a mortgage-backed securities bond. As a result, the original mortgage is no longer held as an asset by the mortgage originator. Mortgage-backed securities generally try to package several different types of mortgage loans into what end up being multibillion-dollar bond issues that in turn are sold back to institutional buyers. In some instances, the buyer of a mortgage-backed securities bond may be the very financial institution that originated the mortgages in the first place.

Subprime loans, including subprime loans originated by banks under

CRA programs, as well as subprime loans generated by mortgage companies specializing in them, were typically included as only a portion of any given MBS package. In other words, a tranche of subprime loans could easily get packaged next to several tranches of different kinds of mortgages. Thus subprime loans packaged in an MBS bond could lie alongside tranches of mortgages sold to well-qualified and high-income mortgage buyers.

Understood most simply, mortgage-backed securities are bonds that pay out the cash flows resulting from the principal and interest payments on the underlying mortgages packaged in the bond. In an MBS "mortgage pass-through" bond, investors are paid all the principal and interest from the underlying pool of mortgages, minus a servicing fee. So, when mortgages in the bond go into foreclosure, the investors owning the bond end up with the losses. Because subprime loans may be packaged into a particular MBS issue, when the subprime loans begin to stop performing then the entire MBS issue may lose market value. MBS bonds experiencing subprime or other losses due to mortgage foreclosures become hard to "mark to market" for a current value. The problem is that investors do not want to take the risk of purchasing the bond when it may be difficult or impossible to estimate exactly how great the losses from mortgage foreclosures will be in that bond. In other words, in an economic downturn, when subprime homeowners are defaulting on monthly payments in great numbers, the entire MBS industry risks melting down.

HOW MORTGAGE-BACKED SECURITIES WORK

Securitization of mortgages into MBS bonds, a process that became a multitrillion-dollar business in the 1990s, increased dramatically the liquidity available to make new home loans. *Liquidity* is simply a term used to mean the amount of money available for any given activity. Mortgage securitization had several important consequences. Because mortgage originators could sell their mortgages to investment bankers creating MBS issues, mortgage originators did not have to hold the mortgage in their mortgage portfolio. As a result, mortgage lenders could more easily engage in riskier lending, including lending to less qualified buyers in the subprime market. By opening up bank CRA-generated and other subprime mortgages to be included in mortgage-backed securities, the Clinton administration advanced a social agenda to extend homeownership into poor inner-city areas where prospective homeowners were typically unqualified to get mortgages. By definition, subprime borrowers are not creditworthy under normal lending standards. The subprime-mortgage market involves providing mortgages to potential homeowners who cannot meet typical lending requirements to verify income, as well as potential homeowners who may have a history of credit problems.

Another important consequence of securitization was that the financial institutions buying MBS securities into their asset portfolio ended up with very complicated instruments, or pieces of instruments, that only financial analysts with advanced expertise in mortgage financing could truly understand. Mortgage-finance experts would analyze MBS issues by examining individual tranches, or parts of the complex security issue, to see how the particular mortgages in that tranche would perform under different interest-rate scenarios.

Just to be clear, a $100 billion MBS issue might get sold to dozens of institutional investors, each of whom bought a part of the total security package, or a particular tranche of the investment, perhaps buying only the "interest payment streams" in the MBS package, while avoiding owing other principal-repayment tranches. Investment bankers sold MBS issues as secure investments because many different kinds of mortgages diversified the investment; the mortgage market as a whole would have to collapse before the entire MBS issue itself would lose value dramatically. Investment bankers also sold the idea that the federal government would never allow mortgages sold by government-sponsored enterprises, or GSEs, such as Freddie Mac and Fannie Mae, to default, given the federal guarantee Freddie and Fannie place on mortgages they underwrite. Freddie and Fannie do not originate loans; instead they buy mortgages from approved lenders, with the intent of either holding the mortgages or packaging them into MBS issues.

In the aftermath of the mortgage bubble bursting, a debate has raged over whether the CRA was responsible for the failure in subprime mortgages that triggered the collapse of the mortgage market. Proponents of the CRA have argued that 50 percent of subprime loans were made by mortgage-service companies not subject to comprehensive federal supervision under CRA rules, while another 30 percent were made by affiliates of banks or thrifts not subject to routine supervision or examinations.[11] Opponents of the CRA frequently argue that in the Clinton administration, Andrew Cuomo as head of HUD and Janet Reno as head of the Justice Department threatened banks with a variety of sanctions unless they loosened underwriting standards in the subprime-mortgage market.[12]

THE ABUSES OF SUBPRIME-MORTGAGE LENDERS

Another necessary condition for the building of the mortgage bubble was unscrupulous mortgage lenders seeing the opportunity to make a quick profit. By preying upon naïve, otherwise credit-unqualified future homeowners to accept mortgages they would never be able to afford, subprime-mortgage originators could make a fast profit originating subprime loans to be sold into MBS securities. There is no question a small army of nonbank mortgage originators moved aggressively into the subprime market during the Clinton administration. At the height of the mortgage bubble, hedge funds and other investors looking for high-yield returns actually favored subprime-mortgage-backed securities. Subprime loans packaged into MBS bonds were typically priced to yield more because of their inherent risk than were conventional mortgage loans sold to credit-qualified homebuyers.

One of the largest subprime-mortgage writers was Countrywide Financial Corporation, a company that in 2006 financed approximately 20 percent of all mortgages made in the United States. Headed by Angelo Mozilo, Countrywide pioneered in providing undocumented loans, where mortgage applicants were not required to provide any loan documentation at all, not even proof of income, and mortgage loans where no down payments were required. To keep the monthly payments low for the first year or so of the mortgage loan, the unregulated subprime market developed a whole set of unorthodox mortgages, such as "interest-only" loans where no principal payments at all were made on the loan for the first year or so, and "balloon" loans where a down payment was postponed to a year or more out in the contract.

Since mortgage lenders priced subprime loans to yield more interest income because of their inherent risk, subprime loans typically paid higher fees to the originator than traditional fifteen-year or thirty-year fixed mortgages. The higher fees gave aggressive loan originators an incentive to sell even a qualified mortgage buyer a nontraditional mortgage. In other words, unscrupulous subprime lenders began pushing subprime-loan offers even when the buyer could qualify for a more traditional mortgage with a more affordable long-term monthly mortgage cost.

Since the loan originator did not plan to own the mortgage for long, the risk of foreclosure could be passed on to the buyer of the mortgage-backed security in which the subprime loan was ultimately bundled as an asset. In the frenzy of the mortgage bubble, many mortgage buyers did not fully understand the exact terms of the exotic mortgage options they were purchasing, and aggressive mortgage lenders motivated by high fees had little economic incentive to be honest. As a result, millions of homebuyers assumed mortgages they could not afford long-term. In the most egregious abuses, the mortgage bubble encouraged reckless practices that amounted to little more than placing unqualified buyers into complex mortgage structures that the mortgage buyers typically did not understand and in the long term could not afford.

A HOUSE OF CARDS

As CNBC reported in a special report titled "House of Cards," first broadcast on February 12, 2009, the best mortgage customer at the height of the mortgage bubble became "anyone with a pulse." [13] CNBC quoted Wall Street mortgage banker Michael Francis, who enlisted lenders on the West Coast to supply him with mortgages to package into MBS bonds. "We removed the litmus test," Francis told CNBC. "No income, no asset. Not verifying income . . . breathe on a mirror and if there's fog you sort of get a loan." [14] Even the credit agencies played along. CNBC interviewed Ann Rutledge, who rated securities for Moodys. When home prices surged, no borrowers defaulted and riskier Triple-B-rated securities made from subprime mortgages began to look as good as the safe Triple-As. "Eventually the market gets smart and says, let's lower the requirements for Triple-A," Rutledge commented. [15] The credit-rating agencies had an incentive to award a mortgage-backed security the best possible rating, CNBC noted, because the agencies were paid for their appraisals by the very investment banks that issued the mortgage-backed securities.

Subprime lenders argued there was no reason to worry. If subprime-mortgage borrowers met hard economic times and struggled to meet monthly payments, they could always resell the home at a profit. The same thinking applied to home-equity loans. If a homeowner with a large outstanding home-equity loan lost a job, the homeowner should still be able to sell the home at a profit. In 2004, homeowners withdrew an estimated $900 billion by refinancing their homes, spending the money on whatever they could buy. "Homes had turned into ATM machines and the economy flourished," CNBC reported.[16]

In the rising real estate market experienced from 2002 through at least 2006, aggressive or outright dishonest subprime-mortgage and home-equity loan tactics often worked. In a declining real estate market, however, holders of subprime and mortgage-equity loans were the first to experience substantial losses. In the down real estate market, such as began developing in the United States in the later months of 2006, many mortgages made under marginal real estate lending practices began to go into foreclosure. Homeowners who bought at the height of the market found themselves stuck with "underwater" loans, where the outstanding mortgage had a higher value than the resell value of the home. Homeowners with underwater loans could not sell the home for enough money to repay their mortgages completely. Many underwater homeowners chose to walk away from the loss rather than sell the home and still owe money on their original mortgage.

Even Greenspan and the Fed were caught by surprise when subprime loans became 20 percent of the mortgage-backed securities market in 2005. "It became a huge revelation," Greenspan admitted to CNBC on camera. When asked if the Fed could have prevented the mortgage bubble from growing, he answered, "The presumption that you could incrementally defuse a bubble was a fantasy. Clearly, you cannot defuse these things unless you hit them right on the head and break the economy, essentially break potential profitability that is engendering that kind of stuff." Reluctantly, Greenspan admitted, "We could have clamped down on the American economy and generated a 10 percent unemployment rate, and I will guarantee we would not have had a housing boom or a stock market boom." The problem was politics. Creating an "ownership society" was a very popular idea as the mortgage bubble grew, among both Republicans and Democrats alike. "Had we tried to suppress the expansion of the subprime market it would not have gone over very well with the Congress, when it looked like we were dealing with a major increase in homeownership which is of unquestioned value to this society," Greenspan told CNBC. "Would we have been able to do that? I doubt it."

Even as the mortgage bubble grew, President Bush continued to brag that his administration deserved credit for expanding the "ownership society" in which millions of Americans previously thought to lack the creditworthiness to own homes were now proud mortgage holders. Greenspan, in his autobiography, amplified this theme, noting that by

2006, nearly 69 percent of all U.S. households owned their own homes, up from 64 percent in 1994 and 44 percent in 1940.[17] Still, Greenspan warned that "as the boom rolled on," evidence of speculation was hard to miss. He noted that by 2005, investors accounted for 28 percent of the homes bought and TV news was carrying reports of "flippers"— speculators in places such as Las Vegas and Miami who bought properties, typically condos, with the intention of selling them for a quick profit. Greenspan argued the real estate boom had peaked by late 2005, "when first-time buyers began to find prices increasingly out of reach." He knew the boom was finally over, Greenspan wrote, when buyers no longer paid above offering prices to bid away a home they wanted to buy.

THE MORTGAGE BUBBLE BURSTS

On January 11, 2008, Countrywide Financial went bankrupt and was forced to sell to Bank of America in a $4.1 billion stock transaction. More than any other, this sale marked the collapse of the subprime-mortgage market and the bursting of the real estate bubble as resale values of homes began to fall dramatically across the country.

The mortgage bubble was doomed to burst when Greenspan and the Fed began raising interest rates late in 2004. At that time, Greenspan and the Fed were worried that low rates had so heated up the U.S. economy that inflation was looming as a potential problem. By raising rates to dampen inflation, Greenspan and the Fed were striking out on a path that would end up bursting the mortgage bubble and sending the U.S. and global economies into a tailspin of a magnitude not seen since the Great Depression of the 1930s.

When Ben Bernanke succeeded Greenspan as chairman of the Federal Reserve on February 1, 2006, he continued Greenspan's policy of tightening credit. Fed-fund rates, at 4.29 percent when Bernanke took over, rose to 5.25 percent in August 2006. Rates stayed at or near that plateau for almost a year. By August 2007, Bernanke and the Fed realized the mortgage bubble had burst and the economy was entering a recession. At that point Bernanke and the Fed began lowering rates, dropping fed-funds rates from the plateau of 5.25 percent in 2006 to 4.24 percent by the end of 2007 and to nearly zero by the end of 2008. Still, the move to drop rates was too little and too late. The damage had already been done.

Subprime mortgages written during the building of the mortgage bubble could not withstand higher rates. The wave of foreclosures that started in the subprime market caused mortgage-backed securities containing the subprime mortgages to lose value. As mortgage rates rose, even qualified buyers had to pay more in monthly payments for the inflated home values they were purchasing at in 2006. As the mortgage market melted down, so too did the assets of financial institutions, simply because bank and investment-firm asset portfolios included trillions in mortgage-backed securities bonds. The collapse of the mortgage market triggered a general economic slowdown that in turn caused the economic recession that officially began in December 2008.

TRACKING THE PEAK IN HOUSING VALUES

Yale economist Robert Shiller created an index of U.S. home prices going back to 1890, estimating the price of a standard home over that period of time. The goal was to track the value of housing as an investment over time, presenting housing values in consistent terms over more than one hundred years and factoring out the effects of inflation.[18] Shiller's analysis demonstrated that home prices peaked in 2006, at prices that began rising dramatically as Chairman Greenspan and the Federal Reserve held interest rates at or near 1 percent in 2003 and 2004. If a standard home sold in 1890 for $100,000, with inflation adjusted to reflect today's dollars, the house dropped to $66,000 in 1920, a level that more or less persisted until the end of World War II and the housing expansion that accompanied the postwar baby boom. In 2006, the standard house was priced at $199,000, up to 199 on the index scale, or 99 percent higher than the standard house in 1890.

What this means is that the housing bubble had approximately doubled the value of the standard home in the United States by 2006. The hard news here is that many homeowners may have to take the estimated price of their home in 2006 at the maximum point of the bubble and divide that value in half to get a true estimate of the home's value in a normal market valuation. As housing markets have adjusted downward since 2006, most homeowners have felt the pain with even a 10 percent drop in values. Underwater mortgages increase when homeowners make small down payments, 10 percent or less, to purchase the home, and the home decreases in value by 10 percent or more. If the housing market in the U.S. does not stabilize until home values reduce to 50 percent of their 2006 peak market value, more than 10 million homeowners in the U.S. will likely have underwater mortgage loans.

As foreclosure rates increased in the depressed nationwide mortgage market, many different government plans were advanced to attempt mortgage modification, or "mo-mod," to increase the likelihood that distressed homeowners might yet keep their homes. In all instances where mortgages were underwater, reducing the outstanding principal on the mortgage meant someone—either the homeowner or the mortgage lender or the taxpayer—had to lose the difference between the original mortgage amount and the reduced mortgage principal under the modified mortgage plan. Another alternative was to modify mortgages with lower interest rates, again with the goal of reducing the monthly mortgage payments in hopes the homeowner could keep the reduced mortgage current. Similarly, reducing the interest rate meant modifying the mortgage contract so the mortgage lender, or the holder of the MBS security into which that loan was packaged, inevitably took a loss.

Another problem was political: those continuing to make their mortgage payments were likely to react negatively to those receiving mortgage modifications. Why should those in foreclosure from loans they could not afford be given preferential treatment over those who were paying their mortgages even if they had to struggle economically to do so?

Politicians favoring mo-mod plans argued that homeowners able to continue making mortgage payments under original terms still benefited, in that reducing the rates of foreclosures would maintain higher home prices in the market as a whole. The problem with that argument is that the home mortgage market might not stabilize until home prices return to the historical standard, as indicated by Shiller's analysis. In other words, regardless of how hard we try to prevent the pain of underwater mortgages, the inevitable consequences of the mortgage bubble bursting will be painful. Home prices may have to reduce by up to one-half from their 2006 peak before mortgage markets in the United States stabilize, no matter how many mo-mod plans we implement.

GOVERNMENT TAKEOVER OF FREDDIE AND FANNIE

On September 7, 2008, the Bush administration assumed complete federal control over Freddie Mac and Fannie Mae, with an announcement that the government would buy, if necessary, the troubled mortgage-backed securities held by the two government-sponsored enterprises, or GSEs.[19] Freddie and Fannie have always enjoyed a hybrid status, partly government controlled and partly private enterprise. The two mortgage giants played a key role in providing a government guarantee to Freddie and Fannie loans that were packaged into MBS issues.

BBC News reported at the time of the government takeover that Freddie and Fannie guaranteed or owned about half of the $12 trillion U.S. mortgage market.[20] According to the *Wall Street Journal*, that amount was about $5.2 trillion. The riskiest loans held by Freddie and Fannie are known as "Alt-A" and subprime mortgages, worth about $780 billion, or about 15 percent of the total $5.2 trillion Freddie and Fannie mortgage-loan portfolio.[21] The takeover had the result of passing to U.S. taxpayers the contingent liability for failures in the entire $5.2 trillion loan portfolio held by the two mortgage giants.

Treasury Secretary Henry Paulson told reporters that "we had no choice" but to bail out Freddie and Fannie because they were "so big" and "so interwoven into our financial markets and our financial system."[22] This theme of "too big to fail" began to dominate the Bush and Obama administrations' justification of government bailouts for financial institutions in 2008 and 2009 as the full dimensions of the financial meltdown were becoming apparent.

OBAMA AND DODD AT TOP OF LIST

The 2008 Obama presidential campaign charged that the failure of Freddie and Fannie led back to a Bush-administration desire to deregulate financial services and the failure of the Bush administration to maintain adequate scrutiny of the operation of both GSEs. While Democrats have wanted to blame the subprime-mortgage meltdown on Republicans because it occurred while George W. Bush was president, Democrats still share the blame for being very cozy with mortgage giants Freddie and Fannie.

Granted, Republicans have pushed for financial-services deregulation since the Reagan administration. Still, the Glass-Steagall Act, a key piece of Depression-era legislation that created walls between banking, insurance, and investment-banking operations, was repealed in 1999 during the Clinton administration. Even here, the bill repealing Glass-Steagall was introduced in the Senate by Republican Phil Gramm of

Texas and in the house by Republican Jim Leach of Iowa, with the additional sponsorships of Virginia Republican representative Thomas Bliley, then chairman of the House Commerce Committee. What became known as the Gramm-Leach-Bliley Act was passed by Republican majorities on party lines in both houses of Congress. Democrats in Congress supported the act only in the final vote, after a conference charged with working out the differences between the Senate and House versions of the bill added language that strengthened the anti-redlining provisions of the Community Reinvestment Act of 1977, a law that continues to enjoy typically more Democratic support than Republican. Rolling back financial-services regulation, in the final analysis, resulted from a bipartisan effort in Congress.

A review of Federal Election Commission records back to 1989 reveals that Barack Obama, in just the first four years of his first term in the Senate, was still the second-largest recipient of Freddie Mac and Fannie Mae campaign contributions, lagging behind only Senator Christopher Dodd, now chairman of the Senate Banking Committee. According to OpenSecrets.com, from 1989 to 2008, Dodd led the list, receiving $165,400 in Fannie Mae and Freddie Mac campaign contributions, including contributions from PACs as well as from individuals, followed in second place by Obama, who received $126,349 in such contributions from 2004 to 2008.

DEMOCRATIC PARTY CONNECTIONS
TO ALLEGED ABUSES AT FANNIE MAE

In the aftermath of the U.S. government takeover of Fannie and Freddie, attention focused on three prominent Democrats who served as Fannie Mae executives: Franklin D. Raines, a former Clinton administration budget director; James A. Johnson, former aide to Democratic vice president Walter Mondale; and Jamie Gorelick, former Clinton administration deputy attorney general. All three prominent Democrats earned millions in compensation while serving as top Fannie Mae executives that was later questioned. Raines earned $90 million in his five years as Fannie Mae CEO, from 1999 to 2004; Johnson earned $21 million in just his last year serving as Fannie Mae CEO (1991 to 1998); and Gorelick earned an estimated $26 million serving as vice chair of Fannie Mae from 1998 to 2003.[23]

Raines's problems began in 2004, when Fannie Mae's regulator, the

Office of Federal Housing Enterprise Oversight, or OFHEO, and the Security and Exchange Commission's top accountant issued reports charging that under Raines's stewardship Fannie Mae had misstated earnings for three and a half years. The $9 billion restatement of earnings required by the OFHEO and SEC ended up wiping out 40 percent of Fannie Mae's originally stated profits from 2001 to mid-2004.[24] Raines resigned from Fannie Mae in December 2004, with a $19 million severance package.[25]

Raines continued playing the victim until April 2008, when he and two other Fannie Mae executives entered into a settlement of a civil lawsuit whose total value was some $31.4 million in connection with their roles in what amounted to an Enron-like accounting scandal. A civil suit accused them of manipulating Fannie Mae books to manufacture earnings from 1998 through 2004, in order to trigger for themselves millions of dollars in otherwise unearned bonuses.[26] In the final settlement, Raines and the others made payments totalling approximately $3 million. The balance of the settlement required the executives to give up sizable portions of their Fannie Mae stock options. None of those accused admitted wrongdoing in the matter.

A controversy broke out in July 2008 when the *Washington Post* reported that Raines had taken calls from Barack Obama's presidential campaign seeking his advice on mortgage and housing-policy matters.[27] After Republican presidential candidate Senator John McCain ran a television advertisement using the *Post* article as a source to claim Raines was an Obama adviser, Raines issued a denial that he was an adviser to Obama or that he had provided the Obama campaign with advice on housing or economic matters.[28] In September 2008, as the controversy continued, the *Post* stood behind its original report, noting that Raines's statement that month contradicted what he had told the newspaper in July.[29]

The Raines scandal represented a triumph for a prominent Fannie Mae whistle-blower, accounting manager Roger Barnes. Since 1999, Barnes had charged that Raines and other Fannie Mae executives had been manipulating earnings through "cookie jar" accounting in order to justify payment to themselves of hundreds of millions of dollars in bonuses. In his twenty-six-page testimony before OFHEO, Barnes detailed multiple deviations from Generally Accepted Accounting Principles, or GAAP, and his repeated efforts to bring these irregularities to the attention of a wide range of Fannie Mae managers and executives, all without positive result.[30]

Barnes said he had left Fannie Mae in October 2003 because he felt "forced out" after being excluded from working on the OFHEO investigation. "As a result of Fannie Mae's refusals to take the concerns I had raised about financial and accounting practices seriously, and the retaliation I faced for raising these concerns, I had no choice but to separate from the Company in October 2003," Barnes had said in his written October 2004 testimony to the Subcommittee on Capital Markets, Insurance, and Government-Sponsored Enterprises of the House Committee on Financial Services. Still, the OFHEO report on the Raines scandal cited Barnes thirty-four times in the first eighty pages of its two-hundred-page report.[31] Barnes, an African-American, as is Raines, reportedly received a $1 million settlement after threatening a whistle-blower lawsuit citing racial discrimination.[32]

James Johnson was appointed to head Obama's vice presidential selection committee, until a controversy concerning an alleged $7 million in questionable real estate loans he received on favorable terms from failed subprime-mortgage lender Countrywide Financial surfaced and forced him to resign from that position. The controversy began when the *Wall Street Journal* reported on June 7, 2008, that Countrywide, led by Angelo Mozilo, had extended millions of dollars in favorable home loans to Johnson and Raines because they were "Friends of Angelo," or "FoA," as such preferential borrowers were known in the inner circles of Countrywide.[33] The *Journal* carefully noted there was nothing illegal about a mortgage firm treating some borrowers better than others. Yet when two top Fannie Mae executives received the preferential mortgage treatment, a political problem was caused for the government-sponsored, shareholder-owned company, as well as for the Democratic Party and the Obama presidential campaign. A lawyer for Johnson told the *Journal* that his Countrywide home-mortgage loans were within industry practice; Raines did not respond to the newspaper's requests for comment.

In 1998, Fannie Mae vice chairman Jamie S. Gorelick received a bonus of $779,625, in connection with a scandal in which certain Fannie Mae employees were found to have falsified signatures on accounting transactions, allegedly in order to manipulate Fannie Mae books to meet 1998 earning targets, which in turn triggered multimillion-dollar bonuses for top executives, including Gorelick's more than three-quarter-million payment.[34] The 1998 bonus reported for then-chairman and CEO Johnson was $1.932 million and for then-chairman-designate Raines was $1.11 million. After leaving Fannie Mae, Gorelick encountered controversy a second time, after a 1995 memo she authored as deputy attorney general at the Justice Department during the Clinton administration surfaced while she was a member of the 9/11 Commission. The memo, calling for what became known as the "Gorelick Wall," appeared to bar federal antiterrorist investigators from accessing various federal records and databases that may have assisted them.[35]

JUST HOW BIG A GLOBAL CRISIS?

U.S. investment bankers sold mortgage-backed securities to overseas institutional investors as well as U.S. investors. Private investors, governments, and, in the Middle East, sovereign-wealth funds bought trillions of dollars of U.S. mortgage-backed securities packaged by Wall Street, regardless of how many subprime loans the mortgage bonds held. So the losses from the U.S. mortgage market meltdown quickly became global, once foreign banks and investment firms had to acknowledge their ownership of U.S. mortgage-backed securities that were now either worthless or nearly so because they had sunk so far below the market values when they were purchased.

At the height of the mortgage bubble, Wall Street was ready and willing to package almost anything into what became known as asset-backed securities, or ABSs. Investment bankers on Wall Street had figured out that they could "securitize," or package into a bond, almost anything that had a regular flow of monthly payments, as long as there was some form of ultimate collateral standing behind the credit. Mortgage-backed securities fall into the broader general classification of "asset-backed" or "collateralized" securities that can be packaged into bonds.

As long as there is a cash flow—the monthly mortgage payments, for instance, on a home—that is backed up by collateral—the home itself, in the case of mortgage securities—then the asset category can be securitized into a multimillion- or multibillion-dollar bond to be sold to institutional investors to hold as an asset. As soon as investment bankers caught on to the idea that they could package mortgages into bonds, they realized many other asset classes were also available to securitize. Car loans, credit-card loans, and student loans were natural follow-on asset categories available for securitization. Like mortgages, these other consumer loans had monthly cash flows and collateral, even if the collateral involved recourse to the assets of the credit-card borrower or a lien on the student's future career.

Nor did Wall Street stop there. Eventually commercial loans to businesses and commercial mortgages became available to securitization. With commercial loans and commercial mortgages, the default problem is very similar to the default problem with mortgages. When the economy turns down, the marginally qualified homebuyer in the subprime market finds it increasingly difficult to make monthly mortgage payments. Eventually, the subprime homeowner who loses a job also loses his home to foreclosure. In hard economic times, the same happens to marginally qualified businesses. When businesses fail, they default on commercial loans as well as their commercial mortgages. The wave of homes in foreclosure throughout the United States beginning in late 2006 was followed by a wave of empty strip malls, closed businesses, and commercial businesses with space to lease.

The ultimate losers in all cases were the investors holding the ABSs into which these complex consumer and commercial credits had been packaged into bonds. Wall Street sold the full variety of U.S.-generated ABSs to international investors, just as Wall Street aggressively sold MBS bonds around the world. Wall Street packaged even state and municipal bonds into ABSs and sold them globally, without worrying about whether the states or municipalities issuing the bonds might ever default, or whether the buyers of these bonds truly understood what they were buying or the risks involved. Insurance companies such as AIG formed derivatives contracts known as credit-default swaps, or CDS, that insured ABS risks against default. So when the ABSs began to fail, AIG was on the hook for potentially hundreds of billions and possibly even trillions in CDS derivative-contract losses.

In late February 2009, a secret seventeen-page report was circulated among European Union finance ministers warning EU governments that toxic assets still held by EU banks and investment firms could still total a massive £16.3 trillion in losses, approximately $24.4 trillion. European Commission officials estimated that "impaired assets" of this magnitude could amount to 44 percent of total EU bank balance sheets. A loss of bank assets of this magnitude was considered potentially destabilizing to the European Union itself and may involve a government-backed bailout effort that stretches across the EU's twenty-seven nation-state members.

A news story on this secret EU report originally appeared in the *Tele-*

graph of London on February 11, 2009. However, the *Telegraph* then sanitized the story and removed the numbers.[36] Nevertheless, a reader posting to a European blog had captured the original story.[37] In the re-written story remaining on the *Telegraph*'s website, the newspaper simply reported that the EU government bailout required for a problem of this magnitude could send the EU into crisis. Omitted was any mention of the quantity of the toxic assets still on EU bank balance sheets; they were described only as "massive."

The meltdown in subprime home loans spread globally as the recession deepened and European banks began experiencing asset losses from the bonds that the banks held on European assets as well as U.S. assets. Predictably, EU banks followed U.S. banks in experiencing a broad range of asset losses from asset-backed securities.

THE MORTGAGE MARKET GONE BUST

The desire to see the poor in America own homes traces back decades, to the Carter administration and the passage of the Community Reinvestment Act. Democrats and Republicans alike supported the cause in their desire to be seen as champions of the American dream of homeownership, extended to all Americans whether or not they could afford a home. Step-by-step, the federal government encouraged the subprime market to develop, first with historically low interest rates that made mortgages extremely affordable and then with the process of securitization, which promised mortgage originators large fees and little or no risk for making even irresponsible home loans to completely unqualified buyers. Looking back to President Lyndon Johnson's Great Society, the "ownership society" proclaimed by President George W. Bush looked like a dream come true.

The problem was that the U.S. mortgage market was heading to a certain crash. If only a few hundred thousand subprime mortgages had been made, the magnitude of the problem would have been insignificant to the U.S. economy, even if all the subprime mortgages failed. But incrementally the United States had developed the largest subprime mortgage market ever seen in the history of the world. When the subprime market finally crashed, it had reached such large proportions that the U.S. economy was thrown into a deep recession that quickly became a global downturn. Once again, a difference in size—which had grown incrementally—became a difference in phenomenon.

Today's mortgage crash is not just a collapse of the mortgage market in the United States. The crisis has become a worldwide crisis in which most, if not all, of the banks and major financial institutions in the U.S. and Europe may be technically bankrupt. The losses in financial institution assets are now measuring in the tens of trillions of dollars. How the U.S. or EU economies will absorb these losses remains to be seen. Nor is the U.S. taxpayer positioned to pay the bill, not when the magnitudes of current and future promised entitlement payments have already bankrupted the U.S. Treasury.

Wall Street has solidly rejected the Obama administration's approach to stimulating the economy, rejecting the proposition that trillions of dollars in deficit spending aimed at creating a massive government apparatus to expand the social-welfare state will create enough jobs to end the recession. Even CNBC's Jim Cramer, usually a reliable cheerleader for the stock market, told NBC *Today* host Matt Lauer that President Obama's economic policy amounted to the "greatest wealth destruction I've seen by a president."[38] Cramer charged that the Obama administration was destroying the savings of millions of Americans. Cramer wondered if President Obama realized that the stock market was "falling apart" and that the administration's agenda "had a big hand in that happening."

In September 2008, the *Wall Street Journal* reported that U.S. mortgage delinquencies had reached nearly 6.6 percent, up sharply from 2 percent in 2005–2006.[39] What the Obama administration risked was a "silent majority" push-back against economic stimulus packages that were perceived as creating an imperial federal government, a "New Deal on steroids," with a welfare state beyond anything FDR had ever imagined in the 1930s.

Middle-class Americans who accepted social-welfare programs when they were perceived as a safety net were much less tolerant when taxes soared and budget deficits were being measured in trillions. With the deepening crisis in home foreclosures, the Economic Panic of 2009 had spread from Wall Street to Main Street.

THREE

Still Dependent on Foreign Oil

Why do we believe so much false bad news about the environment, resources and population?

—Economist Julian Simon, *Hoodwinking the Nation,* 1999[1]

For decades, environmentalists in the United States fought hard to restrict oil and gas exploration. In recent years, "global warming" enthusiasts such as former vice president Al Gore joined the environmentalists in the campaign to limit oil and gas exploration in the United States, believing that the production and use of "fossil fuels" exudes harmful carbon dioxide. The scare is that "greenhouse gases" as a result of human activity cause the temperature of the earth to warm up, such that the resultant dramatic climate changes cause undesirable effects, such as a projected rising of the oceans. Radicals in the environmental or climate-change movements appear at times to be opposed to industrial activity, or possibly even anticapitalist, in their core beliefs.

As a result of litigation and organized political activity launched by environmental and global-warming activists, oil and natural-gas exploration and development in the United States has failed to keep up with U.S. demand over the past few decades. The United States, for instance, has not built a new refinery in more than three decades, largely because of the NIMBY, or "Not in My Back Yard," syndrome, which has led many Americans to see refineries as dirty, or polluting, rather than as signs of robust economic activity capable of creating jobs and building wealth in a community.

Yet the fault for U.S. dependence on foreign oil does not lie strictly with environmentalists and climate-change activists. As long as Americans continue to believe in peak-oil theories, oil companies can more easily charge a premium for what is perceived to be a diminishing commodity. Moreover, the primary responsibility of the boards of directors of U.S.-based multinational oil companies is to maximize profits at those companies internationally, and not specifically to reduce U.S. dependence on oil, or to educate the U.S. public on the abundance of oil worldwide.

U.S. dependence on foreign oil has not been accidental, and it figures as squarely into the Economic Panic of 2009 as a major contributor to our negative balance of trade with China. As a consequence of our dependence on foreign oil, U.S. capital is leaving the country in massive amounts at a time when major U.S. financial institutions and key corporations, including Chrysler and General Motors, faced insolvency from lack of capital. Ironically, the Economic Panic of 2009 has positioned China and the Middle Eastern oil countries to be major players in the America-for-sale chapter in U.S. economic history, soon to be written as the next chapter in the global economic crisis.

U.S. DEPENDENCE ON FOREIGN OIL

Every day, the United States consumes approximately 21 million barrels of oil, and imports about 13 million barrels, which constitutes more than 60 percent of the total oil consumed in the United States.

According to the Energy Information Agency, the percentage of foreign oil consumed in the United States has grown steadily from approximately 35 percent during the Nixon administration, in 1973.[2] To gain a historical perspective, remember that during World War II, U.S. oil production fueled virtually the entire Allied war effort. The trend is definitely not in favor of a positive U.S. balance of trade.

In 2008, the top-five oil exporters to the United States were Canada, at 1.886 million barrels a day; Saudi Arabia, 1.541 million barrels a day; Mexico, 1.220 million; Nigeria, 1.102 million; and Venezuela, .980 million.[3] Of these, only Saudi Arabia, Nigeria, and Venezuela are members of the Organization of the Petroleum-Exporting Countries, or OPEC. Approximately 11 to 12 percent of all oil consumed in the United States, about 2 million barrels a day, comes from Persian Gulf states.

Because of the economic slowdown, total petroleum-products consumption in the United States declined in 2008 by almost 1.2 million barrels a day, or 5.8 percent from the 2007 average, the largest annual decline since 1980.[4] Still, three of the top-five oil importers remain within the Western Hemisphere: Canada, Mexico, and Venezuela.

Oil importation represents a massive and continuing transfer of U.S. wealth overseas that we can reverse only if we resolve to reduce our dependence on foreign oil.

With oil at $40 a barrel, the price in late 2008 and early 2009, the United States was sending more than $520 million a day overseas, with some $80 million a day going to the Persian Gulf. With oil at $147 a barrel, the all-time high, in July 2008, some $1.9 billion was sent overseas each day, with approximately $294 million a day sent to Persian Gulf states. In sum, our dependence on foreign oil creates a continuing negative strain on our balance of trade and a resultant outflow of dollars into the foreign-exchange reserves of oil-producing countries. Moreover, our dependence on foreign oil provides a continuing cash-flow influx to Persian Gulf oil-producing countries, allowing these governments to amass more billions into sovereign-wealth funds.

Remember, the United States is also dependent on Middle Eastern governments, largely through their agents in London, to join countries such as China and Japan to purchase the trillions of dollars in U.S. debt that the U.S. Treasury must sell to finance federal budget deficits. Moreover, Middle Eastern sovereign-wealth funds are positioned to make massive capital investments and purchase key U.S. assets, including financial institutions, U.S. infrastructure projects, and corporations, even if dollar-rich countries in the Middle East and China are temporarily holding off on making direct equity investments into the United States until U.S. equity markets stabilize.

So the U.S. Treasury is in a double bind to finance trillions of dollars in federal budget deficits while also seeing billions of dollars flowing out of the U.S. to oil-producing countries. Buttressing failing U.S. financial institutions with hundreds of billions of dollars in borrowed funds is a short-term strategy to restore the capital these companies need to survive long-term. In other words, the Treasury now has to solve two problems: induce China and the Middle Eastern petrodollar countries to continue to buy U.S. debt while figuring out a way to stem the flow of dollars into the foreign-exchange reserves of other countries.

SOVEREIGN-WEALTH FUNDS

The Middle Eastern oil-producing countries have been unusually focused on accumulating petrodollar earnings in sovereign-wealth funds, whereas other oil-producing countries, such as Canada and Mexico, have not. Sovereign-wealth funds in six Persian Gulf countries, including Kuwait, the United Arab Emirates, and Qatar, have now amassed $1.7 trillion, according to figures compiled by *BusinessWeek* in 2008.[5] Estimating accurately the total sovereign-wealth funds in the Middle East is hard to do, largely because countries such as Saudi Arabia do not have the same types of public-disclosure requirements as apply in the United States. Conceivably, the oil-producing countries in the Middle East have several trillion in petrodollar earnings accumulated in various, largely secretive government-investment structures that stand ready to make investments around the world as opportunities arise.

Increasingly, U.S. investment bankers are traveling to the Middle East to meet sovereign-wealth-fund managers, getting ready to introduce the U.S. public to a new cast of Middle Eastern investment bankers with Islamic names who head these Islamic government investment funds. Equity investments by sovereign-wealth funds differ from traditional private or public investment in that the equity invested is not owned by a private investor or public holder of listed common stock, but rather by a foreign government that owns the stock resulting from the investment as a government equity.

Not surprisingly, China followed the lead of the Middle Eastern petrodollar countries in utilizing foreign-exchange reserves to create its first sovereign-wealth fund, the China Investment Corporation, on September 29, 2007.[6] By 2009, Chinese sovereign-wealth funds were estimated to be the same size as similar funds in the Middle East, totaling approximately $2 trillion.

DUBAI INVESTS IN CITIGROUP AND NASDAQ

In November 2007, the Abu Dhabi Investment Authority, or ADIA, placed a $7.5 billion capital infusion into Citigroup in exchange for an ownership position of approximately 4.9 percent in the bank.[7] ADIA is an investment arm of the Abu Dhabi government, with an estimated $1 trillion under management. Abu Dhabi is the second most populous city in the United Arab Emirates, after Dubai, and the seat of the Abu Dhabi government. According to the *Wall Street Journal*, the investment made ADIA one of the largest shareholders of Citigroup,[8] exceeding the stake held by Saudi Prince Alwaleed bin Talal, reputedly one of the largest shareholders of Citigroup before the Abu Dhabi investment.[9]

At the time Abu Dhabi made the investment, Citigroup was trading at $30.70 a share, considerably off the stock's high of $57 a share, set in late December 2006. At the end of 2008, subprime-mortgage losses had forced Citigroup into dire straits, more than could be overcome by the Abu Dhabi investment. The federal government in November 2008 injected Citigroup with a total of $45 billion in bailout funds plus a $300 billion guarantee against anticipated losses in troubled bank assets.[10]

Unfortunately, government bailouts and guarantees, even of this magnitude, were not enough to solve Citibank's problems.

On February 20, 2009, when Democratic senator Christopher J. Dodd of Connecticut, the powerful chairman of the Senate Banking Committee, told Bloomberg Television that nationalization of troubled banks such as Citigroup might be necessary, Citigroup began trading at under $2 share. "I don't welcome that [nationalization] at all," Dodd told Bloomberg, "but I could see how it's possible it may happen. I'm concerned that we may end up having to do that [nationalize some large banks like Citigroup], for at least a short time." [11]

The price of Citigroup shares plummeted for a simple reason: if Citigroup were nationalized, holders of Citigroup common stock stood to lose their entire investment. What this means for Abu Dhabi is that a $7.5 billion investment when Citigroup was trading at $30.70 was worth approximately $500 million when Citigroup was trading around $2. This was a dramatic loss in principal that no investor could afford to take lightly, regardless how wealthy. The pain was not reduced by the fact that the investor in this case was a government entity. In the Middle East, the sovereign-wealth funds and the investments the funds make are ultimately owned by the ruling families themselves.

Dubai, the largest of the emirates in the U.A.E., fared better than Abu Dhabi. In September 2007, through a series of complex transactions, Dubai acquired 19.9 percent of NASDAQ in New York, placing the Arab government in an ownership position of the key U.S. stock exchange.[12] The transaction was made through Borse Dubai, a holding company 100 percent owned by the government of the Emirate of Dubai and controlled by Mohammed bin Rashid al-Maktoum, the head of the Dubai ruling family. Dubai had just acquired a major equity stake in a cornerstone of U.S. financial-industry infrastructure. While Dubai was not insisting NASDAQ operate according to Islamic law, there appeared to be no provisions in the transaction that would prohibit that requirement from being imposed sometime in the future.

U.S. TREASURY NEGOTIATES WITH MIDDLE EASTERN GOVERNMENTS

Foreign investments in U.S. companies are subject to approval from the Committee on Foreign Investment in the United States, or CIFUS, organized within the U.S. Treasury. Even approval by CIFUS is no guarantee the foreign investment will be well received by the U.S. public. In 2006, a national outrage broke out over port security and potential terrorist threats when a Dubai company, Dubai Ports World, proposed to take over operation of several major U.S. ports as part of an acquisition involving the London-based Peninsular & Oriental Steam Navigation. By the closing months of 2007, however, the U.S. economy had been deteriorating so rapidly that Middle Eastern investments aimed to bail out failing U.S. financial institutions received almost no public outcry. Suddenly the American public perceived the infusion of foreign capital from the Middle East as welcome.

In early 2008, the U.S. Treasury began discussions with Dubai and Abu Dhabi to establish ground rules for the U.A.E. governments to invest in U.S. financial institutions while reassuring the U.S. government that the investments by the Muslim states would not impose restrictions usually dictated by Islamic law. In March 2008, the *Wall Street Journal* reported that Abu Dhabi sent a three-page letter to U.S. Treasury Secretary Henry Paulson and other Western finance officials spelling out a set of principles that would guide Abu Dhabi's investing philosophy.[13] Specifically, Abu Dhabi pledged it would not use its investment money to achieve political goals in the United States. The letter was also sent to the finance ministers of the other Group of Seven industrialized nations (G7), the International Monetary Fund (IMF), the World Bank, the Organisation for Economic Co-operation and Development, and the European Commission.

As the Obama administration took office, a key goal was to stabilize the economy, in full recognition that Middle Eastern sovereign-wealth funds were unlikely to invest more capital in failing U.S. financial institutions until a bottom in the toxic-asset crisis had been reached. The equation was simple: U.S. petrodollars flowed into Middle Eastern sovereign-wealth funds; now, with trillions of dollars lost in U.S. financial institution capital, the U.S. government was positioning for petrodollars held by Middle Eastern governments to return to the United States, returning as investments in struggling U.S. financial institutions.

Still, Middle Eastern sovereign-wealth-fund investments in U.S. companies remains a double-edged sword: the United States needs the equity capital, yet the concern remains that with the investment will come a political agenda that may be laden with religious overtones. In either case, the result is the same. U.S. banks and brokerage firms could easily end up being owned by Middle Eastern governments. So too could major U.S. corporations, including those with national security implications. Following that could be U.S. infrastructure, as increasingly cash-strapped state governments invite foreigners to invest in public-private partnerships to convert U.S. highways to a next generation of toll roads.

AN ENERGY POLICY DOOMED TO FAIL

The United States is caught in a dependence on carbon-based fuels against which environmentalists and climate-change activists have waged war for decades. At the same time, alternative technologies, such as wind turbines or solar panels, have not proved sufficiently robust to replace carbon based fuels in anything but marginal applications. The only possible conclusion is that the United States currently has an energy policy that is doomed to perpetuate the flight of U.S. capital to foreign oil-producing states. What is hard to comprehend is how U.S. thinking about oil has become so confined into the narrow terms of the current debate. Looking at the hard evidence, the United States can increase the amount of domestic oil we produce, thereby reducing our dependence on foreign oil. Natural gas and atomic energy are two energy alternatives that are robust, even if strong opposition from environmentalists and climate-change activists is certain, especially in the case of nuclear energy.

The housing bubble and the energy crisis are both crises of our own making. Pain from the bursting of the housing bubble will not subside until housing prices retreat to more normal levels, down from the artificial peak reached in 2006. Pain from the energy crisis will not subside until the United States expands utilization of existing domestic oil and natural gas resources while building more nuclear energy plants. Research and development should continue to see if wind power, solar energy, or biofuels can be made to handle economically a large percentage of U.S. energy needs.

How and why have public-policy makers allowed the United States to become increasingly dependent upon foreign oil? Much of U.S. energy policy is based on questionable presumptions, such as the assumption that the world has hit "peak-oil" production.

THE "PEAK OIL" HOAX

An underlying argument in the energy debate is the theory of peak oil, which postulates that oil is a finite resource that we have begun to exhaust; oil-production rates, then, are inevitably bound to decline.[14] Peak-oil theories support the arguments of environmentalists and radical global-warming activists: If we are bound to run out of "fossil fuels," then why not look for energy alternatives now?

The running-out-of-oil scare began in 1956, when M. King Hubbert, a geophysicist working in the Shell Oil research lab in Houston, published a graph that predicted U.S. oil production would peak in the 1970s. Hubbert's then-unproven assertion was based primarily on an understanding of a normal bell-shaped distribution curve, which he postulated represented the predicted U.S. experience with oil production. In simple terms, the graph showed almost no oil production in the early 1900s, with the curve rising to a peak in the early 1970s; after that the curve drops off gradually, until there is no more oil production in the United States by 2050. Because a normal curve rises on the page like a mountain, the analysis became known as "Hubbert's Peak." The name also stuck because "peak" suggests we will reach a high point of oil production from which we will inexorably fall back to zero, the same place where we began prior to 1859 and the historic Drake well in Pennsylvania.

A central problem with Hubbert's argument is that oil production did not peak in the 1970s, as predicted. Still, peak-oil adherents have refused to accept conflicting evidence as proof that the theory itself is flawed. Since Hubbert's Peak was first postulated, believers have simply moved out the date of peak production to accommodate conflicting evidence. Believers insist that their revisions are minor corrections and that Hubbert's basic concept is inevitable. Hubbert's Peak has become a tautological extension of fossil-fuel oil theory itself. In other words, if we assume fossils (or biological material of some sort), are responsible for the production of oil, and there were only so many fossils (or only so much biological material available), then there can be only a finite amount of oil. Thus with increased exploration and development we are bound to experience a decline in the rate of oil production sooner or later. Put simply, the logic of the fossil fuel argument dictates we will run out of oil.

Unfortunately for the adherents of peak-oil theory, the Energy Information Administration of the U.S. Department of Energy documents that the world's proven oil reserves totaled 1.3 trillion barrels in 2009, the largest amount ever in human history, despite oil consumption having doubled worldwide since the 1970s.[15] These data hardly support a contention that world oil reserves are being exhausted, a necessary corollary of peak-oil theory. Most Americans conditioned to thinking the United States is running out of oil would be surprised to know that we still *export* some 1.6 million barrels of oil a day,[16] despite importing some 13 million barrels a day. Today the United States still ranks as the world's third-largest *producer* of oil, producing 8.3 million barrels of oil a day in 2006, behind Saudi Arabia at 10.7 million barrels and Russia at 9.7 million barrels. This means the U.S. still produces more oil than four of our top-five oil-importing countries—China, Mexico, Venezuela, and Nigeria—as well as more oil than Iran, the United Arab Emirates, Kuwait, or Iraq.[17]

A further indication that peak-oil theory is a hoax occurred in 2008, when oil prices spiked to an all-time high of $147 a barrel, only to recede to under $40 before the end of the year. When oil prices spiked, peak-oil theorists claimed the dramatic price increase was proof that oil-production rates had slowed to create disequilibrium with increasing world oil demand.

The truth was that in both instances oil prices were largely determined by supply and demand. Oil traders, including those speculators bidding in the oil futures markets, had not realized until after July 2008 that worldwide oil demand was decreasing dramatically due to the worldwide economic recession, or else they underestimated the severity of the downturn. But by the end of 2008, even the speculators had realized that oil demand had subsided dramatically worldwide.

What was clear in July 2008 was that even at $147 a barrel there was no shortage of oil in the United States—no rationing or gas lines at service stations. There was no proof that oil was in irreversibly short supply.

ALTERNATIVE ENERGIES: WIND, SOLAR, AND BIOFUELS

Today wind and solar power contribute minuscule amounts of the electricity and total energy consumed by the United States. Even enthusiastic proponents of wind and solar power estimate it would take four more decades of development before we could switch away from coal, oil, natural gas, and nuclear power plants to meet even 69 percent of U.S. electricity and 35 percent of total U.S. energy needs.[18] The Energy Department released an enthusiastic report in May 2008 claiming it was technically feasible to harness enough wind power to provide up to 20 percent of the nation's total electricity needs by 2030.[19] Yet converting to wind or solar power requires huge tracts of land, involving tens of thousands of square miles that would have to be covered with photovoltaic panels or wind-turbine farms. Even then, a score of problems persist, creating technical challenges for successfully integrating intermittent wind and solar power into a nationwide power grid that requires energy on a twenty-four-hour basis. The U.S. power grid consists of some two hundred thousand miles of power lines divided among some five hundred owners, with every addition to the grid likely to provoke legal challenges from property owners.[20]

Another problem is that the wind does not always blow and the sun does not always shine. So wind-turbine farms and solar panel fields need conventional hydrocarbon-powered generators to meet grid requirements that do not vary with wind ar sun intensity. Also, wind-turbine-generated or solar-generated electricity cannot be stored on an industrial basis. So when wind turbines or solar panels generate excess electricity, the only economical alternative is to sell that electricity off to grid competitors, often at a loss. Additionally, NIMBY objections surface whenever government officials propose to create wind turbine farms or solar panel fields. Memorable here are the objections that Senator Ted Kennedy, a typically environmentally sensitive advocate of hydrocarbon alternatives, voiced when Massachusetts proposed allowing wind turbines off his beloved Cape Cod.

A 2007 study titled "Calculating the Real Cost of Industrial Wind Power,"[21] produced in Bruce County, Ontario, Canada, examined data from wind power generated on an industrial basis in Europe over the last ten years. The study concluded, "As the public increasingly learns the real costs of wind turbine development, publically subsidized industrial wind projects are rapidly becoming unacceptable." The study noted that in Denmark, which has one of the world's highest concentrations of wind turbines, approximately 80 percent of the wind energy that is produced has to be sold to Denmark's neighbors Norway and Sweden "at a price far below the cost of production in order to stabilize the grid because it is produced during periods of low consumer demand." Conversely, the study observed, Denmark is frequently forced to buy hydro and nuclear power from its neighbors. "The net outcome," the Ontario study concluded, "is that Denmark with the highest amount of installed wind energy has the highest consumer electricity charges in Europe. Danish households already pay 100 percent more for their electricity than other European customers."

Nor are biofuels necessarily energy efficient. The production of ethanol may burn up more hydrocarbon fuel than it saves. Consider the different uses of hydrocarbon fuels needed to convert corn into ethanol. Corn has to be planted, grown, and harvested. Then corn needs to be transported to an ethanol plant and converted to ethanol through a chemical process that relies on hydrocarbon fuels.

An analysis conducted by David Pimentel, professor of ecology and agriculture at Cornell University, and Tad Patzek, professor of civil and environmental engineering at the University of California, Berkeley,[22] came to this conclusion by taking into account the production of pesticides and fertilizers needed to grow the crops, the running of farm machinery and irrigation, the grounding and transporting of the crop, and the fermenting and distilling of ethanol from the water mix. They concluded that corn requires 29 percent more hydrocarbon energy than the fuel produced, switchgrass requires 45 percent more, and wood biomass requires 57 percent more. The same conclusions held for soybean plants used to produce biodiesel fuel (27 percent more hydrocarbon fuel used than produced) and sunflower plants (118 percent more hydrocarbon fuel used). The analysis did not factor in the additional costs of federal and state subsidies that are passed on to consumers in the form of additional taxes.

"The United States desperately needs a liquid fuel replacement for oil in the near future," Pimentel was quoted as saying, "but producing ethanol or biodiesel from plant biomass is going down the wrong road, because you use more energy to produce these fuels than you get out from the combustion of these products." He went on to add: "The government spends more than $3 billion a year to subsidize ethanol production when it does not provide a net energy balance or gain, is not a renewable energy source or an economic fuel. Further, its production and use contribute to air, water and soil pollution and global warming." Pimentel had nothing positive to say about the endeavor: "Ethanol production requires large fossil energy input, and therefore, it is contributing to oil and natural gas imports and U.S. deficits." He further added that the vast majority of tax benefits and subsidies went not to farmers but to large ethanol-producing corporations.

What the debate here highlights is that wind turbines, solar panels, and biofuels are alternative energy sources that may be renewable but should not be accepted uncritically as a panacea for U.S. dependence on foreign oil anytime soon. *Renewable energy* is a promising term in that it implies we will never run out, regardless of how much we use. *Alternative energy* is also an alluring phrase, suggesting we should not get stuck in traditional energy solutions when options exist that may be superior. The problem is that both agendas largely have only political suasion behind them, not demonstrated proof that wind turbines, solar panels, or biofuels could find a market without the benefit of government subsidies.

THE PICKENS ENERGY PLAN

Billionaire oilman T. Boone Pickens has invested $2 billion to build the world's largest wind farm in Pampa, Texas, a small town in the Texas panhandle.[23] Pickens has created a website to promote his "Pickens Plan" solution for a U.S. energy policy that will wean the U.S. from dependence on foreign oil.[24] So far, Pickens has spent approximately $58 million to broadcast a series of television commercials promoting his agenda. Pickens will lose his investment unless Dallas agrees to create the necessary connections to transmit the electricity generated by the Pampa wind-turbine farm to the city.

One commercial begins by tracking U.S. oil imports from 42 percent in 1970 to "almost 70 percent" today, and still "climbing every minute." Pickens's somewhat inflated numbers also assert that "over $700 billion leaves this country to foreign nations every year," an amount "four times the cost of the Iraqi War." Pickens, typically a strong financial supporter of Republican candidates, made a point of "sitting out" the

2008 presidential campaign. He then formed strong ties with the incoming Obama administration to advance the Democtatic Party's alternative energy agenda.

The comprehensive Pickens Plan involves using solar power as well as wind to provide electricity to cities. He then wants to switch eighteen-wheeler commercial trucks to natural gas, with a goal of converting 300,000 of the nation's fleet of 6.5 million long-haul trucks. Pickens believes electric batteries will be the ultimate solution for automobiles. He openly acknowledges that billions of dollars will have to be spent to modernize electric grids throughout the country, to modify long-haul trucks as well as to provide a natural-gas infrastructure of service stations around the country, and to create a new generation of battery-powered cars.

The "pillars" of the Pickens Plan, listed on his website, include:

- Create millions of new jobs by building out the capacity to generate up to 22 percent of our electricity from wind. Add to that with additional solar capacity;

- Build a twenty-first-century-backbone electrical grid;

- Provide incentives for homeowners and the owners of commercial buildings to upgrade their insulation and other energy savings options; and

- Use America's natural gas to replace imported oil as a transportation fuel.

The Pickens Plan is reminiscent of many initiatives that have been discussed since the administration of Jimmy Carter in the 1970s. Anyone who has driven through California has seen hundreds of abandoned wind turbines that were built from the 1970s onward as a result of various tax-incentive subsidies that attempted to promote the alternative-energy or renewable-energy agendas of past decades.

Still, Pickens pleads, "I've been an oilman all my life. But this is one emergency we can't drill our way out of." [25] The truth is that if the federal government or the state of Texas does not spend hundreds of millions of dollars to connect the Pickens-built wind farm to the electrical grid in Dallas, Pickens is left with a lot of wind turbines blowing in the wind in the dusty Texas panhandle, facing approximately a $2 billion loss on his wind-turbine adventure. [26] When we examine the amount of money Pickens has at stake in this venture, it is no wonder he has pumped millions into running a television campaign promoting a vision of alternative energy that features wind turbines.

Granted, wind turbines and solar panels have been proven to have limited applicability to generating electricity. Yet if we return to the principle that a difference in scale is a difference in phenomenon, going from 1 percent of all electricity generated by wind and solar power to perhaps 20 percent will require not just an expansion of wind and solar technology, but an entirely different electrical grid system. Even then, the expanded wind and solar power system may not work. To power New York City by wind power may require dedicating a landmass equivalent to the state of New Jersey for the purpose. Even then, an electric grid powered by wind turbines or solar panels would require extensive hydrocarbon fuel backups to prevent the grid from collapsing when the wind stopped blowing or the sun stopped shining. Ironically, the backup may end up expending more hydrocarbon fuel than would have been expended if the traditional power grid had just been upgraded to "twenty-first-century standards" by bringing more nuclear power online.

Another truth is that Pickens is a peak-oil-theory believer who, as a result, sees no long-term future for oil. Even if Pickens's motivation derives entirely from this intellectual conviction, his proposition that wind and solar power will be more than a marginal addition to the U.S. power equation in the twenty-first century remains to be proven. Once the nation starts down the path of alternative or renewable energies, billions of dollars could well be spent constructing another technology that was doomed from the start, another version of Howard Hughes's *Spruce Goose*. To return to our analysis that size matters, solar and wind energy would need to be several orders of magnitude more powerful to produce the energy an industrialized nation like the United States needs to operate.

THE GLOBAL-WARMING HOAX

The earth has warmed considerably since thousands of years ago, when North America was largely covered by glaciers and mammoths roamed free. Yet, proving that cavemen and their carbon fires were responsible for the retraction of the glaciers and the disappearance of the mammoths is a stretch. The argument over global warming is not whether the earth has warmed in recent decades, but whether human activity is responsible. Truly, when we look back over millions of years of geological history, the earth has gone through many warming and cooling cycles, most of which occurred long before evidence that human beings existed at all.

In March 2008, more than a hundred internationally prominent environmental scientists presented research papers to the 2008 International Conference on Climate Change in New York City, arguing that global warming is a natural process, not likely the result of human activities. The conference was organized by the Heartland Institute[27] to provide public refutation to Al Gore and the United Nations International Panel on Climate Change, or IPCC.[28] Both had contended that the science on global warming is "settled," with an "established scientific consensus" that human beings are at fault for causing the earth to warm dangerously.

Environmental scientist Dr. S. Fred Singer kicked off the conference by releasing a report titled "Nature, Not Human Activity Rules the Climate," summarizing the three-year international scientific research project conducted by the Nongovernmental International Panel on Climate Change, or NIPCC, which Singer headed.[29] "There are many factors that affect the climate," Singer told World Net Daily. "What we can now exclude by scientific evidence is the argument that greenhouse gases are an important factor in causing global warming." Singer and the NIPCC agreed that global warming occurred in the twentieth century but disagreed with the claim that human activity was responsible, arguing instead that natural phenomena were likely the dominant causes.

The NIPCC scientists contended that the U.N. agenda "is largely hypothetical and not sustained by observations," and is driven by complex mathematical models. The computer models utilized by advocates of climate change, the NIPCC scientists claimed, are only valid in a "virtual computer world" and fail to produce reliable real-world predictions that can be empirically verified.

"Computer models undoubtedly have their place as a way of projecting possible consequences when one or more variables are changed," the NIPCC scientists wrote. "However, models do not represent reality, yet the IPCC persists in treating them as if they do." The NIPCC report presented scientific evidence that solar-wind variability is a primary cause of climate change, a better explanation for twentieth-century warming than greenhouse gas effects. Moreover, the NIPCC report argued that the IPCC's estimates of future human-generated carbon dioxide emissions are too high. Besides, higher concentrations of carbon dioxide have been beneficial to plant and animal life.

"Global warming is attributable to natural causes," Singer told reporters, "so in that sense global warming is unstoppable, regardless of what measures Al Gore or the U.N. want to impose on us with new international governmental regulations."

On November 17, 2007, in Valencia, Spain, the IPCC released a report titled "Climate Change 2007," which argued that "much of the observed increase in globally averaged temperatures since the mid-20th century is very likely due to the observed increase in anthropogenic GHG [i.e., greenhouse gas] concentrations." [30] The United Nations has utilized the IPCC to launch an aggressive agenda, largely supporting the Kyoto Protocol, calling for the establishment of a global response to climate change. At the core of the U.N. agenda is an array of recommended governmental policies designed to reduce carbon dioxide emissions produced by burning carbon-based fuels. These policies include the creation of an international carbon market to impose economic penalties for noncompliance.

"Al Gore and the U.N. have a fixation with the argument that we cause global warming," Singer said. "Besides that, look at the billions of tax dollars going into various schemes like subsidizing biofuels. We're being charged twice by the global-warming alarmists—once in new taxes the U.N. is planning to impose on us and then again as consumers who will ultimately have to bear the cost of these new global taxes."

Interestingly, after a series of severe winters and unseasonably cold summers experienced in the U.S. since 2005, global-warming alarmists shifted the ground of their concern from the more limited topic of global warming to the broader topic of climate change. In other words, when computer models that had predicted global warming and a resulting disastrous rise in sea levels failed to be accurate, global-warming theorists refused to admit that the evidence disproved their theory. Instead, global-warming theorists, like the peak-oil theorists before them, just shifted their ground, arguing that the real concern was that increased emissions of greenhouse gases produced dramatic and dangerous climate changes that might just include global warming, in certain instances.

That the antipathy toward carbon-based fuels is a political and not a scientific agenda is made clear by the Obama administration's determination to impose a "cap-and-trade" carbon-emissions tax on the United States.

A "CAP-AND-TRADE" CARBON-EMISSIONS TAX

A cap-and-trade emissions control scheme is necessary to impose on the U.S. economy only if global warming and climate change can be attributed to human activity by irrefutable scientific evidence. Otherwise, what amounts to a significant drag on the U.S. economy should be avoided.

The concept advanced by the Obama administration is similar to the cap-and-trade program introduced in the Clean Air Act of 1990 to reduce sulfur emissions that cause acid rain.[31] The idea, derived from global-warming activists, is to reduce the amount of carbon-dioxide emissions a company is allowed to make. The "cap" is the enforceable maximum limit of carbon dioxide a particular company will be allowed to emit. Under the assumption that it will be easier for some companies to reduce their carbon emissions than other companies, a cap-and-trade system allows companies that are able to reduce their carbon emissions below their allowance to sell their extra permits to companies having a more difficult time reducing their carbon emissions. If the federal government auctions the carbon emissions permits to the companies struggling to reduce carbon emissions, a revenue stream is created for the U.S. Treasury to collect. A goal might be to reduce carbon emissions by U.S. companies to 80 percent of some specific target level, perhaps the 1990 level of U.S. carbon emissions, by the year 2050.[32]

Economist Peter Orszag, currently the director of the Office of Management and Budget in the Obama administration, testified before Congress on cap-and-trade in 2008, when he was the director of the Congressional Budget Office. From his testimony, it was clear Orszag believed global climate change resulting from human causes was a serious, perhaps even catastrophic problem. "Human activities are producing increasingly large quantities of greenhouse gases, particularly CO_2," he testified. "The accumulation of these gases in the atmosphere is expected to have potentially serious and costly effects on regional climates throughout the world."

Admitting that a cap-and-trade program amounts to a "carbon tax," Orszag argued it was a "market-oriented" approach to reducing carbon emissions that would be more efficient in reducing carbon-dioxide emissions than a "command-and-control" approach, as typified by a system of government regulations that would require across-the-board emission reductions by all firms. Orszag estimated a cap-and-trade emissions program could generate as much as $145 billion a year in revenue for the federal government. Acknowledging that cap-and-trade would function as a tax that corporations would most likely pass on to consumers in the form of higher prices, Orzag testified that "price increases would be essential to the success of a cap-and-trade program because they would be the most important mechanisms through which businesses and households would be encouraged to make investments and behavioral changes that reduced CO_2 emissions."[33]

Whenever the government creates a scarce resource, in this case the right to emit carbon, and then mandates that businesses buy or trade permits, costs are inevitably passed on to all consumers in the form of higher prices. Congressional Budget Office estimates suggest price hikes from a 15 percent reduction in emissions would cost the average family in the bottom quintile of income earners about 3.3 percent of its after-tax income every year. The middle three quintiles would lose between 2 percent to 2.7 percent of their income. The top quintile of income earners would pay a 1.7 percent tax. That all income earners, even those in the bottom quintile, would be impacted by the higher prices resulting from the cap-and-trade permit system belies President Obama's frequent campaign promise that in an Obama administration tax increases would not affect 95 percent of working families.[34]

Critics point out that cap-and-trade will increase gasoline prices and the cost of energy in the twenty-five states that get more than 50 percent of their electricity from coal. Businesses that emit carbon dioxide, including manufacturing companies, will face yet one more cost of operations in paying cap-and-trade costs, at a time when they are trying to compete in a global economy where multinational corporations are free to outsource operations to cheap-labor countries, such as China, that appear to have no intention of implementing cap-and-trade emission schemes. Moreover, the imposition of what may well amount to a cap-and-trade tax may further depress the economy at a time when families are struggling just to keep their jobs and homes and meet monthly living expenses, including those involved in raising children. Proponents of cap-and-trade schemes typically assume that the economic costs of what they perceive as the "climate-change catastrophe" produced by man-made carbon-dioxide emissions far outweigh the economic cost of the scheme itself.

As Congress prepared to take up the cap-and-trade debate as part of the Obama administration's proposed $3.6 trillion federal budget for 2009, Senate staffers briefed by the White House were told the cap-and-trade legislation could amount to as much as a $2 trillion tax over the next eight years, considerably more than the $646 billion the White House had estimated publicly. "The last thing we need is a massive tax increase in a recession, but reportedly that's what the White House is offering: up to $1.9 trillion in tax hikes on every single American who drives a car, turns on a light switch or buys a product made in the United States," Michael Steele, a spokesman for Republican House Minority Leader John A. Boehner of Ohio, told the *Washington Times*. "And since this energy tax won't affect manufacturers in Mexico, India and China, it will do nothing but drive American jobs overseas." [35]

WHY WE WILL NEVER RUN OUT OF OIL

What is typically ignored in the argument over U.S. dependence on foreign oil is that oil and natural gas remain so abundant that it is unlikely the world will ever run out. Not to base U.S. energy policy on a determination to develop and utilize more U.S based carbon fuel resources is irresponsible in the face of the evidence that abundant carbon fuel resources remain available to the United States at home.

Economist Julian Simon, formerly a professor of business administration at the University of Maryland and a senior fellow at the Cato Institute, was famous for taking a contrarian position on energy resources, arguing that our perception of scarcity was not validated by the current or historical factual record of energy abundance.

In an essay titled "When Will We Run Out of Oil? Never!," [36] Simon argued against Malthusian fears that peak-oil theorists were right and that sooner or later the pumps would run dry, as environmental alarmist Paul Ehrlich frequently argued. [37] Simon traced fears of energy-resource exhaustion back to an 1865 book by W. Stanley Jevons, one of the nineteenth century's greatest social scientists, titled *The Coal Question: An Inquiry Concerning the Progress of the Nation, and the Probable Exhaustion of our Coal-mines*. [38] Jevons argued that Great Britain's industrial progress would grind to a halt because industry would soon use all available coal. Jevons further concluded that there was no chance oil would be an alternative resource able to solve the problem.

"What happened?" Simon asked. "Because of the perceived future need for coal and because of the potential profit in meeting that need, prospectors searched out new deposits of coal, investors discovered better ways to get coal out of the earth, and transportation engineers developed cheaper ways to move the coal." [39] Simon traced similar fears in the

United States back to an 1885 U.S. Geological Survey report declaring there was "little or no chance" oil would ever be found in California. In 1939, the U.S. Department of the Interior argued U.S. oil resources would be exhausted in thirteen years; then, when that prediction proved a false alarm, the department revised its estimate and declared that it was starting in 1951 that U.S. oil would be exhausted in thirteen years.

Simon argued that gloomy predictions about running out of oil, coal, or any other energy resource, including natural gas, were typically wrong for several reasons, including these:

- Energy resources such as oil, coal, and natural gas typically exist in quantities much larger than initially estimated;

- Advances in technology make exploration and recovery of previously difficult-to-develop oil, coal, and natural gas resources more efficient and economically affordable;

- Improvements in productivity lead to more efficient use of oil, coal, and natural gas resources over time;

- Alternative sources of energy are found, even while oil, coal, and natural gas resources remain abundant;

- Previously dominant energy resources, such as oil, coal, and natural gas, become less dominant as more efficient energy resources, such as nuclear power become safer, cheaper, and more reliably introduced.

Simon's energy-resource analysis essentially maintains that we will be running automobiles with nuclear batteries long before we run out of oil. Another point consistent with Simon's analysis is that technologies have been developed permitting the clean burning of coal, while coal resources in the United States remain among the most abundant on the earth. In the final analysis, nuclear power is the final inexhaustible energy resource.

Moreover, the development of nuclear power plants to provide electricity to U.S. cities would serve the dual purpose of providing infrastructure jobs that conceivably could match the jobs created by President Eisenhower's decision to build the interstate highway system, while providing cheap, safe, and efficient energy to satisfy our municipal needs indefinitely. Today, the U.S. Navy runs ships around the world predominately on nuclear power, without any history of life- or environment-threatening accidents. Simon wrote: "Of course nuclear power can replace coal and oil entirely, which constitutes an increase in efficiency so great that it is beyond my powers to portray the entire process on a single graph based on physical units." [40]

Since the 1980s, France has built a network of modern nuclear power plants needed to power its major cities for the foreseeable future. Today, approximately 80 percent of France's electricity is generated by fifty-nine nuclear plants across the country that are at least a generation more advanced than the nuclear power plants operating today in the United States. [41]

As with the *Exxon Valdez* oil spill, the nightmare scenarios with nuclear power are now decades old. The Three Mile Island accident occurred in Pennsylvania in 1979 and the Chernobyl reactor meltdown occurred in the Soviet Union in 1986. The world has experienced no similar incidents with nuclear energy since then.

"FOSSIL FUEL" THEORY VS. ABIOTIC OIL

For generations, Americans have been conditioned to think of oil and natural gas as "fossil fuel." The "Dino the Dinosaur" advertising symbol was so popular that in 1932 Sinclair Oil registered the brontosaurus as a trademark. The dinosaur identification with "fossil fuels" persists in common parlance, even though most scientists today are more inclined to argue that minute biological material, including plankton, produces oil, rather than to attribute the origin of oil to dinosaurs or ancient decayed forests. Even the simplest analysis reveals that the "fossil fuel" theory taken literally must be wrong, largely because fossils are not typically the ancient animal or plant, but the image of the animal or plant that was formed and preserved in rock. Petrified wood, for example, is not the original ancient tree itself, but rather the minerals that have filled the original tree cell structure and hardened into metamorphic rock.

The alternative theory, the abiotic or nonorganic theory, is that oil originates from natural chemical processes that take place in the mantle of the earth on a constant basis continuing even today. The abiotic theory of oil's origin has predominated among Russian and Ukrainian geologists and petrochemists since the end of World War II.

While it is not the purpose of this book to argue the theory of abiotic oil at length, consider the commonsense point that it is not the case that all the dinosaurs herded to Saudi Arabia and died in a big heap at the end of the Mesozoic Era. That is not the reason Saudi Arabia has abun-

dant oil while many Middle Eastern neighbors are relatively oil defi-
cient. The bedrock under Saudi Arabia is deeply fractured along fault
lines that map directly onto Saudi Arabia's major oil fields. The tectonic
evidence supports the argument that Saudi Arabia's oil has seeped upward from the mantle of the earth into the sedimentary layers that have
been confused for generations as being responsible for creating the oil in
the first place.

An important, but neglected, study of the bedrock underlying the
Saudi oil fields provides strong evidence that the oil fields result from
fractures and faults in the basement rock, not from a disproportionately
large deposit of biological material in ancient times uniquely on the Arabian Peninsula. The study, published in 1992 by geologist H. S. Edgell,
argued that the Saudi oil fields, including the giant field at Ghawar, were
"produced by extensional block faulting in the crystalline Precambrian
basement along the predominantly N–S Arabian Trend which constitutes the 'old grain' of Arabia." [42] Precambrian rock dates back geologi-
cally some 4.6 billion years, to the origin of the earth, until some 570
million years ago, hardly the era in which petrogeologists think biological material was deposited to later form oil. Moreover, dinosaurs did
not roam the earth until much later, during the Mesozoic Era, beginning 250 million years ago, a considerable distance in time from the
Precambrian period.

Edgwell's study supports the argument that oil in Saudi Arabia is
abundant because the fault patterns in the underlying bedrock permit
oil from the earth's mantle to seep upward, into the many porous sedimentary strata lying above.

Abiotic-oil theories are often characterized by detractors as assuming there is an endless fountain of oil, if only we dig deep enough. Abiotic oil theory may argue that oil is under constant production in the
mantle of the earth, but abiotic oil theorists typically make no assumption that oil resources are without limit. After all, the earth itself is finite, so all resources on the earth are finite. The point of abiotic-oil
theories is to argue that oil may be much more abundant than traditional petrogeologists trained in the biological theory of oil's origin
imagine.

The importance, then, of the abiotic theory is to direct our attention
to exploring for oil deeper within the earth, at levels several miles below
the earth's surface, where modern drilling technology makes oil exploration and recovery economically feasible.

Moreover, more than three-quarters of the earth's surface is water. Oil geologists are finding large quantities of oil on the shelf area offshore from continents around the world, suggesting oil might be found even in the depths of the ocean. Underwater deep drilling draws an obvious advantage of being able to reach depths not easily accessible to onshore drilling, simply by beginning the drilling at the sea bottom below the water's surface.

Peak-oil theory is inherently flawed in that logically it must make an assumption about how much oil and natural gas are available on earth, in order to make projections about when the available resources will reach diminishing rates of production. With three-quarters of the earth covered by water and yet largely unexplored for oil and natural gas, so far we may have discovered only a fraction of the available total oil and natural-gas resources on this planet.

THE LOST CITY HYDROTHERMAL FIELD

An article published in the February 1, 2008, issue of *Science* provided additional scientific evidence supporting the abiotic theory for the origin of oil. The article, written by Giora Proskurowski of the School of Oceanography at the University of Washington in Seattle, reported samples of hydrogen-rich fluids venting at the bottom of the Atlantic Ocean in the Lost City Hydrothermal Field.[43] Proskurowski and his associates concluded the hydrogen-rich fluids were produced by the abiotic synthesis of hydrocarbons in the mantle of the earth. Lost City is a hypothermal field some 2,100 feet below sea level that sits along the Mid-Atlantic Ridge at the center of the Atlantic Ocean, noted for strange ninety- to two-hundred-foot white towers at the sea bottom.

In 2003 and again in 2005, Proskurowski and his team descended in a scientific submarine to collect liquid bubbling up from Lost City sea vents. Proskurowski found hydrocarbons containing carbon-13 isotopes that appeared to have been formed from the mantle of the earth, rather than from biological material settled on the ocean floor. Carbon-13 is the carbon isotope scientists associate with abiotic origin, compared to carbon-12, which scientists typically associate with biological origin. Proskurowski argued that the hydrocarbons found in the natural hydrothermal fluids coming out of the Lost City sea vents are attributable to abiotic production by Fischer-Tropsch, or FTT, reactions. The Fischer-

Tropsch equations were first developed by German scientists in the Weimar Republic. The Nazis later used the FTT equations to produce synthetic oil from coal.

The Lost City explorations do not establish conclusively whether there is a large quantity of oil and natural gas recoverable from below ocean floors. Still, the research gives impetus to the additional exploration needed to determine just how much oil and natural gas can be found under the ocean floors. If we are finding significant quantities of oil right now along the continental shelves around the world and in the Gulf of Mexico, we might also find significant quantities of oil under the oceans. As deep-earth drilling technologies advance, oil and natural gas available under the oceans should become more economical to explore and recover.

The Lost City research also provides further scientific support for Cornell University physicist Thomas Gold, an influential champion of abiotic oil theory. In his book titled *The Deep Hot Biosphere: The Myth of Fossil Fuels*, Gold argued that because oil is found in sedimentary rock does not mean oil was formed by biological processes within that sedimentary rock.[44]

THE JACK FIELD AND OFFSHORE DRILLING

Oil imported to the United States from Mexico comes primarily from Mexico's giant Cantarell oil field, in the Gulf of Mexico off the Yucatan, and one of the largest oil-producing complexes in the world.

The Cantarell field was discovered in 1976, supposedly after a fisherman named Cantarell reported an oil seep in the Campeche Bay. Exploration yielded surprising results. It turned out that Mexico's richest oil-field complex was created 65 million years ago, when the huge Chicxulub meteor impacted the earth at the end of the Mesozoic Era. In a seminal 1980 paper, University of California at Berkeley physicist Luis Walter Alvarez, working with his son Walter Alvarez, suggested that an impact meteor was responsible for the extinction of the dinosaurs. Many scientists now believe that the Chicxulub meteor impact was also the culprit responsible for creating the Cantarell oil field.

The Chicxulub meteor impact crater is massive, estimated to be 100 to 150 miles wide. The seismic shock of the meteor fractured the bedrock below the gulf and set off a series of tsunami activity that caused a huge section of land to break off and fall back into the crater underwater. Traditionally, oil exploration in the continental U.S. has tended to stay close to the surface, dictated by the idea that sedimentary layers close to the surface of the earth would contain the biological material needed to produce oil.

If Mexico can discover a massive oil find in the Gulf of Mexico, why shouldn't the United States be able to do the same?

In September 2006, Chevron Corporation and two oil-exploration companies announced that a giant deep-oil reserve had just been discovered in the Gulf of Mexico. Known as the Jack Field, the area some 270 miles southwest of New Orleans was estimated to hold as much as 15 billion barrels' worth of oil reserves. Chevron had discovered the huge oil reserve by drilling some seven miles below the surface of the Gulf of Mexico. The *Wall Street Journal* reported that this find alone could boost the nation's current oil reserves by as much as 50 percent.[45]

A few months earlier, in March 2006, Mexico had announced the discovery of a new huge oil find, the Noxal field in the gulf, some sixty miles from the port of Coatzacoalcos on the coast of the Veracruz state. Estimated to contain as much as 10 billion barrels of oil, the find could well be larger than Cantarell.[46] Like the Jack Field find, Noxal is a deep-water find, relying on new deep-water-drilling technology.

Then, in July 2006, Cuba announced plans to hire the communist Chinese to drill for oil off Key West. This move was made possible by the 1977 agreement under President Jimmy Carter that created for Cuba an "Exclusive Economic Zone" extending from the western tip of Cuba up north, virtually to Key West, Florida.[47]

In November 2007, Brazil announced the discovery of a huge offshore oil field that could contain as much as 8 billion barrels of oil, enough to expand Brazil's proven reserves of 14.4 billion barrels by 40 to 50 percent.[48] The "ultradeep" Tupi field was found a total of 4.48 miles below the surface of the Atlantic Ocean. Sergio Gabrielli, the chief executive officer of the state-run oil firm Petrobras, told Brazil's President Luiz Inacio Lula da Silva that reserves in the pre-salt area off Brazil's coast are much larger even than the Tupi field, possibly containing as much as 80 billion barrels in oil reserves. By specializing in advanced ultradeep offshore oil exploration, Brazil has moved from being a country dependent on ethanol for its gasoline consumption to becoming a net exporter of oil within less than a decade. Felipe Cunha, an oil analyst with the São Paulo–based brokerage Brascan, proclaimed the find, saying, "If the best-case scenario happens, this discovery would make Petrobras' reserves overcome those of Shell and Chevron and put Petrobras behind only Exxon and British Petroleum."[49]

For decades, the debate has raged in Washington, D.C., and in states along both the Atlantic and Pacific coasts of the United States, regarding offshore drilling, with Republicans and oil companies typically pushing for expanded drilling and Democrats and environmentalists doing their best to prohibit it. If the experience in recent years with offshore drilling is any indication of future success, the United States should be able to increase dramatically domestic oil reserves by expanding offshore exploration, in the Gulf of Mexico as well as along both coasts.

The same debate restrains aggressive development of the oil and natural-gas resources known to be available in the Arctic National Wildlife Refuge, or ANWR. Truly, the size of ANWR compared to Alaska is comparable to the size of a postage stamp placed on a football field. Environmental scares remain associated in the public mind with traumatic news events, such as the *Exxon Valdez* oil spill, which occurred in Alaska's Prince William Sound on March 24, 1989. Environmentally sound oil and natural-gas exploration and development techniques have advanced considerably over the two decades since the *Exxon Valdez* oil spill. When Hurricane Katrina hit the southern coast of the United States on August 28, 2005, for example, considerable damage was done to New Orleans. Yet the hundreds of oil rigs in the Gulf of Mexico in the path of the tremendously powerful hurricane generated no oil spills or other environmental disasters.

THE BAKKEN FORMATION

Technological innovation also supports Julian Simon's contention that oil resources in the United States may be more abundant than were initially assumed.

A shale formation stretching from North Dakota to Montana has an estimated 3.0 to 4.3 billion barrels of technically recoverable oil, according to a U.S. Geological Survey (USGS) assessment released in April 2008. Known as the Bakken Formation, this find would make the recoverable oil in North Dakota and Montana the largest U.S. oil reserves outside Alaska. The USGS assessment evidenced a 2,800 percent increase in the amount of oil recoverable from the Bakken Formation, compared to the agency's 1995 estimate of 151 million barrels of oil. According to the USGS, the increased estimate resulted largely from new advances in drilling and production technologies. By the end of 2007, approximately 105 million barrels of oil had been produced from the Bakken Formation. "The Bakken Formation estimate is larger than all other current USGS oil assessments of the lower forty-eight states and is the largest 'continuous' oil accumulation ever assessed by the USGS," the agency announced in April 2008.[50]

The Bakken Formation lies in "Williston Basin," a geological formation in the north-central United States, underlying much of North Dakota, eastern Montana, northwestern South Dakota, and southern Saskatchewan and Manitoba, Canada, according to the U.S. Department of Energy's Energy Information Administration, which cited the success of horizontal drilling and fracturing efforts in Montana as the reason a decision was made to reevaluate the 1995 estimate of only 151 million barrels.[51]

The USGS announcement was projected to give "a significant boost to North Dakota's already-booming oil industry," according to a press release from the office of Democratic senator Byron Dorgan of North Dakota.[52] "The oil industry in North Dakota has already seen substantial growth," Dorgan said. "The Bakken Shale should attract significant new investment to this region. This is an exciting time for North Dakota's oil industry. We're going to see new growth that will boost our economy and help our country shed its dependence on foreign oil."

Abiotic oil is not an endless resource that promises, like an energy "fountain of youth," to provide an easy solution to U.S. dependence on foreign oil. Yet if U.S. petrogeologists were to take abiotic oil theory seriously, we could expect to find abundant oil and natural-gas resources not only offshore but at deep-earth levels in the continental U.S. itself.

PROJECT "DEEP TREK" AND THE EMERGENCE OF NATURAL-GAS TECHNOLOGIES

In 2002, the Department of Energy established "Deep Trek," a project aimed at developing high-technology capabilities for deep-earth drilling of abundant natural-gas resources yet untapped in the continental United States. Although more than 70 percent of the natural gas produced in the United States comes from wells 5,000 feet or deeper, only 7 percent comes from natural-gas formations below 15,000 feet. Yet an estimated 125 trillion cubic feet of natural gas is believed to be trapped at these greater depths.

The technological problem is that for wells deeper than 15,000 feet, half of the drilling costs can be spent penetrating the last 10 percent of the well's depth. Deep Trek has sponsored the development of a new drilling called IntelliPipe, which turns oil and gas drills into high-speed data transmission tools capable of sending data from the bottom of a well up to 200,000 times faster than mud-pulse and other down-hole telemetry technology industry in common use today.[53] Similar to the case with oil, the Energy Information Administration estimates world reserves of natural gas in 2009 at 6,254 trillion cubic feet, more reserves than ever before in human history, despite worldwide consumption doubling since the 1970s.[54] Deep-earth finds of natural gas are likely to increase these reserve estimates dramatically, once the technology develops more completely.

As a measure of the importance of deep-earth natural gas in the United States, consider that we will have imported approximately 369 billion cubic feet of natural gas in 2009.[55] Natural-gas consumption in the United States is projected to increase from about 22 trillion cubic feet in 2006 to 23 trillion by 2030.[56] Currently, most of the demand for natural gas in the United States is met with domestic production and imports via pipelines from Canada. Yet the development of liquefied natural gas (LNG) technologies has opened up a new technological horizon. The Federal Energy Regulatory Commission is currently reviewing forty LNG terminals in North America to expand the seven import and one export LNG terminals currently operating in ports on the East Coast, the Gulf Coast, Puerto Rico, and Alaska.[57]

Remember, only a few decades ago, natural gas was considered a waste product that many oil wells burned off, not a valuable energy resource that could challenge oil and coal for its clean-burning energy efficiency.

STILL DEPENDENT ON FOREIGN OIL

As the United States nears a 70 percent dependence on foreign oil, a crisis occurs in the massive wealth transfer involved in sending hundreds of billions of dollars overseas to increase the foreign-exchange reserves of the oil-producing states. Truly, by continuing our dependence on foreign oil, the United States is expending capital that is not easily renewed on oil that is immediately consumed.

The immediately available solution to reducing U.S. dependence on foreign oil is to drill and to drill now.

FOUR

Exporting Jobs While Importing an Underclass

Our political, business, and academic elites are waging an out-right war on Americans, and I doubt the middle class can survive the continued assault by forces unleashed over the past five years if they go unchecked.

—Lou Dobbs, *War on the Middle Class*, 2006[1]

As a result of "free trade" policies since the administration of President George H. W. Bush, the U.S. has lost millions of jobs to outsourcing, as U.S.-based multinational corporations have pursued cheap foreign labor. At the same time, U.S. immigration policy has shifted in favor of open borders since at least the administration of President Ronald Reagan.

The basic formula is that the United States has exported high-paying manufacturing jobs to foreign nations, while a Spanish-speaking underclass from south of the border has been imported to compete at lower benefits and wages for low-skilled jobs in the United States. The loser in this equation is the U.S. middle class, and, as a result, the U.S. consumer, ironically the very engine that has propelled the growth in the global economy.

President Reagan expressed his determination to "do something" about immigration when the Immigration Reform and Control Act (IRCA) passed in 1986. The act combined a pathway for citizenship for those illegal immigrants already in the country with tough new regulations designed to punish employers who hired illegal aliens and to secure our borders. What happened with IRCA has become typical of all the immigration legislation passed since the Immigration and Nationality Act of 1965. First, far more illegal aliens became legalized than the proponents of the law ever projected. Second, the enforcement provisions of the law were either ignored or not enforced. All immigration laws passed since the Reagan administration have followed this path: regardless of how tough the border security or other enforcement provisions of the bill are written, pathway-to-citizenship and guest-worker provisions end up allowing millions of illegal aliens to become citizens, as enforcement provisions against illegal immigrants are largely ignored.[2]

Similarly, free-trade agreements have given the green light to U.S.-based multinational corporations to pursue cheap labor worldwide in the effort to increase profits in the immediate term. As a result, millions of manufacturing jobs have been lost, and the United States has entered a dangerous cycle of large and increasing negative international-trade balances. Free-trade agreements, sold on the basis that an expansion of U.S. exports would increase U.S. jobs, have instead resulted in a dramatic decline of real income for the vast majority of workers in the United States.

U.S. JOBS OUTSOURCED TO CHINA

The U.S. government does not collect statistics directly measuring jobs outsourced to China or to any other foreign country. The government collects statistics on jobs gained or lost, but when jobs are lost, tracking where those jobs go is beyond current government data-collection abilities. Most likely, the government has no interest in detailing for Americans the millions of jobs that are being outsourced worldwide to workers making slave or near-slave wages. When we hear elected government officials make the claim that U.S. workers need to be competitive in a global market, the argument usually reduces to an assumption that U.S. workers are paid too generously. A global labor market with no restrictions on the ability of multinational corporations to seek the cheapest labor available anywhere in the world unleashes a worldwide race to the bottom for workers' wages and benefits. Those negotiating our free-trade agreements have intentionally removed or diluted the "anti-dumping" provisions typically placed in classical international trade agreements to prevent the intentional exploitation of labor to produce goods for the U.S. market, which undercut U.S. workers. Instead we have created tax incentives that encourage U.S. corporations to manufacture goods in foreign countries where wages, benefits, and taxes are lower than in the United States.

But it's obvious that manufacturing jobs are being transferred to China from the statistics the government does collect: in 2007, China overtook the United States to become the world's second-largest merchandise exporter after the European Union.[3] China's net exports contributed to one-third of its gross domestic product growth in 2007. The Chinese government estimates that more than 80 million Chinese are now employed in the foreign-trade sector.

Our trade deficit with China has grown from $84 billion in 2000 to $256 billion in 2007. This reflects imports from China growing nearly 250 percent, from $100.1 million in 2000 to $243.5 in 2005; U.S. exports to China in 2005 stood at only $41.8 billion, despite a nearly 400 percent increase since 2000. Moreover, the gap is widening. The Congressional Research Service (CRS) noted the trend, reporting the "U.S. trade deficit with China in 2006 was about 24 percent higher than it was in 2005."[4]

Since 2000, the U.S. manufacturing sector has lost approximately 4 million manufacturing jobs, nearly 25 percent of the total manufacturing workforce, according to the Bureau of Labor Statistics.[5] While economists argue that not all these jobs were lost to outsourcing, U.S.-based multinational corporations have invested heavily in transferring manufacturing to other countries.

The CRS, in evaluating the trade deficit with China, conceded that China's real competitive advantage is an underclass labor force with a cost advantage over higher-priced U.S. labor. Writing in March 2006, the CRS reported that China has a poor record of adopting or enforcing internationally recognized standards for working conditions and environmental regulation.[6] Moreover, multinational corporations and their supporters typically turn a blind eye toward China's continuing use of political and religious prisoners to produce goods for foreign sale. Similarly ignored is China's use of near-slave labor, with workers paid as little as fifty cents an hour to produce goods for the U.S. market.

Further proof that U.S.-based multinational corporations have outsourced jobs to China in the hundreds of thousands comes from an analysis of how the Economic Panic of 2009 has impacted the Chinese economy. The slowdown in exports contributed to the closing of at least 67,000 factories across China in the first half of 2008, according to a report published in the *New York Times*.[7] In October 2008, hundreds of angry workers protested in a near riot that lasted for several days outside a large toy factory that was forced to shut down in Zhang Mu Tou, in Guangdong Province of southern China. It was one of a series of violent or near-violent outbursts China experienced as the export market for Chinese manufactured goods dried up.[8] Approximately 3,600 toy factories closed doors in China in 2008, about half the industry's total.[9]

Clearly, China's economic growth was a miracle not of a surge in economic development in China per se, but a surge in manufacturing jobs in China resulting from a massive outsourcing of manufacturing jobs from the United States. With the economic downturn in the United States, the demand for cheap goods made in China declined, with drastic effects on the Chinese worker and economy. With the U.S. middle class in economic distress, China's U.S. consumer market is in peril.

CHINA'S UNFAIR ADVANTAGES

If labor in China were not being exploited, why else would any U.S.-based multinational corporation bother traveling to China to make goods that would have to be transported thousands of miles to the United States? The truth is that labor costs still remain the most expensive part of manufacturing, so reducing labor costs is necessary if corporations are to increase marginal rates of profit without raising prices.

A near-constant complaint of the U.S. government is that China manipulates its currency vis-à-vis the dollar to make its exports cheaper and imports more expensive than they would be under a floating system. The threat of congressional legislation led China in July 2005 to appreciate its currency by 2.1 percent and to switch to an exchange-rate system based on a basket of currencies, including the dollar. Many U.S. policy makers, however, continue to charge that these reforms have not gone far enough and have warned of potential congressional action if China fails to make further reforms. We need look no further than the website of Democratic senator Charles Schumer of New York to find charges that China is unfairly manipulating the yuan for trade advantages[10] and that the Bush administration was responsible for a growing number of manufacturing jobs lost to China.[11] Still, despite the fundamental unfairness of China's decision to manipulate the yuan, the multi-national corporations have sufficient strength to force politicians on both sides of the aisle to vote for free-trade measures that continue to send jobs to China. The gamble is that cheap goods from China and un-restrained free trade will continue to fuel economic growth in both countries.

The United States welcomed China into the World Trade Organiza-tion in 2001 without requiring that the "free-trade" agreements with China also be fair-trade agreements. Classically trained international-trade economists would never have predicted the comparative advan-tages of a country like China are the following:

- China subsidizes the yuan, keeping China's currency artificially low, in order to advantage Chinese exports;

- China commonly uses near-slave employees paid under a dollar an hour and charged for their room and board in employment com-pounds of thousands of workers who are routinely fired when they are "too old," sometimes defined as being only twenty years old;

- China regularly exports defective products, including toys with lead paint and poisonous food for pets and people;

- China allows manufacturing companies to pollute the environment, without requiring the types of expensive environmental protection systems required of companies in the United States; and

- China applies a tax structure that adversely impacts imports to China, reimbursing to the manufacturer in China the value-added tax, or VAT, on goods made in China for export, while imposing a VAT on goods imported to China.

Still, with the United States depending on China to buy U.S. Trea-sury debt to finance our federal budget deficits, the U.S. government can ill afford to be heavy-handed with China in pushing for "fair trade" ad-justments or human-rights reforms within China.

In December 2006, in an unusual move, the Bush administration sent virtually the entire economic "A-team" to visit China for a "strate-gic economic dialogue" in Beijing. Treasury Secretary Henry Paulson and Federal Reserve Chairman Ben Bernanke led the delegation, along with five other cabinet-level officials, including Secretary of Commerce Carlos Gutierrez. Also in the delegation were Labor Secretary Elaine

Chao, Health and Human Services Secretary Mike Leavitt, Energy Secretary Sam Bodman, and U.S. Trade Representative Susan Schwab.

China listened politely, but at the end of the meeting, Schwab said, the delegation only "asked and received assurances" that economic reform was not stalling, adding that it was "clear there are voices in China" that want to turn back the clock.[12] The U.S. delegation was so concerned not to offend the Chinese that Bernanke's spoken remarks before the Chinese Academy of Social Sciences omitted a warning contained in his prepared text that China's intentionally undervalued currency was an "effective subsidy" of Chinese exporters.

CHIMERICA

Noted Harvard economist and bestselling author Niall Ferguson sent tremors through world financial markets in February 2009 when he announced in a speech in Ottawa, Canada, his studied conclusion that the global economic crisis had only just begun. Before the economic crisis is over, Ferguson warned, there would be civil violence and governments would be toppled. Disagreeing with Bernanke's assertion that the U.S. economic recovery could begin in 2009, Ferguson told the Canadians, "There will be blood." [13] Ferguson warned the economic downturn was "a crisis of globalization" that would not soon end.

"A crisis of this magnitude is bound to increase political as well as economic [conflict]. It is bound to destabilize some countries," he warned. "It will cause civil wars to break out that have been dormant. It will topple governments that were moderate and bring in governments that are extreme."

Ferguson explained his view that the current crisis is a crisis of debt leveraging: "It's a crisis of excessive debt," he explained, "and the deleveraging process has barely begun. U.S. consumers are not going to suddenly bounce back and hit the shopping malls just because they get a tax cut."

Ferguson is well known for creating the term *Chimerica*, a combination of China and America that he concocted to criticize the phenomenon of the U.S. selling massive quantities of U.S. Treasury debt to China as a means of financing massive U.S. budget deficits. In his bestselling 2008 book, *The Ascent of Money*, Ferguson explained that the dual country of Chimerica "accounts for over a tenth of the world's land surface, a quarter of its population, a third of its economic output and more than half of global economic growth in the past eight years." He noted that for a while the combination of China and America looked like "a marriage made in heaven." Why? "The East Chimericans [China] did the saving" while "the West Chimericans [America] did the spending." Chinese imports kept down U.S. inflation while Chinese savings kept down U.S. interest rates. Cheap Chinese labor kept down U.S. wage costs. "As a result, it was remarkably cheap to borrow money and remarkably profitable to run a corporation." Ferguson concluded that "thanks to Chimerica, U.S. corporate profits in 2006 rose by the same proportion above their average share of GDP." [14]

Ferguson, however, argued that the Chinese savings rate was recycled back into the United States to permit excess borrowing on cheap credit terms. "Chimerica—or the Asian 'savings glut,' as Ben Bernanke called it—was the underlying reason why the U.S. mortgage market was so awash with cash in 2006 that you could get a 100 percent mortgage with no income, no job or assets," he wrote. Ferguson also attributed cheap credit to the bubbles created in the hedge-fund and derivatives markets, as well as the surge of the Dow Jones Industrial Average to a height exceeding 14,000 in July 2007. Ferguson also worried about the surge in sovereign-wealth funds accumulated in China by the negative balance of trade derived from China's massive exports to the United States and in the Middle East from petrodollars. He cited a Morgan Stanley forecast predicting that within fifteen years, sovereign-wealth funds could end up with assets of $27 trillion, just over 9 percent of global financial-wealth funds. Ferguson contemplated that the sovereign-wealth funds were positioned to be major acquirers of U.S. banks and investment firms, once global financial markets stabilize. [15] Until financial markets stabilize, the sovereign-wealth funds will most likely stand back, fearing that a move by the United States to nationalize banks could wipe out all private investors and that a drop in the dollar resulting from massive U.S. deficit spending could depreciate the value of all dollar-denominated investments.

In February 2009, Hillary Clinton made clear on her first visit to China as secretary of state that the United States continued to depend on China as a buyer of U.S. Treasury debt. China and America are "truly going to rise or fall together," Clinton said in China. "Our economies are so intertwined. The Chinese know that in order to start exporting again to its biggest market, the United States has to take some drastic measures with the stimulus package. We have to incur more debt. The Chinese recognize our interconnection." Clinton went on Chinese television and virtually pleaded with the Chinese to continue buying U.S. Treasury debt. "It's a good investment, it's a safe investment," she insisted.[16]

INDIA AND THE OUTSOURCING OF TECHNICAL JOBS

In the middle of the Economic Panic of 2009, a little-noticed story highlighted the incentive for U.S. corporations to outsource jobs to India. JPMorgan Chase, the nation's second-largest bank, grew significantly from acquiring, with the assistance of government guarantees, what was left of Washington Mutual and Bear Stearns, two financial-services giants rocked by the subprime-mortgage crisis. In March 2009, as JPMorgan Chase was struggling to absorb the acquisitions, *Business-Week* picked up a story from the *Economic Times* of India reporting that the bank planned to increase its spending on outsourcing to India by 25 percent, to nearly $400 million. To bring down the cost of integrating different information technology systems, or IT systems, in the acquired banks, JPMorgan Chase sought the cost savings of using lower-cost but highly skilled IT services in Mumbai. Before this decision, JPMorgan Chase was already outsourcing $250–300 million in IT and back-office projects to India, in addition to the bank's own captive IT center operating from Mumbai. The *Economic Times* of India reported that similar opportunities existed with other bank mergers forced as a result of the economic downturn, including the merger of Bank of America and Merrill Lynch. The decision to use computer-trained offshore labor in India was expected to save outsourcing banks 30–40 percent in costs over using comparable computer talent based in the United States.[17]

India competes with cheaper labor not just in computer services, but in a wide range of service jobs, ranging from 800-number call services, with American companies having their help and customer-service lines answered not in the United States but in Mumbai, to accounting and legal work, with Indian-trained accountants and paralegals more than capable of doing the intensive research and staff work needed to advise accounting professionals and lawyers in the United States. English proficiency is more likely to be found in India than any other developing country. Graduates of Indian universities typically have been given world-class instruction and emerge with fundamental language and mathematical skills, as well as technical proficiency. Management consulting firm

McKinsey & Company has predicted that white-collar offshoring of U.S. jobs is capable of increasing at a rate of 30 to 40 percent per year. Forrester, a world-class research firm based in Cambridge, Massachusetts, predicted that through 2015 approximately 3.3 million service jobs will have moved offshore, including 1.7 million "back office" jobs such as payroll processing and accounting, and 473,000 jobs in IT.[18]

What outsourcing to India demonstrates is that modern telephone, video, and computer technologies, enhanced by the Internet, permit U.S. corporations to operate with their workforce dispersed internationally. Because service labor in India is well trained and relatively cheap, U.S. corporations are willing to overcome the inconveniences of distance, language, and time. With the Internet, where workers are located becomes relatively unimportant for many businesses. Service work performed in India is at no disadvantage because of the time difference or geographic distance. Time differences between the United States and India can actually become a benefit, as when Indian workers perform technical work overnight so that the work is available when U.S. managers begin their days, or when 800-number service centers operate through the U.S. night, a more difficult and expensive time for U.S. service-center workers to operate.

What is important is the cost of labor. The global market operates to the detriment of the U.S. worker, endangering by its very nature the U.S. middle-class lifestyle.

OUTSOURCED WHITE-COLLAR JOBS CHALLENGE FREE-TRADE ASSUMPTIONS

Beginning in 2004, economists began reporting on a series of studies challenging fundamental assumptions that free trade would necessarily benefit the U.S. economy. Basically, the studies demonstrated that advances in telecommunications, including broadband and the Internet, had created an international market where highly skilled white-collar U.S. workers were being undercut in wages and benefits by highly skilled white-collar workers in other countries. When globalization affected only the 25 percent of the U.S. workforce that is blue-collar, economists were willing to argue that the cut in U.S. wages and benefits resulting from free trade was outweighed by the advantage of having lower-cost foreign-made goods sold in the U.S. marketplace. Yet, this logic is short-sighted. *BusinessWeek* pointed out the problem: "If blue- and white-collar employees alike are thrown into the global labor pool, a majority of workers could end up losing more than they gain in lower prices." [19]

In 2004, Forrester Research found that among the thousand largest U.S. corporations, the number that were engaging in some form of off-shore outsourcing was projected to rise from 37 percent to 54 percent within four years.[20] Researchers Ashok Deo Bardhan and Cynthia Kroll at the University of California's Fischer Center for Real Estate and Urban Economics estimated that 14 million white-collar jobs in the United States involve work that could be shipped electronically and were vulnerable to being outsourced to foreign countries.[21] The jobs most vulnerable to this new "second wave" of outsourcing included medical-transcription services, stock-market research for financial firms, customer-service call centers, legal online database research, as well as payroll and other back-office activities. Salary differences were found to be the driving reason for the outsourcing. A telephone operator paid a U.S. wage of $12.57 an hour was paid under $1.00 an hour in India. Health-record technologists and medical transcriptionists paid $13.17 an hour in the United States were paid between $1.50 and $2.00 an hour in India. Legal assistants paid $17.86 an hour in the United States were paid between $6.00 and $8.00 in India. The University of California researchers concluded that Forrester's 2002 estimate that 3.3 million jobs in the United States would be lost to outsourcing by 2015 was conservative.

The researchers pointed out that between 25,000 to 30,000 American jobs had been outsourced to India in June 2003 alone.

These new data prompted economist Paul Samuelson, the author of one of the leading economics textbooks used in universities across the country for decades, to be troubled. Samuelson commented that the issue of "good American jobs" being lost to outsourcing to low-cost labor countries including China or India is "a hot issue now, and in the coming decade, it will not go away." [22]

H-1B VISAS

Another battleground of the globalists has been to push for unlimited H-1B visas, which were originally designed for technical workers who wanted to work temporarily in the United States without having to apply for U.S. citizenship or permanent resident status. The H-1B visa was created by Congress to bring foreign technical labor into the United States to supplement U.S. workers in a wide range of areas, including mathematics, social and physical sciences, medicine and health, education, law, computer sciences, and engineering, to mention just a few. The idea was that foreign talent with advanced skills could be recruited to come to the United States to work for a while in areas where the supply of available U.S. workers with the required skills failed to fill the demand.

H-1B visas have become a way for top U.S. corporations to recruit cheaper foreign workers to come to the United States and undercut technically skilled labor that might compete for the available jobs at higher wage and benefit costs. Perhaps not surprisingly, one of the most outspoken advocates of allowing an unlimited number of H-1B visa applicants to come to the United States has been Bill Gates, the founder and chairman of Microsoft and one of the richest people in the world. In 2005, ZDNet.com reported that Gates "slammed" the federal government's limits on temporary visas for technical workers, saying he would scrap the system altogether if the decision were up to him. "The theory behind the H-1B visa—that too many smart people are coming—that's what's questionable," Gates was quoted as saying at a panel discussion at the Library of Congress. "It's very dangerous. You can get this idea that the world is very scary; let's cut back on travel . . . let's cut back on visas."

In 2005, H-1B visas were capped at 65,000.[23]

Gates, who began his career in personal computers after dropping out of Harvard College, owes his billionaire status to the millions of Americans who bought his software products for decades. But with his enthusiastic support of H-1B visas, Gates demonstrated that Microsoft, one of the most profitable companies in the country, was more committed to those profits than to the American worker. How is it possible that Gates could not find qualified U.S. workers to take openings for technical jobs at Microsoft? Why is it that U.S. highly trained workers might not make the same or better contribution an H-1B visa worker might make? When Gates retired as Microsoft chairman, his fortune was estimated at $50 billion.[24]

In 2008, *BusinessWeek* examined Mumbai-based companies that provide technical workers to U.S. companies. The investigation concluded that many of the estimated 500,000 foreign workers in the United States under H-1B visas were typically underpaid, in comparison with comparable U.S. workers.[25] The conclusion was not unanticipated. The motivation to hire H-1B workers for U.S. corporations is that the foreign workers are not just well trained, but also cheaper.

Why else would U.S. companies go to the extent of hiring H-1B workers over comparably trained and qualified U.S. workers, if the H-1B workers did not represent a cost savings?

THE MYTH OF THE "JOBS AMERICANS WON'T DO"

There are many jobs that cannot be outsourced to foreign labor. For example, many menial jobs such as janitorial work or localized work such as construction have to be done here. So, those promoting free trade have argued for free and open labor mobility across borders, so lower-skilled workers in foreign countries can move here to compete for lower-skilled jobs. In the United States, illegal immigration has been justified by arguing that "guest workers" from south of the border are needed to do the low-paying, menial jobs that "Americans won't do." The truth is that the U.S. open border with Mexico permits millions of underclass workers to depress wages and benefits in lower-skilled jobs that Americans typically do perform but at higher wages and benefits than the immigrants typically demand. Once again, free trade translates into a rush to the bottom for wages and benefits.

When we examine job statistics, we find there is no job an American will not do. Moreover, there is no job classification in which foreign-born workers are the majority. Even in the low-paying, menial-job categories, Americans still hold most of the jobs. Yet, the millions of illegal immigrants competing for low-paying jobs do manage to depress wages for all workers in the lower-skilled job categories. This is the real impact of open borders and unlimited illegal immigration on the job market. Wages are depressed by increasing the job pool with millions of impoverished and largely uneducated immigrants who are grateful to work in the United States for lower wages and benefits than the average American worker expects.

Jeffrey Passel, a senior research associate at the Pew Hispanic Center, noted that in March 2005 there were approximately 7.2 million "unauthorized migrants," or illegal immigrants, working in the civilian U.S. workforce, accounting for about 4.9 percent of the 148 million workers in the United States.[26] He reported that a higher percentage of illegal immigrants tended to take less-skilled jobs than did native-born workers.

Here are three of the lower-skilled job categories, with the percentage of illegal aliens taking these jobs listed first, and the percentage of native-born Americans in these occupations listed second:

- 31 percent of all illegal immigrants working take service-occupation jobs (compared to 16 percent of native-born Americans);

- 19 percent of illegal aliens are in construction and extractive jobs (compared to 6 percent of native-born Americans);

- 15 percent of illegal aliens are in production, installation, and repair jobs (compared to 10 percent of native-born Americans).

To some, these numbers may sound as though illegal aliens are necessary for these jobs to get done. Yet illegal immigrants compose a relatively small percentage of the U.S. workforce, only about 4.9 percent. So, even if a higher percentage of illegal aliens take construction jobs, the majority of construction workers are still likely to be U.S. workers. A simple example makes the point: Let's say there are 5 illegal immigrants and 95 native-born workers in a group. In that group, illegal aliens make up 5 percent of the total sample of 100. If 100 percent of these 5 illegal aliens work in construction, we have 5 illegal aliens in construction. If only 10 percent of the native-born workers in this sample work in construction, we have 10 native-born construction workers. Thus, of our 15 construction workers, one-third are illegal immigrants and two-thirds are U.S. workers. Because the population of U.S. workers is larger, U.S. workers remain the majority of construction workers in the example even though a larger percentage of the available illegal immigrants work in construction.

Steven Camarota of the Center for Immigration Studies makes a related point.[27] The highest percentage of immigrants in any job category, including both legal and illegal immigrants, involves "farming, fishing & forestry," in which 44.7 percent of the workers are immigrants. The next-highest proportion is construction. Yet even there, only 26.1 percent of the workers are immigrants. Camarota concludes, "It's simply incorrect to say that immigrants only do jobs natives don't want. If that were so, then there should be occupations comprised almost entirely of immigrants."[28]

Calculating the unemployment rate among native-born Americans, Camarota further demonstrated that there are available, unemployed

Americans in every job category in which immigrants hold jobs. In the three classifications where immigrants have the highest proportion of all jobs, there is still substantial native-born unemployment: in fishing, farming, and forestry, where immigrants (both legal and illegal) hold 44.7 percent of the jobs, the native-born unemployment rate is 12.8 percent; in construction and extraction, in which immigrants hold 26.1 percent of the jobs, the native unemployment rate is 11.3 percent; and in building cleaning and maintenance, in which immigrants hold 38.8 percent of the jobs, the native-born unemployment rate is 10.5 percent. Not only do Americans work in all job categories, but there are available native-born Americans who are unemployed and available to go to work in these job categories.[29]

Camarota conducted a detailed analysis of 473 separate occupations, proving that "there are virtually no jobs in which a majority of workers are immigrants, let alone illegal aliens. The overwhelming majority of workers in almost every single occupation, even the lowest-paid, are native-born."[30] Moreover, Camarota's study showed that less-educated native-born Americans are facing increasing competition from the poorly educated immigrants flooding the country. Alarmingly, Camarota found that an increasing number of the less-educated native-born Americans have simply dropped out of the workforce. Some 7 million Americans without a high-school diploma have simply stopped looking for work. "Even if half or two-thirds of this group did not wish to work, there is still a huge pool of native-born unskilled adult labor numbering in the millions."[31]

"The findings of this report call into question the idea that America is desperately short of less-educated workers," Camarota wrote. "In 2005, there were 3.8 million unemployed adult natives (18 to 64) with just a high school degree or less and another 19 million not in the labor force. Moreover, between 2000 and 2005 there was a significant deterioration in the labor market prospects of less-educated adult natives."[32] The conclusions are clear: America still has millions of less-educated and/or low-skilled workers to compete for the only jobs that immigrants are qualified to take. When immigrants are willing to work at below-market wages, often without benefits, the immigrant workers place a squeeze on the bottom tiers of American workers.

The United States has opened the southern border with Mexico under the banner of NAFTA free trade, with the result that the invasion of a Spanish-speaking underclass has undercut wages and benefits for Americans competing for lower-skilled jobs in the workforce. In other words, underclass immigrants pouring into America across the border with Mexico threaten employment prospects for America's own poorly educated workers. Less-educated Americans also tend to be the poorest Americans. The increasing numbers of immigrants competing for the available lower-skilled jobs is a certain promise for the expansion of federal and state social-welfare programs, especially in an economic downturn such as the one that officially began in December 2008.

MEXICAN CONSULATE OFFICES IN THE U.S. AND NORTH AMERICAN INTEGRATION

In April 2008, the fourth annual summit meeting of the Security and Prosperity Partnership of North America, or SPP, was held in New Orleans, with President Bush meeting with Mexico's President Felipe Calderon and Canada's Prime Minister Stephen Harper. In the first public event, Bush and Calderon reopened a Mexican consulate office. The Mexican government had closed the consulate in 2002 due to budget cuts in Mexico. The New Orleans *Times-Picayune* had reported that the rebuilding of damaged areas after Hurricane Katrina led to an influx of 30,000 Mexican nationals in southeastern Louisiana. Prior to the reopening of the New Orleans consulate, those nationals had to rely on the Mexican consulate in Houston.[33]

The New Orleans consulate was the forty-eighth that Mexico had opened in the United States. A key purpose of the Mexican consulates has been to protect the rights under Mexican law of the millions of Mexican citizens, including both legal immigrants and illegal immigrants, currently living in the United States. The U.S. government admits that as many as 10 million Mexican citizens currently live in the United States. Thus, approximately 10 percent of Mexico's population now lives here, without any requirement that they renounce their Mexican citizenship or become U.S. citizens. By 2010, some 20 percent of Mexico's population may be living in the United States, if immigration numbers remain at or around the 2006 level. New Orleans mayor Ray Nagin and Louisiana governor Bobby Jindal both attended the official ceremony opening the consulate office, not only to accompany the presidents of the United States and Mexico but also to emphasize the importance of the consulate and Mexican workers to the economies of the city and the state.

The press covering the Mexican consulate reopening was dominated by Mexican radio, print, and television news reporters, with U.S. coverage limited primarily to pool reporting from the White House press corps. At the opening ceremony, President Bush stressed, "I chose New Orleans for our meetings with Mexico and Canada because I wanted to send a clear signal to the people of my country that New Orleans is open for business." While Bush did not mention the SPP by name, he commented that the reopening of the consulate was "a good sign, because we celebrate the values that cause Mexico and the United States to be friends—values like family and culture." Calderon also neglected to mention SPP by name, commenting only that he believed the reopening of the consulate would lead to greater security and prosperity between the two nations.

The three governments engaged in a public-relations campaign to reposition the New Orleans SPP meeting away from the controversial North American integration focus of the previous three annual SPP summits. Billed instead as a "North American Leaders" summit, the emphasis was on creating more photo opportunities designed to show President Bush meeting separately in bilateral meetings with the leaders of Mexico and Canada. Deemphasized was the trilateral cooperation that has been the centerpiece of previous SPP summit meetings. Since being first declared at the trilateral summit in Waco, Texas, on March 23, 2005, the SPP has received increasing attention from critics who see it as a NAFTA-plus arrangement that could easily lead to the creation of a North American Union by pursuing the same path of regulatory and bureaucratic integration used in Europe to create the European Union. A White House press release noted that Bush, Caldron, and Harper planned to "review progress and continued cooperation under the Security and Prosperity Partnership," yet even the logo used to depict the summit dropped any reference to the SPP, instead showing a riverboat and the flags of the United States, Canada, and Mexico.

Another clue to the downplaying of North American integration can be gleaned from a paper titled "Saving the North American Security and Prosperity Partnership," published in March 2008 by the Fraser Institute in Canada.[34] Blaming "left-wing economic nationalists in Canada and right-wing protectionists in the United States" for attacking SPP, the authors of the report, Fraser Institute political scientist Alexander Moens and intern Michael Cust, lamented: "Neither Prime Minister Stephen Harper nor President George W. Bush seem willing to invest new political capital in the talks at this point to overcome the loss of momentum." The solution, the authors argued, was a public-relations makeover in which the goals of North American political and economic integration would remain the same but the SPP designation would be changed. Trilateral arrangements between the three nations would continue to advance but the leaders of the three countries would have more deniability that their goal was North American integration. Rather than operating under the auspices of the SPP, the authors proposed any reference to the name "North American Union," or NAU, should also be dropped, in favor of a declaration that the three countries now want to create a "North American Standards and Regulatory Area," or NASRA.

Moens and Cust acknowledged that the attacks of SPP critics "are starting to hurt." One Canadian commentator had declared the SPP "dead" and "defunct," while another had stated that it had "collapsed under a heap of conspiratorial rubbish." But the authors argued that the SPP was in fact "far from dead." Acknowledging it was operating under a "low profile," Moens and Cust stressed that trilateral talks in the bureaucratic working groups constituted under SPP by the three governments should continue working. "Its critics may have tarnished the 'SPP brand,' " they conceded, "but the precise areas of its work—to follow where NAFTA left off and to do so by incorporating post-9/11 security criteria as well as public safety and quality of life (pandemic illness and food safety)—are key Canadian interests." The Fraser Institute paper also encouraged the SPP working groups to develop "a better communications strategy" so that the public "can begin to understand its benefits."

The authors, however, were opposed to expanding the list of SPP advisers to include public-interest groups or the media, preferring to stay with the closed-door advice offered by the thirty corporations self-picked by chambers of commerce in the three countries to serve as members of the North American Competitiveness Council, or NACC.

THE FREE-TRADE AGENDA

At the conclusion of the SPP summit in New Orleans, President Bush and Secretary of Commerce Carlos Gutierrez attended a private cocktail party sponsored by the New Orleans Chamber of Commerce, at which they openly proclaimed their determination to continue with the Security and Prosperity Partnership and NAFTA. Key to understanding the comments at the cocktail party was the decision of the House of Representatives to table the Bush administration's proposed Colombia free-trade agreement. "Unfortunately, we had a setback," Bush admitted in his remarks that evening. "The free-trade agreement with Colombia is dead, unless House Speaker Nancy Pelosi changes her mind." The Bush administration was coming under fire from Democratic Party presidential contenders Senators Barack Obama and Hillary Clinton, who were arguing that NAFTA and other free-trade agreements needed to be renegotiated. At that time, Obama and Clinton were arguing that NAFTA needed to be more fair to U.S. workers who saw high-paying jobs replaced by lower-paying service jobs as the Bush administration continued the Clinton administration's movement of the U.S. economy into a global economy.

Gutierrez told the business leaders at the private cocktail party that the Bush administration intended to push the SPP agenda by fighting for new free-trade agreements with South Korea and Panama, despite Speaker Nancy Pelosi's decision to kill the administration's proposed Colombia free-trade agreement in the House. Preceding Gutierrez and Bush to the podium, Mayor Ray Nagin and Governor Bobby Jindal both emphasized that the economic future of the city lay with international trade and the anticipated deepening and widening of the Panama Canal. New Orleans anticipates a huge influx of millions of containers from China and the Far East once Panama builds a new canal capable of accommodating the new generation of "post-Panamax" ships, which can transport as many as 12,500 containers each.

Stressing SPP themes, Bush told the group, "the meeting gives three friends the chance to come together to discuss our commitment to security and prosperity, to reconfirm the need for the three of us to work in harmony together for the good of our peoples. It's a chance to talk about how we can best protect our people and extend prosperity." The audience received his comments enthusiastically. "One of the best ways to do this is through trade," Bush continued. "The people in Louisiana understand the benefits of free trade firsthand. Many sectors of the economy were hit hard by Katrina. Exports here in New Orleans are a source for jobs and hope. Exports through Louisiana exceeded $30 billion for the first time ever in 2007. But the fundamental is whether we're going to be a nation that continues to relate to free trade." Bush indicated he continues to "strongly support" NAFTA, noting that "exports between the three countries have more than tripled under NAFTA and our economies have grown by more than 50 percent.

"Tomorrow, we will be meeting with the business leaders of the North American Competitiveness Council to listen to their specific recommendations," Bush said, reinforcing the importance of continuing the SPP agenda at the New Orleans summit, even if the three leaders had reached a decision to give SPP less public fanfare. "The United States has an opportunity to continue the trading agenda. As a matter of fact, we have an opportunity with three important countries—Colombia, South Korea and Panama." Bush left no doubt where he stood on free trade. "If we turn down this deal with Colombia," he emphasized, "it would send forth a message that America cannot be counted on. If the Colombia deal doesn't go forward, it will embolden the voices of false populism in our neighborhood and it will make it harder for President [Alvaro] Uribe to do what is necessary to make Colombia a safe place in which to live."

FREE TRADE OR A NORTH AMERICAN UNION?

A legal case that demonstrated the extent to which U.S. laws are being compromised by the political and economic agenda to integrate with Mexico involved a man named José Medellín. At issue was a death-penalty verdict in Texas for Medellín, who confessed in 1993 to partici-pating in the rape and murder of two teenage girls, Jennifer Ertman and Elizabeth Pena of Houston. Both were sodomized and raped for over an hour by Medellín and eight of his Mexican illegal-alien gang members.

The girls made a fatal mistake. After a pool party that ended late, they decided to take a shortcut home by the railroad tracks, trying to make one of the girls' midnight curfew. In their hour-long torture, one of the girls was hit so hard her teeth were knocked out of her head. Me-dellín and his gang buddies strangled the girls to death with their belts. Medellín then boasted of keeping a Mickey Mouse watch from one of the girls to give to his girlfriend as a souvenir of their crime. Medellín and four of his cohorts were convicted of capital murder and sent to Texas's death row. While Medellín was still pleading for his life, one of these criminals had already been executed for the crime.

Almost unbelievably, the Bush Justice Department argued in 2008 at the U.S. Supreme Court that a Mexican murderer on death row should be given a new trial at the demand of the U.N.'s International Court of Justice in the Hague. Why? All because Medellín was not allowed to first call the Mexican consulate when he was arrested. In other words, the Bush administration argued Medellín's confession should be thrown out because years after the crime he complained that his civil rights had been violated when the Mexican consulate was not invited to take on his defense. The Supreme Court had already rejected Medellín's complaint once and the Texas appellate court had ruled that under the U.S. Constitution, the president of the United States has no authority to tell Texas criminal courts to stand down so international law could apply to determine the outcome of the case.

Medellín appealed the Texas appellate court decision and the case was sent back to the U.S. Supreme Court for a second time. In 2008, President Bush instructed the solicitor general to argue alongside Medellín's attorneys that international law has supremacy over U.S. criminal law, and thus U.S. treaty obligations under the Vienna Convention trump Texas criminal law. If President Bush's argument had prevailed, Medellín's confession could have been thrown out, with the result that there might not have been enough evidence to retry him. He might have been released despite his confession to the heinous crime.

What was at stake was the very foundation of U.S. judicial sovereignty. The World Court hates the death penalty, and Mexico was loath to see even one of their worst criminals in the United States be put to death for capital crimes. Fortunately, the U.S. Supreme Court rejected President Bush's arguments and Medellín was executed despite the strong protests of the Mexican government. Yet, we still have to ask: If Medellín's appeal had been successful, would law-enforcement officers in the United States have to call the Mexican consulate every time a Mexican, either legally or illegally in the United States, is arrested?

Borders opened under the banner of free trade end up producing situations where the sovereignty of U.S. law is ultimately challenged.

MEXICAN TRUCKS

In 2009, one day after signing the $410 billion Omnibus Funding Bill, which contained provisions ending the Department of Transportation's eighteen-month-long Mexican-truck-demonstration project, the Obama administration announced intentions to restart the program as soon as possible. Debbie Mesloh, a spokesperson for the Office of the U.S. Trade Representative, told the Associated Press that President Obama has asked the office to work with Congress, the DOT, the State Department, and Mexican officials on legislation to create "a new trucking project that will meet the legitimate concerns" of Congress and the United States under NAFTA.[35] The Obama administration's determination to see Mexican long-haul rigs roll throughout the United States is a slap in the face for labor unions, such as the Teamsters, who supported candidate Obama in the 2008 presidential election, in part on his promise to renegotiate NAFTA to preserve U.S. jobs.

The sudden and sharp policy reversal was also a blow to many Democrats in Congress, including Senator Byron Dorgan, Democrat of North Dakota, and Representative Peter DeFazio, Democrat of Oregon. Both had fought hard to have language inserted into legislation stopping the DOT Mexican truck-demonstration project, out of concerns that Mexican trucks do not conform to U.S. safety regulations.

After the Senate passed the Omnibus Funding Bill with the language ending the truck-demonstration project, the Mexican government put immediate pressure on the Obama administration to reinstate approval for Mexican trucks to operate throughout the United States. "Mexico still believes that the United States' noncompliance on this issue, more than fourteen years overdue, is a violation of the North American Free Trade Agreement," Ricardo Alday, embassy spokesman, said. Alday insisted Mexico is willing to work with Congress and the U.S. "in finding a solution that honors its international obligation."[36]

The Mexican truck issue became rancorous when Bush administration secretary of transportation Mary Peters fought off repeated efforts by Congress to confine Mexican trucks to a narrow twenty-mile commercial area north of the southern border. Still, the Bush administration pressed forward, arguing that under NAFTA the United States was required to open all its roads to Mexican trucks. The so-called demonstration project was begun by the Bush administration to allow one hundred Mexican trucking companies the right to operate their long-haul rigs throughout the United States. DOT hoped to prove Mexican trucks and Mexican truck operators could comply with U.S. safety regulations.

But questions persisted. World Net Daily reported that after the DOT Mexican truck-demonstration project had begun, an examination of the Federal Motor Carrier Safety Administration database revealed hundreds of safety violations by Mexican long-haul rigs rolling on U.S. roads under the project.[37] World Net Daily also reported that in a contentious Senate hearing in March 2008, Senator Dorgan, in tight questioning, got Peters to admit that Mexican drivers were being designated at the border as "proficient in English" even though they could explain U.S. traffic signs only in Spanish. Listening to her testimony, Dorgan accused Peters of being "arrogant" and in reckless disregard of a congressional vote to stop the Mexican trucking demonstration project by taking funds away.[38]

Opposition in the House was led by Representative DeFazio, who in September 2007 accused the Bush administration of having a "stealth plan" to allow Mexican long-haul rigs on U.S. roads. "This administration [of President George W. Bush] is hell-bent on opening our borders," DeFazio then said, "but has failed to require that Mexican drivers and trucks meet the same safety and security standards as U.S. drivers and trucks."[39]

Previously, Peters had argued that the wording of the Dorgan amendment did not prohibit the Transportation Department from stopping a Mexican truck-demonstration project that DOT has already begun, even if the measure prohibited DOT from starting any new Mexican truck-demonstration project. Despite strong congressional opposition, the DOT under President Bush had announced it planned to extend the Mexican truck-demonstration project for another two years, in an attempt to force the incoming Obama administration to comply with a departmental decision that had been finalized before Obama's secretary of transportation, Ray LaHood, took office.

During the presidential campaign, candidate Barack Obama was under fire when his campaign economic adviser, Austan Goolsbee, an economics professor at the University of Chicago, traveled to Canada to reassure Canadians that Obama's campaign rhetoric against NAFTA was just that—campaign rhetoric. In the Ohio and Pennsylvania Democratic primaries, Obama pledged to renegotiate NAFTA, part of his appeal to Ohio and Pennsylvania workers who lost manufacturing jobs under the free-trade agreements negotiated by Presidents Clinton and George W. Bush. Once candidate Obama was elected president, Goolsbee was quietly invited to join the administration. Goolsbee took a leave of absence from the University of Chicago after President Obama appointed him to serve as chief economist and staff director of the newly created Presidential Economic Recovery Advisory Board, chaired by former Federal Reserve chairman Paul Volcker.[40] President Obama also appointed Goolsbee to the Council of Economic Advisors, which is charged with assisting in the development of White House economic policy.

Then, in his first trip to a foreign nation, President Obama traveled to Canada, where he used a press conference with Canadian prime minister Stephen Harper to backtrack on his promise to renegotiate NAFTA. The *Guardian* in London reported that Obama's comments in Canada "muddied his position" on NAFTA.[41] Obama responded to a question at the joint press conference with Harper by saying, "Now is a time where we have to be very careful about any signs of protectionism." Translated, this meant that any renegotiation of NAFTA by the Obama administration might involve fine-tuning some of the side agreements, not renegotiating NAFTA itself in any fundamental way.

Also, there was the issue of the "Buy American" provision that was inserted into the Obama administration's $787 billion economic stimulus plan. Canada was concerned that the provision could hurt Canadian steel exports to the United States and the EU objected that the provision was antithetical to the spirit of the Transatlantic Economic Council, which President Bush signed into effect with the EU in April 2007. The Obama administration did not object when language was added to the economic stimulus bill to specify that the Buy American provision would be interpreted as meaning buy American only when doing so is consistent with U.S. international trade obligations. In other words, the "Buy American" language in the bill didn't mean "buy American" if there was a free-trade agreement that overrode that obligation.

DO FREE-TRADE EXPORTS CREATE U.S. JOBS?

Free-trade advocates inevitably argue that eradicating trade barriers between nations expands international trade, with the result that new jobs will be created in the United States. The North American Center for Transborder Studies, a partnership of six universities in the United States, Mexico, and Canada, and based at Arizona State University, released a report titled "North America Next: Report to President Obama on Building Sustainable Security and Competitiveness," advising President Obama prior to that first foreign trip, to Canada. The report claimed that 40 million jobs were created in the United States, Canada, and Mexico—after NAFTA was signed into law by President Clinton—from 1993 to 2007. The report estimated a $7.2 billion annual output loss, or the equivalent of 62,000 jobs, between just two border sister cities in 2007, due to border congestion, traffic, and paperwork.[42] Typically, the study failed to articulate the methodology by which these job estimates were derived, nor did it indicate whether the job creation was a *net* of 40 million, after taking into account the jobs lost from NAFTA or other free-trade agreements such as those under the World Trade Organization.

When we look at the international-trade statistics between the United States, Canada, and Mexico, we see that while the dollar volume has gone up since 1993, so too has the negative balance of trade the United States now holds with the other nations. According to the U.S. Census Bureau's Foreign Trade Statistics,[43] in 1993 the United States enjoyed a nearly $1.7 trillion favorable balance of trade with Mexico, exporting approximately $41.6 billion and importing approximately $39.9 billion. By 2008, the trade balance had reversed, such that the United States had a negative $64.4 billion trade balance in Mexico's favor, after the U.S. exported approximately $151.5 billion to Mexico and imported $215.9 billion. With Canada, the United States in 1993 already had a $10.7 billion negative trade balance, which had expanded to $74.2 billion by the end of 2008.

What these data suggest is that the net new jobs created under NAFTA in North America are likely being created in Mexico and Canada, not in the United States.

The same pattern holds generally for U.S. international trade under free-trade agreements. China entered the World Trade Organization in December 2001. In 2001, the United States had a negative $83.1 billion trade balance in favor of China, which had expanded to a negative $266.3 billion by 2008. In international trade under free-trade agreements, the overall volume of trade has grown significantly, but typically to the detriment of the U.S. worker, as U.S. imports far exceeded exports to key international trading partners, including Mexico, Canada, and China.

Free-trade advocates typically point only to an expansion of international trade and an overall international creation of jobs as their measure of success. What is neglected is an industry-by-industry analysis to track the loss of U.S. jobs to foreign workers in the process. For instance, since 1990 more than 1 million U.S. jobs have been lost in the textile and apparel industries to foreign labor, representing a contraction of approximately 70 percent of the labor force in these industries.[44]

While the impact of foreign trade is a complex phenomenon that will reflect differences in various industries, today we face the possibility that entire industries may be nearly wiped out in the United States as multinational corporations seek cheaper labor costs in foreign countries. Anyone objecting to the loss of U.S. jobs is tagged pejoratively as a "protectionist," as if caring about preserving American jobs in the era of expanding international trade is inherently wrong.

On March 28, 2007, free-trade advocate Alan S. Blinder, a professor of economics at Princeton who formerly served as Federal Reserve Board vice chairman and has been a perennial adviser to Democratic presidential candidates, shocked the investment world by allowing the *Wall Street Journal* to publish his suddenly developed reservations about international trade.[45] Blinder told the *Journal* that a new industrial revolution in communication technology that allows services to be delivered from afar will put as many as 40 million American jobs at risk of being shipped out of the country in the next two decades. That number was more than double the number of workers employed in manufacturing in 2008.

The *Journal* registered its surprise at these comments by observing that Blinder wrote in 2001, "Like 99 percent of economists since the days of Adam Smith, I am a free trader down to my toes." What Blinder did not address was how many of the 40 million jobs lost in the United States would ever be replaced and whether the new jobs created in the U.S. economy would pay anywhere near what the lost jobs had paid or provided in terms of benefits.

UNDEREMPLOYMENT, STRUCTURAL UNEMPLOYMENT, AND CHRONIC UNEMPLOYMENT

A typical argument advanced by free-trade advocates is that the United States has matured from a manufacturing economy to a service economy, as if the shift represented an upgrade in U.S. employment possibilities. Somehow, the idea is that manufacturing is tough, menial work, while service work is more elevated or refined, as if providing a service where one human being helps or assists another human being is on a higher plane than simply making something in a factory. Manufacturing jobs outsourced to China then can be seen as sparing U.S. workers the menial labor demanded from factory jobs, while the immigrant Hispanic labor imported across the border with Mexico attracts low-skilled, low-paid labor to do the jobs "Americans won't do."

But what exactly does "service economy" mean? A "service job" ranges widely, including employment in health care, legal services, computer and data-processing services, recreation, engineering and architecture, accounting, finance, insurance, real estate, as well as wholesale and retail trade, to mention just a few. Yet at the lower end of the pay scale, service jobs include many relatively menial jobs, such as basic janitorial or sanitary services. Looked at economically, moving to a service economy often means a worker must exchange a manufacturing job that may pay in excess of $35 an hour for a relatively unskilled service job that may pay less than $15 an hour, with considerably reduced benefits. The reality is that not all displaced manufacturing employees have the educational background to compete for the higher-skilled and higher-paying service jobs, nor are all displaced manufacturing workers able to complete the job-retraining courses needed to compete for the higher-paying service jobs.

What is clear is that the United States has been losing manufacturing jobs steadily since the end of World War II. In 1945, at the conclusion of the war, the service industries accounted for only 10 percent of nonfarm employment, compared to 38 percent for manufacturing, according to the U.S. Bureau of Labor Statistics. The crossover point came in 1982, when for the first time services surpassed manufacturing as the largest employer among major industry groups. By 1996, services accounted for 29 percent of nonfarm employment, and manufacturing, at 15 percent, had reduced to being somewhat smaller than retail trade.[46] By 2008, manufacturing was less than 10 percent of nonfarm employment, and service-producing employment had risen to approximately 84 percent.

In a global economy, U.S. employment has undergone what economists call "structural" changes. Structural changes occur not when particular workers are laid off temporarily, or when workers have to change from one manufacturing job to another manufacturing job. Translated into layman's terms, structural employment changes occur when the very structure of the economy results in loss of jobs or reductions in wages for particular types of workers. The workers are available and ready to work, but the problem is that the jobs are gone.

When manufacturing jobs in the United States are lost to countries with underclass labor costs, or when an immigrant underclass is allowed to migrate freely into the United States to compete for low-skilled jobs, the employment changes that result are structural in nature. The middle class in the United States under globalization has lost both high-paying technical jobs and high-paying manufacturing jobs to underclass foreign labor, while lower-skilled and lower-paid U.S. workers have been forced to compete with immigrant labor for low-skilled and low-paying manual jobs in the U.S. economy. Foreign labor working for a U.S.-based multinational corporation in a foreign country and immigrant foreign labor migrating into the United States both compete with U.S.

citizens for jobs that Americans controlled domestically before global-ization.

We can see manifestations of these changes in various government data: The Bureau of Labor Statistics reports that the percentage of married-couple U.S. families with two wage earners has grown in the past four decades. In 1967, 55.1 percent of U.S. families had two wage earners or more, a percentage that had grown to 61.7 percent by 2006.[47] Within married couples, more women are working, often to support a lifestyle that a single worker used to be able to support. Clearly, as real incomes have stagnated or declined since 2000, an increasing number of families have found themselves under distress, especially as costs have skyrocketed across the board for family basics including automobiles, homes, food, energy, and college education.

An extensive social science literature has been developed to study the "working poor," those marginal workers in a service economy who end up not earning enough to sustain a decent standard of living for them-selves or for their families. In 2004, David Shipler wrote *The Work-ing Poor: Invisible in America*, in which he described the working poor: "The man who washes cars does not own one. The clerk who files cancelled checks at the bank and has $2.02 in her own account. The woman who copyedits medical textbooks has not been to a dentist in a decade."[48]

The Bureau of Labor Statistics has projected that of the thirty occu-pations with the largest growth potential between 2004 and 2014, two-thirds will not have any educational requirement, except for moderate or short-term on-the-job training.[49] These jobs include retail salesper-sons, food-preparation workers (including fast-food workers), janitors, sanitation workers, waitresses, receptionists, security guards, truck drivers, delivery assistants, and landscaping workers or groundskeepers. None of these jobs are expected to be high paying. To fill these jobs, there will not even be a requirement to have passed grade school, let alone hold a high school diploma. Many will have no English language requirement at all, or, if there is an English language expectation, suc-cessful applicants may not be required to read English, as long as they can speak and understand it minimally. The Bureau of Labor Statistics report concluded that "professional occupations are projected to grow the fastest, chiefly because they are concentrated in some fast-growing sectors, such as health care and social assistance as well as professional, scientific, and technical services, while production occupations are projected to decline, mainly because seven-tenths of employment in these occupations is in the declining manufacturing sector." [50] Few displaced manufacturing workers will have the educational requirements needed to take advantage of opportunities in professional occupations, including health care or scientific/technical fields.

As the United States approached double-digit unemployment in 2009, a little-noticed but important category of unemployment statistics demonstrated the growing problem of structural unemployment: Unemployment statistics collected by the U.S. Department of Labor are intentionally designed to underreport unemployment. Only those actively looking for work are considered "unemployed" by the department. Meanwhile, millions of former workers who have simply given up searching for employment are ignored in the statistics by being completely left out of the numbers of "unemployed" stated in the monthly reports. Between December 2008, the date the recession officially began, and February 2009, the U.S. lost approximately 4,384,000 jobs, with more than half the losses coming in the four months since November 4, 2008, the day candidate Obama became President-elect Obama. By February 2009, the number of jobless families in the United States had risen to 12.5 million.

But this was only part of the story. In March 2009, the Labor Department estimated that the total number of unemployed had swelled to more than twice that number, topping 25 million families, once the Labor Department added three categories: 1) those working part-time because full-time work is unavailable; 2) those who want a job but have not looked for work in the past twelve months; 3) those who were looking for work but got discouraged or stopped looking for a job for other reasons. [51]

By the time unemployment becomes chronic unemployment and the person simply drops out of the labor force, the U.S. Department of Labor no longer considers the person unemployed.

GLOBALISTS ADMIT U.S. WORKERS ARE SUFFERING

An important article was published in *Foreign Affairs* magazine in 2007 by Kenneth F. Scheve, a political science professor at Yale University, and Matthew J. Slaughter, an economics professor at the Tuck School of Business at Dartmouth and a senior fellow for business and globalization at the Council on Foreign Relations. [52] Scheve and Slaughter argued that as a result of globalization, income in the U.S. has become "extremely skewed." Incomes for most workers have stagnated, or in many cases fallen, they argued. The numbers are "stark," Scheve and Slaughter had to admit. Less than 4 percent of workers were in educational groups that enjoyed increased real-money earnings from 2000 to 2005; only workers with doctorates and professional graduate degrees saw increases in real-money earnings, while the earnings of all other classes of workers fell. In other words, when the earnings were put in "real dollars," a standard that was designed to factor out inflation, globalization turned out to have caused the vast majority of U.S. workers, some 96.6 percent, to see their earnings fall between 2000 and 2005. The only workers to experience income gains under globalism were at the very top, those with doctorates or top professional degrees, including in law and business. Ironically, these highly educated workers were also likely to be the most successful competitors for jobs managing or advising multinational corporations outsourcing jobs to foreign workers.

Scheve and Slaughter appeared worried not so much because of the income inequality itself, but because the income inequality risked causing a populist backlash against globalism. U.S. trade policy risks becoming more protectionist, they cautioned, "because the public is becoming more protectionist, and the public is becoming more protectionist because incomes are stagnating or falling." Scheve and Slaughter's analysis is particularly troubling to supporters of globalism, who typically respond that what is needed is more education of the public in general and job retraining in labor sectors where jobs are lost because of global outsourcing or competition from an underclass of illegal immigrants freely crossing our open southern border. "Significant payoffs from educational investment will take decades to realize," Scheve and Slaughter admitted, "and trade adjustment assistance is too small and too narrowly targeted on specific industries to have much effect."

The authors found that an increasing number of Americans are asking themselves, "Is globalism good for me?" Increasingly the conclusion is that it is not. Scheve and Slaughter believe the solution lies in a "new deal" for globalization under which payroll taxes, which contain a Social Security and a Medicare portion paid half by the worker and half by the employer, would be eliminated for all workers earning below the national median-income level. Their argument was that by rewriting the tax code to redistribute income to those earning less than the median, globalism can be "saved." Scheve and Slaughter argued that public-opinion data suggest Americans "would be more inclined to back trade and investment liberalization if it were linked to more support for those hurt in the process."

Scheve and Slaughter admitted that increasing gaps between the small educated minority in countries affected by globalization and the masses of workers are a worldwide phenomenon. "Poor income growth has co-incided with the integration into the world economy of China, India, and central and eastern Europe." Yet Scheve and Slaughter seemed at a loss to explain the data, arguing only that economists "do not under-stand exactly what has caused this skewed pattern of income growth and to what extent globalism itself is implicated, nor do they know how long it will persist." Still, the authors conceded that "it is plausible there is a connection."

Clearly, Scheve and Slaughter are in the doctorate-educated group, and their data show they should be among the privileged who can an-ticipate economic gains under globalism. The full impact, however, hits that 96.6 percent of workers who are struggling economically under globalism. What should be apparent is that globalism has permitted multinational corporations to conduct a worldwide search for labor that will push labor costs as low as possible. In this dynamic, U.S. middle-class workers who have enjoyed an improving standard of living since the end of World War II suddenly find themselves competing for jobs with the impoverished peasants flooding the cities in China, college graduates in India with advanced technical skills and the ability to speak English, as well as uneducated Spanish-speaking workers fighting their way to cross the border illegally in search of any possible job that will enable them to earn enough to support themselves well enough to also send some money back home to the poor families left behind.

Income statistics produced by the Census Bureau show a widening of the gap between the top 20 percent of wage earners in the United States and the bottom 20 percent. In 2006, the top fifth of U.S. households claimed 50.4 percent of all income, up from 45.6 percent in 1985. Mean-while, in 2006, the bottom fifth of U.S. households earned 3.4 percent of all income, down from 3.9 percent in 1984.[53] The *Wall Street Journal* reported that the income gap was also apparent in the countries where labor benefits from increased global trade, including China and Mexico. "As trade, foreign investment and technology have spread, the gap be-tween economic haves and have-nots has frequently widened, not only in wealthy countries like the U.S. but in poorer ones like Mexico, Ar-gentina, India and China as well," the *Journal* wrote. "Many econo-mists now say that the biggest winners by far are those with the education and skills to take advantage of new opportunities, leaving many lagging far behind. Incomes of low-skilled workers may rise, but incomes of skilled workers rise a lot farther."[54] The overwhelming evidence is that even in developing countries, less-skilled workers are not benefiting from globalization.

EXPORTING JOBS WHILE IMPORTING AN UNDERCLASS

The United States has exported jobs and imported an underclass over enough decades that incrementally the nation is at risk of becoming a dual country, in at least two senses of that term:

- The loss of jobs and the widening income gap have created a dual nation of the relatively wealthy, consisting largely of the highly educated, those with top professional skills, and the managers/owners of multinational corporations, and the relatively poor, consisting of everyone else;

- With 10 percent of Mexico's population living in the United States under the protection of some fifty Mexican consulate offices that protect the rights of these Mexican nationals to live in the United States under Mexican law, the United States has in effect already merged with Mexico, such that U.S. sovereignty is subject at any time to challenge by Mexicans objecting to U.S. law being applied to them.

These trends were not obvious with the loss of a few jobs outsourced to Mexico, China, or India. Yet in the Economic Panic of 2009, the difference in scale became more apparent as a difference in phenomenon. When average middle-class working Americans were losing jobs, homes, and retirement funds, the reality of the global economy became painfully clear. When millions of Mexico's underclass began living openly in the United States and relying on generous social-welfare benefits, including free education of children in Spanish at public schools and free primary care at hospital emergency rooms, the reality of a historically unprecedented migration from Mexico made U.S. citizens aware that for the first time in our history a substantial percentage of another country's citizenry was living in our midst.

That a fundamental change had occurred in the United States was obvious when candidate Barack Obama openly railed against NAFTA and job outsourcing while competing in the Democratic primaries of states such as Ohio and Pennsylvania, although he abandoned these concerns once he was in the White House. When millions of illegal immigrants marched under the Mexican flag in a dozen U.S. cities during the 2006 May Day protests, average U.S. citizens watching the news reports on television saw proof with their own eyes that millions of Mexican citizens were living as such in U.S. cities. Multinational companies based in the United States now assert their supposed right to seek cheap labor wherever cheap labor is available, anywhere in the world. Mexican nationals and their supporters assert that "No Human Being Is Illegal" when pressing their supposed right to move to the United States, work here, and accept generous social-welfare benefits, whether the Mexican nationals have immigrated to the United States legally or illegally.

Since the end of World War II, the United States has built the most economically successful and robust middle class in the history of the world. There is now a risk that the U.S. middle class will not survive another generation of globalist thinking that has no regard for preserving U.S. workers, jobs, or sovereignty. Ironically, by exporting U.S. jobs and importing a foreign underclass, globalists have undercut the U.S. middle class that was the very engine of global economic growth. Without the U.S. consumer, the world economy has gone into recession. The Economic Panic of 2009 reaches deeply into China, India, and Mexico precisely because the world economy is dependent upon the U.S. middle class having sufficient economic wealth to purchase the cheap goods produced by foreign labor.

Ironically, if globalists continue their disregard of the U.S. middle class, globalists will manage to destroy the engine upon which global economic growth depends.

Part II

AMERICA FOR SALE

If Princeton economist Alan Blinder is correct, the United States will outsource an estimated 40 million jobs in the next two decades, largely to China and India. In the process, the middle class will continue losing ground, as the income gap accelerates with those at the top serving multinational corporations and foreign investors.

The future of the United States is being driven to accept globalist solutions by economic crises: a declining dollar, large and growing trade deficits, the bursting of the mortgage bubble, and trillions of dollars in federal budget deficits.

Saddled with a negative net worth, given the Social Security and Medicare liabilities already owed to the retiring baby-boom generation, the United States continues to resort to deficit spending, trying to stimulate the economy with debt while expanding social-welfare programs, with even more debt.

Capital accumulation has now transferred from the United States economy to the Middle Eastern petrodollar nations and China, which has accumulated an unprecedented nearly $2 trillion in foreign-exchange reserves, largely as a result of its favorable balance of international trade with the United States.

If the Middle Eastern petrodollar nations and China should stop purchasing U.S. government-issued debt, the U.S. federal government would have no recourse to obtain the deficit financing needed to keep the government in operation, unless the Federal Reserve contrives to buy trillions of dollars in U.S. Treasury–issued debt securities, or the Treasury just starts printing money.

A bankrupt U.S.A. is by definition an "America for Sale."

Influential globalists have advanced a one-world currency and one-world government for decades. Under a plan to convert the United States from a manufacturing and producing nation to a nation of consumers, the transportation infrastructure of the United States is being reconfigured to accommodate the demands of international free trade. The myth of "free-trade" prosperity is exposed by a nation increasingly dependent on imports to survive. Meanwhile, the plan to destroy the dollar is well advanced, with China already trying to replace the dollar as the world's reserve currency.

As a bankrupt nation, the United States is being forced into a global economy and one-world government, whether the U.S. citizenry likes it or not.

Since the end of World War II, globalist economists, political thinkers, and business leaders have planned for a transformation into a world-power configuration in which the United States and the dollar are no longer dominant.

As globalist interests gain control of key U.S. assets and infrastructure, the momentum will accelerate to create a North American market dominated by North American multinational corporations, moving forward to create a North American currency. Ultimately the regions will be collapsed into a one-world government with a one-world currency.

Can a nation such as the United States survive as a sovereign nation, or will the need for foreign capital force the nation to compromise or abandon our sovereignty, just to allow our economy to survive?

Can the United States remain strong against a nation such as China, which is utilizing our foreign-reserve currency to build a strong military of its own? Could China pressure U.S. foreign policy at any time simply by selling U.S. Treasury debt securities on the open market at a deep discount?

If the United States does not fight the battle to preserve U.S. sovereignty, Americans could well end up living in a second-rate country where U.S. banks, highways, and major corporations are owned by foreigners, including many who may be our enemies.

Will Islamic countries investing in U.S. banks, brokerage firms, and major exchanges ultimately require that our financial laws be modified to comply with Islamic law?

As Chinese firms install radio-frequency identification chips, or RFID technology, along major U.S. transportation corridors such as Interstate 35 simply so the Chinese can monitor the progress of Chinese containers moving throughout the United States, have we created an infrastructure that could be diverted to serve the needs of the nuclear terrorists of the future?

How will the United States limit technological espionage if foreign nations are permitted to own controlling positions in important U.S. technological firms, or to own or operate key U.S. infrastructure including highways and ports?

FIVE

Meet the Globalists

Sovereignty is an anachronistic concept; it has been inherited
from an age where kings ruled over their subjects.

—George Soros, *The Age of Fallibility*, 2006[1]

A key argument in Christopher Booker and Richard North's book
The Great Deception: The Secret History of the European Union
is that the intellectual elite pushing the concept of a "United States of
Europe" knew deception was key to their success.[2] Those advocating a
European regional government clearly understood their intent was to
transplant the sovereignty of European nation-states with a suprare-
gional governmental structure that ultimately would function as a European government, complete with a European parliament, a European
judiciary, a European president, a European currency and central bank,
a European bureaucracy, and a European foreign policy. Yet, the architects of the EU realized their ability to deny their true intent was critical
to their success.

The incremental steps taken to form what became the EU were intentionally presented to the people of Europe as no more than economic
agreements designed to facilitate free trade, promote European economic competitiveness, and generate growth in the European gross domestic product, or GDP. Yet today the EU is firmly in place, along with
the euro, the European Central Bank, and a robust EU bureaucracy lo-

cated in both Brussels and Luxembourg. Veteran EU politician Javier Solana has even been appointed EU foreign-policy chief, charged with the mission of formulating an EU foreign policy that would supersede the foreign policies of the twenty-seven EU member states.

Today globalism is typically promoted in the United States on the same premises under which Europe was sold the European Coal and Steel Community created by the Treaty of Paris in 1951: namely, that free trade will result in economic prosperity. Those arguing for globalism understand that with free-trade economic agreements inevitably come the regional and global political structures needed to regulate free trade and settle trade disputes. From the beginning, the architects of globalism planned for the path to one-world government to begin in the call for global free trade.

The architects of global free trade have not limited their activities to published writings. Today they create, fund, and operate political organizations with a mission to advocate and encourage the creation of the regional and global governance structures necessary for free trade to operate successfully.

The easiest way to make the argument that global governance inevitably lies behind global free-trade activism is to examine the writings and political activities of the globalists themselves. The goal here is to hold the globalists responsible for the regional and one-world governments they intend to create.

Intellectually, globalists put America up for sale decades ago, once they decided to worship at the altar of free trade.

GEORGE SOROS

In his many books, billionaire hedge-fund manager George Soros has made clear that he views economic globalism as an accomplished fact. Financial markets became "truly global in the early 1990s after the collapse of the Soviet Union," Soros wrote in his book *On Globalization*.[3] Yet, Soros warns, "While markets have become global, politics remain firmly rooted in the sovereignty of the state."[4] He is up-front that the formation of international institutions of governance has lagged behind the development of global markets: "The development of international institutions has not kept pace with the growth of global financial markets. Private capital movements far outweigh the facilities of the International Monetary Fund and the World Bank."[5] Soros has offered many different proposals for overhauling the International Monetary Fund, the World Bank, and the World Trade Organization. Yet his conclusion is always the same: global financial markets require a new generation of world-governance organizations capable of imposing global political control over global economics.

From this lofty perspective, Soros demands we transcend nation-states to somehow become global citizens. In an explanation he frequently repeats, Soros argues that sovereignty "became the cornerstone of international relations with the Treaty of Westphalia in 1648." Then, Soros continues, after thirty years of religious wars, "it was agreed that the ruler had the right to determine the religion of his subjects." In the Soros version of world history, all this changed when the French Revolution overthrew King Louis XVI "and the people seized sovereignty." In principle, Soros insists, "sovereignty has belonged to the people ever since." [6] Yet in Soros's view, the sovereign people are the people of the world, not the people of any particular nation-state. "The world order needs a major overhaul," Soros has proclaimed. What exactly this means has a lot to do with transcending nation-states. "I am not advocating a radically new world order," he explained, "only a change of attitude; from the single-minded pursuit of national self-interest to showing some concern for the common interests of humanity." [7]

That Soros derives his perspective from globalism is indisputable. "Globalism has made the world increasingly interdependent," he insists.[8] And again, "Although it would be utopian to replace the people's sovereignty with something else, that principle, on its own, is inadequate for today's increasingly interdependent world." [9] Keeping with the theme, Soros characterizes himself as a "stateless statesman." [10]

Much of Soros's intellectual framework is based on his education at the London School of Economics, where he was deeply influenced by philosopher Karl Popper's call for an "Open Society." While Popper refused to give his call for an Open Society a precise definition, Popper railed against ideologies that proclaimed a person could become free only by becoming a true believer. Popper identified Hitler's Nazism and Stalin's communism as enemies of the Open Society. The Open Society is best understood as a type of intellectual and political freedom in which all ideas are constantly able to be challenged, based on the premise that there is no "political truth" as such, only a value relativism in which all ideas must be subject to constant challenge.

In a revealing passage, Soros identifies his antipathy to George W. Bush in terms fashioned from Popper's Open Society philosophy: "When

I heard President Bush say, 'Either you are with us or you are with the terrorists,' I was reminded of Nazi propaganda." [11] Fundamentally, Soros criticized the "Bush agenda" as being "nationalistic," too focused on pursuing narrowly defined U.S. nation-state interests.[12] Soros was particularly vituperative toward Vice President Dick Cheney, whom he demonized as "the power behind the throne" and characterized as having worked mostly successfully with Defense Secretary Donald Rumsfeld "in imposing their views on Bush." [13]

Asking how he came to have a position of influence on world affairs, Soros honestly admitted, "I have made a lot of money." [14] Nor has Soros been shy about spending his money to advance his political agenda. Since founding the Open Society Institute in 1979, Soros has spent hundreds of millions of dollars funding this flagship organization, which in turn has funneled millions to organizations dedicated to advancing causes of the political Left, including MoveOn.org and the Center for American Progress. In 2004, Soros admittedly spent several hundred million dollars in the attempt to prevent George W. Bush from having a second term as president. Soros was an early supporter of Barack Obama, holding a fund-raiser at his home and donating the maximum legal amount even before Obama was elected to the U.S. Senate. In 2006, Soros urged Obama to run for president. When Obama declared his candidacy, Soros organized a meeting with other financiers in Soros's Wall Street office.[15] His strong and early financial support of candidate Obama has given Soros a strong voice in the Obama White House.

ZBIGNIEW BRZEZINSKI

A foreign-policy expert and former national security advisor to President Jimmy Carter, Zbigniew Brzezinski agrees with Soros in viewing a global world as an interdependent world. "The quest for a wise foreign policy must begin with the realization that 'globalization' in its essence means global interdependence," he wrote in his 2004 book, *The Choice: Global Domination or Global Leadership.*[16] Brzezinski cautions America against pursuing a foreign policy based on national-security interests. Instead he prefigures President Obama's argument that the United States must think beyond national interests in foreign policy, because an "anxious America, obsessed with its own security, could find itself isolated in a hostile world." [17]

What Brzezinski counsels is a move away from American hegemony toward a globalism in which international agencies of governance assume more responsibility for maintaining world order. Recommending a "gradual and controlled devolution" of U.S. world power, Brzezinski looks forward to a new world order with "an increasingly formalized global community of shared interest, with supranational arrangements increasingly assuming some of the special security roles of traditional nation-states." [18] Brzezinski's antipathy to the continuance of nation-states, including the United States of America, could not be more clear.

Brzezinski is outspoken in how enthusiastically President Bill Clinton supported globalism as national policy. "Globalism became Clinton's pet project," Brzezinski wrote. [19] And again: "President Clinton was especially relentless in preaching the historical inevitability, social desirability, and need for American political leadership of mankind's march into the era of globalization." [20] To prove his point, Brzezinski cited several Clinton statements endorsing globalism. "Today we must embrace the inexorable logic of globalism—that everything, from the strength of our economy to the safety of our cities, to the health of our people, depends on events not only within our borders, but half a world away," Clinton told an audience in San Francisco in 1999, in a speech quoted by Brzezinski. [21]

The attraction of globalism, according to Brzezinski, was that "it appealed to the key power elites that shared common interests, it offered a critique of what ought to be rejected, and it postulated a better tomorrow." [22] Yet Brzezinski worried that globalism was producing a wave of anti-American reaction, in that U.S. hegemony was seen to be placing a self-serving U.S. sensibility on globalism. "The 'Made in the U.S.A.' label is thus quite visibly and unavoidably imprinted on globalization," he wrote. [23]

The immediate solution, Brzezinski argued, was for the United States to foster a strong alliance with the European Union. "Only the two sides of the Atlantic working together can chart a truly global course that may significantly improve the world state of affairs," he wrote. By developing a strong transatlantic alliance, he hoped, the world could move incrementally into a globalism that did not necessarily have U.S. dominance stamped on its character.

Brzezinski has consistently counseled that U.S. foreign policy must transcend national-security interests defined from the perspective of the United States seen as a nation-state, to reach a level in which U.S. foreign policy is determined by a global perspective of shared interests that encompasses the interests of all peoples and regions of the world. "A genuine U.S.-EU transatlantic alliance, based on a shared global perspective, must be derived from a similarly shared strategic understanding of the nature of our era, of the central threat that the world faces, and the role and mission of the West as a whole," he insisted.[24] He urged the United States and EU to unite into a transatlantic alliance, arguing: "The level playing field is a reality only between the United States and Europe. When the two agree, together they can dictate to the entire world the rules governing global trade and finance."[25]

Still, Brzezinski insisted that as the only true world superpower since the fall of the Soviet Union, the United States should not exert global power in a narrowly defined, self-interested manner. "The ultimate objective of American policy should be benign and visionary: to shape a truly cooperative global community, in keeping with long-range trends and with the fundamental interests of humankind,"[26] he wrote, expressing a perspective that has remained remarkably persistent since the 1960s, when Brzezinski first began the writings that set him on the path to the Carter White House and a role as a top foreign policy consultant to Barack Obama.

From his early writings, Brzezinski's sympathy for the extreme political Left and his antipathy for the nation-state was obvious. In his 1970 book, *Between Two Ages: America's Role in the Technetronic Era*, Brzezinski explained that the nation-state became "a new deity" after Christianity subsided as the "most active" of the "universal religions." However, Brzezinski argued that the nation-state was gradually losing its sovereignty: "The nation-state as a fundamental unit of man's organized life has ceased to be the principal creative force."[27] Brzezinski saw the international banks and the multinational corporations replacing the nation-state in their ability to establish a psychological identity for human beings as a new internationalism began to arise.

Writing his 1970 book from his position as director of the Research Institute on Communist Affairs and a professor of government at Columbia University, Brzezinski's admiration for Marxism was obvious. Clearly seeing a progression to history, Brzezinski claimed "Marxism represents a further vital and creative stage in the maturing of man's universal vision."[28] He further asserted that "in the gradual evolution of man's universal vision Marxism represents as important and progressive a stage as the appearance of nationalism and of the great religions."[29]

MANAGEMENT-CONSULTANT GLOBALISTS

Those who doubt economic globalism has been predicated upon the fading away of the nation-state need only consult a vast body of literature that has grown up among management consultants over the past two decades. During the Clinton administration several influential business consultants began preaching the gospel of globalism openly and loudly. Notable among them was Peter Drucker, one of the most important management consultants of his generation.

Arguing that the world is moving into a "post-capitalist" era, Drucker held that the nation-state had to transform into a "post-capitalist polity," in which power has to be shared with the transnational governmental authorities needed to regulate a global economy.[30] While Drucker expressed doubts that the nation-state would be quickly or easily replaced, he believed that a global economy made the nation-state a less effective economic regulator. The problem, in Drucker's view, was that corporations had become transnational, such that even a megastate, such as the United States, could only partly regulate a company that operated globally. "Successful transnational companies see themselves as separate, nonnational entities," Drucker wrote in *Foreign Affairs* in 1997. "This self-perception is evidenced by something unthinkable a few decades ago: a transnational top management. The world's best-known international management consulting firm, McKinsey & Co., for instance, though headquartered in New York, is headed by an Indian."[31]

Another person fulfilling Drucker's prediction was Kenichi Ohmae, a Japanese-born, MIT-trained nuclear engineer who became a senior partner at McKinsey & Company, where he directed the firm's practice in Japan and the Asian Pacific. In his 1990 book, *The Borderless World: Power and Strategy in the Interlocking Economy*, Ohmae left no doubt that he considered the nation-state to be an anachronism, much as did George Soros.[32] "Governments that continue to think and behave like saber-rattling, mercantilist ruling powers of centuries past discourage investment and impoverish their people," he wrote. "Worse, they isolate their citizens from the emerging world economy, which, in turn, effectively dooms them to a downward spiral of frustrated hopes and industrial stagnation."[33] In his 1995 book, *The End of the Nation State: The Rise of Regional Economies,* Ohmae was even more explicit.[34] There he explained that the forces of the global economy "*have* raised troubling questions about the relevance—and effectiveness—of nation states as meaningful aggregates in terms of which to think about, much less manage, economic activity." [35] He argued that the four "I's"—industry, investment, individuals, and information—flow so unimpeded across national borders that the very notion of sovereignty is "in serious need of redefinition or, perhaps, replacement." [36]

Ohmae was harsh in his criticism, charging that "the nation state has become an unnatural—even a dysfunctional—organization for thinking about economic activity." [37] And again: "In a borderless economy, any statistical regime that takes the nation state as its primary unit of analysis is—and must be—badly out of date." [38] He questioned economist John Maynard Keynes's assumption that nation-state governments should and could regulate national economies by traditional rules that specify that if demand increases, so does supply. Or, if supply increases, so do jobs. "In a borderless economy an increase in demand in one country may boost supply—and with it, the number of jobs—in another." Lower interest rates in a global economy may not increase supply at home, but might end up driving "supply-nurturing capital abroad to other countries where the promised returns look more attractive." [39]

Ohmae ridiculed the 1980s, when a prominent American business leader such as Lee Iacocca could talk openly of "Buy American" as a key component of his strategy to save Chrysler from bankruptcy. "Today few people still think in these terms," Ohmae said dismissively. "The world has moved a long way toward a fully borderless economy— in the sense that economic borders between nations are far less important than they used to be." [40] In other words, Ohmae viewed nation-state boundaries as artificial given that information technology permits worldwide markets to develop. According to the principles of supply-side economics, manufacturing and assembly could be geographically dispersed, as long as parts made anywhere in the world were delivered to the place of assembly on time. And the production of goods need not reside geographically in the markets where the goods are sold, as long as cost-efficient transportation allows the multinational corporations producing the goods to deliver them to market without wiping out the labor savings gained by diversifying jobs to low-cost labor markets. Generally, the supply-side formula worked, largely because labor costs tend to be the single greatest cost in producing goods and getting them to market.

Ohmae hypothesized that the optimal global business unit in the borderless world was a region-state, defined "through its consumption and its capacity for interaction with the global economy." [41] In other words, the nation-state was too limiting a geographical definition of the activity that went on in the global economy. The region-state, in Ohmae's analysis, was hypothesized to derive a more efficient geographical definition of how worldwide markets need to operate for maximum cost efficiency, competitiveness, and productivity. The region-state, in Ohmae's view, would need a large, computer-literate population "capable of providing some service to the global community," along with "an international airport and a capacity for international freight-handling" and "a highly developed cybernetic infrastructure." [42] He saw the movement toward region-states beginning in 1957 with the establishment of the European Economic Community, and he credited the euro as being the first regional currency. He saw the next emergence of a region-state market developing in the Western Hemisphere in two stages. First, he saw North America developing into a region-state, such as the North American Union, through the influence of NAFTA. Second, he saw a separate region-state that would develop in South America, through the Mercado Comun del Sur, or MERCOSUR.

Region-states, in Ohmae's analysis, entailed the inevitable "voluntary devolution of power and control from central nation-state authorities" to region-state governments that superseded the sovereignty of the nation-states composing the region-state. [43] Region-states, not nation-states, were the fundamental units of government needed, in his analysis, to regulate a one-world economy—at least, that is, until a one-world government could exert supremacy over the region-states, on the way to producing worldwide information sharing, technological expertise, competitiveness, and productivity, all within a global, cost-effective structure.

DAVID ROCKEFELLER

In his *Memoirs*, American banker David Rockefeller proclaimed himself to be a "proud internationalist." [44] In a much-quoted passage, Rockefeller posited: "Some even believe we are part of a secret cabal working against the best interests of the United States, characterizing my family and me as 'internationalists' and of conspiring with others around the world to build a more integrated global political and economic structure—one world, if you will." He could not have been more direct in posing this question, nor could he have been more direct in responding.

"If that's the charge, I stand guilty, and I am proud of it."[45] He noted that "populists" believe in conspiracies and that he had earned the distinction of being "conspirator in chief." Then he affirmed that that designation was also deserved. "Populists and isolationists ignore the tangible benefits that have resulted from our active internationalist role during the past half-century."[46] Put simply, the businesses the Chase bank financed under David Rockefeller's leadership had operated in dozens of countries, even if the corporations were headquartered in the United States. To Rockefeller and the multinational corporations he owned or financed, U.S. laws and regulations were roadblocks on the path to profits. The U.S. dollar itself simply introduced currency risk as another business risk Rockefeller's multinational corporations needed to manage.

Rockefeller characterized opponents as wanting "to wall off the United States by rejecting participation in such constructive international activities as the World Trade Organization and the North American Free Trade Agreement, eviscerating the World Bank and the International Monetary Fund, and assaulting the United States." All these approaches Rockefeller rejected. "The free flow of investment capital, goods, and people across borders will remain the fundamental factor in world economic growth and strengthening of democratic institutions everywhere," he wrote. Rockefeller insisted the United States cannot escape from global responsibilities: "In the twenty-first century there can be no place for isolationists; we must all be internationalists." Rockefeller left no doubt that he considered the United States of America instrumental in his vision of the future world, but only as an agent of change while the one-world economy and government took shape.

Rockefeller was a globalist from the political Right, in sharp contrast to globalists such as George Soros and Zbigniew Brzezinski. What the globalists agreed upon was that the United States, as a nation-state, could not be allowed to stand in the way of the formation of a one-world economy and a one-world government. Still, the political Left and Right had many points of specific disagreement on globalism. For the political Left, globalism promised to unite a worldwide proletariat, where workers could unite as transnational supporters of political parties seeking to expand international government power in the interest of creating a global social-welfare state. From the political Right, globalism promised to bring the interests of multinational corporations to the forefront. The political Right was as concerned with regional and global government as was the political Left, yet from the Right the requirements were that regional and global government needed to set "integrated and harmonized" worldwide administrative rules and regulations so the multinational corporations could operate globally. These regulations would also allow them to pursue cheap labor wherever labor efficiencies could be found in the world, utilize natural resources on an affordable basis, and develop an international transportation system for the cheap delivery of goods. The political Right felt social-welfare benefits would flow naturally from multinational businesses operating in a favorable one-world economy that set the rules so global corporations could maximize profits, increase productivity, and enhance competitiveness.

JOSEPH STIGLITZ

A critic of globalization, Nobel Prize–winning Columbia University professor of economics Joseph Stiglitz served on President Clinton's cabinet as chairman of the Council of Economic Advisors, until he stepped down in 1997 to become the chief economist for the World Bank. Although Stiglitz shared the sympathies of the political Right in promoting globalism, he had reservations. Stiglitz worried that allowing multinational corporations to pursue their global business interests under one-world government would leave the poor behind.

Stiglitz criticized globalism predominately because the economic benefits of a world economy have not so far been equally shared with emerging economies in the Third World. In his 2002 book, *Globalization and Its Discontents*, Stiglitz argued that a "growing divide between the haves and have-nots has left increasing numbers in the Third World in dire poverty, living on less than a dollar a day." [47] He noted that despite the promises made that a world economy would reduce poverty, "the actual number of people living in poverty has actually increased by almost 100 million," as total world income increased by an average of 2.5 percent annually. [48] Rather than reduce poverty, international organizations such as the IMF and World Bank have had the reverse effect of dramatically increasing the debt of Third World countries. In his follow-up 2006 book, *Making Globalization Work*, Stiglitz noted that the world's developing countries owed $1.5 trillion to creditors, including international banks such as the IMF and World Bank. Despite repeated rounds of international debt forgiveness, "the level of indebtedness by low-income countries has continued to increase." [49]

Stiglitz's solution was not to end globalism, but to insist that one-world government operate according to democratic principles whereby the developing countries of the Third World would have an equal voice.

In his analysis of the problem, Stiglitz agreed with Ohmae. Nation-states were incapable of governing or regulating a world economy effectively. While nation-states have been weakened by free trade, "there has yet to be created at the international level the kinds of democratic global institutions that can deal effectively with the problems globalization has created." [50] Stiglitz was forthright in his conclusion that world government was needed to regulate a world economy. "Unfortunately, we have no world government, accountable to the people of every country, to oversee the globalization process in a fashion comparable to the way national governments guided the nationalization process," he wrote in *Globalization and Its Discontents*. "Instead, we have a system that might be called *global governance without global government*, one in which a few institutions—the World Bank, the IMF, the WTO—and a few players—the finance, commerce, and trade ministries, closely linked to certain financial and commercial interests—dominate the scene, but in which many of those affected by their decisions are left almost voiceless." [51]

In writing *Making Globalism Work*, Stiglitz argued that economic globalization has outpaced political globalization. [52] He insisted that "we will have to think and act more globally," developing a "sense of global identity" to replace the national identities common to a previous era in which nation-states were the appropriate entity to govern and regulate the economy. [53] Here Stiglitz embraced Brzezinski's admonition that global-thinking elites would need to accept principles of social justice that transcend narrowly defined national interests. Stiglitz has repeatedly argued that a system of international one-world governance would involve changing voting-rights organizations including the U.N., the IMF, the World Bank, and the WTO, so that the United States no longer has effective veto power and the effective decision making is shared more democratically, giving developing countries a participatory voice.

Responding to the global Economic Panic of 2009, Stiglitz chaired an eighteen-member U.N. commission charged with drafting a proposal for reforming international financial institutions, including the IMF and World Bank, to be voted on by the 192-member U.N. General Assembly. Predictably, Stiglitz's commission recommended replacing the G20 organization, in which a group of the world's twenty largest economies set global economic policy, with a new Global Economic Council. The proposed council would include representatives from the developing economies of the Third World, to introduce more democratization into global economic decision making. It would also create a new global reserve currency system that would provide support to developing countries, so that the distribution of the global reserve currency would not be subject to veto by the industrialized countries that dominate international organizations such as the IMF, World Bank, and WTO. According to the *Financial Times,* Stiglitz's proposal stressed that a global response to the world financial crisis "must encompass more than the G7 or G8 or G20, but the representatives of the entire planet, from the G192." [54]

FORMAL GROUPS AND SECRET MEETINGS

Interestingly, Zbigniew Brzezinski and David Rockefeller worked together to found the Trilateral Commission in 1973. Among the founding group were Paul Volcker and Alan Greenspan, both of whom later became chairmen of the Federal Reserve. David Rockefeller advanced the idea to form what became the Trilateral Commission at the 1972 meeting of the Bilderberg Group, a highly secretive group that was organized by Prince Bernhard of the Netherlands and took its name from the Netherlands hotel where the group first met in 1954. Other groups thought to promote one-world government interests include the Council on Foreign Relations, which David Rockefeller chaired from 1970 until he retired as chairman in 1985, and the World Economic Forum, which Brzezinski has characterized as "a party congress for the new global elite: top politicians, financial tycoons, captains of commerce, media moguls, academic heavyweights, and even rock stars." [55]

The Trilateral Commission has come under criticism since it was first disclosed that some twenty-five commission members played key roles in the Carter administration. In its first two months in office, the Obama administration appointed nine Trilateral Commission members, virtually 10 percent of the commission's current list of U.S. members. [56]

The Trilateral Commission members of the Obama administration include:

- U.S. Treasury Secretary Timothy Geithner;

- Ambassador to the United Nations Susan Rice;

- National Security Advisor Thomas Donilon;

- Chairman, Economic Recovery Committee, Paul Volcker;

- Director of National Intelligence Admiral Dennis C. Blair;

- Assistant Secretary of State, Asia and Pacific, Kurt M. Campbell;

- Deputy Secretary of State James Steinberg;

- State Department Special Envoy Richard Haas;

- State Department Special Envoy Dennis Ross; and

- State Department Special Envoy Richard Holbrooke.

Many other incidental links exist between the Obama administration and the Trilateral Commission:

- Secretary of State Hillary Clinton is married to Trilateral Commission member William Jefferson Clinton;

- Treasury Secretary Geithner came to national prominence working for former Nixon secretary of state Henry Kissinger at Kissinger Associates in New York, and Kissinger is a Trilateral Commission lifetime trustee;

- Trilateral Commission member Brent Scowcroft, former national security advisor under Presidents Gerald Ford and George H. W. Bush, has been an unofficial adviser to Obama and a mentor to Defense Secretary Robert Gates;

- Trilateral Commission member Robert Zoellick is currently president of the World Bank; Lawrence Summers, White House economic adviser, was mentored during the Clinton administration by Trilateral Commission member Robert Rubin, former Treasury secretary under President Clinton.

Yet, in fairness, it must be pointed out that many Trilateral Commission members also served in the administration of President George W. Bush, including:

- Richard Armitage, U.S. Secretary of State, 2001–2005;

- Robert Blackwill, U.S. Ambassador to India, 2001–2003, and U.S. National Security Council Deputy for Iraq, 2003–2009;

- Meghan O'Sullivan, special assistant to the president and deputy national security advisor for Iraq, 2005;

- General Joseph W. Ralston, NATO Commander, 2003, and special envoy for countering the Kurdistan Workers Party, 2006; and

- Timothy Geithner, who was president of the New York Federal Reserve from 2003 to 2009.

The list of Council of Foreign Relations members who have served in presidential administrations since the group was founded in 1921 is far too lengthy to mention.

Beginning with the World Economic Forum in January/February, an annual meeting cycle continues with Bilderberg and G20 meetings in April/May, followed by World Bank and IMF annual conferences in September. In each venue, many if not most key meetings are held behind closed doors. Still, the World Economic Forum is widely reported in the international press, and organizations such as the IMF and World Bank publish scores of documents that make apparent their promotion of the global economy. The Council on Foreign Relations publishes the quarterly *Foreign Affairs* magazine, in which those who hold or have held government policy jobs, academics, and a variety of nongovernmental officials openly debate a wide range of views on international politics. Still, what emerges from virtually all meetings of these groups is a consensus for globalism that soon begins showing up in the policy positions articulated by politicians in office, including recommendations made by the president of the United States to Congress.[57]

That there are closed-door conferences of global activists cannot be denied. In his *Memoirs*, David Rockefeller writes what reads almost like a confession to having joined the Pesenti Group in 1967, a select private meeting organized by Carlo Pesenti, the owner of a number of prominent Italian corporations. Founding members of the Pesenti Group included Jean Monnet, Robert Schuman, and Konrad Adenauer, key members of the elite that for decades worked separately and in unison to create the European Union. Rockefeller was typically the only American attending the Pesenti Group meetings, although he disclosed that Henry Kissinger joined the group for dinner when the group met in Washington while Kissinger was national security advisor to President Nixon. Rockefeller noted that all the members of the Pesenti Group were committed to European political and economic integration. He withdrew from the group when it developed a concern about the Soviet threat and the rise to power of communist political parties in France and Italy. Rockefeller related that he enjoyed the discussions, but that he ultimately withdrew after his Chase bank associates feared his membership would be construed as "consorting with reactionaries."[58] No published meetings of Pesenti Group meetings can be found.

Rockefeller also played a key behind-the-scenes role in advancing the Security and Prosperity Partnership of North America (SPP) agenda. A Council on Foreign Relations report, "Building a North American Community," published in May 2005, argued that the Security and Prosperity Partnership of North America, sealed by President Bush with Mexico and Canada on March 23, 2005, should become by 2010 a "North American economic and security community, the boundaries of which would be defined by a common external tariff and an outer security perimeter."[59] The Council of the Americas, founded by David Rockefeller in 1965, played a major role in creating the North American Competitiveness Council, or NACC, under the SPP.

The NACC consisted primarily of thirty multinational corporations handpicked by the chambers of commerce in the United States, Mexico, and Canada, designated to serve as advisers to the bureaucratic trilateral working groups constituted under the SPP. At the SPP summit meetings held in Montebello, Quebec, in August 2007, and in New Orleans in April 2008, the NACC was the only group to meet behind closed doors with the three heads of states, the various cabinet ministers in attendance, and the SPP working-group bureaucrats. No press representatives were allowed to attend the meetings and no transcripts of the discussions were ever produced. Yet, the SPP website, maintained for the U.S. government by the U.S. Department of Commerce, posts various "Reports to Leaders" that document more than 250 memoranda of understanding or other agreements signed by the working-group bureaucrats, even though virtually none of the agreements are published on the website (www.spp.gov).

Truthfully, penetrating closed-door meetings and documenting secret closed-to-the-press international conferences are not necessary to prove that the devotees of globalism include an influential group of current and former government officials, intellectuals and academics, leaders of nongovernmental organizations, a worldwide business elite, and many prominent members of the mainstream media. Just read their many published books and the reports emanating from the meetings that are largely open to the public, including the World Economic Forum. There is no conspiracy when the globalists have been writing openly for more than four decades about their intentions.

In his book *Superclass: The Global Power Elite and the World They Are Making*, David Rothkopf, a former managing director of Kissinger Associates and the deputy undersecretary of commerce for international trade policy in the Clinton administration, wrote openly about the many internationalist meetings he has attended, including those of the Bilderberg Group.[60] He quoted one regular Bilderberg attendee as saying, "I've been to most of the last twelve [meetings]. It's nothing. It's a group of 120 very senior people. By senior I mean old. I'm not joking about them being old, by the way. Rockefeller is in his nineties." [61] The regular attendee also commented that "Oprah Winfrey has more influence than anyone who goes to Bilderberg at this point." [62] Similarly, he quoted a regular attendee of Trilateral Commission meetings as saying about the same: "It's a bunch of has-beens who do not have power except to convene themselves—and to feel a little bit more important because they have convened themselves." The attendee commented that the Trilateral Commission meetings typically consist of "useless presentations and levels of abstraction that are unconnected with reality." [63]

"Davos Man" is a term coined by the late Harvard University political science professor Samuel Huntington to describe a group of globalist international elites who have no allegiance to any country. The Davos Man, as described by Huntington, views national boundaries as inevitably vanishing, sees nation-state governments as harmful vestiges of the past, and believes national laws and administrative regulations are as detrimental to the world economy as are national currencies.[64]

Groups promoting globalism will remain suspect as long as their doors remain closed, their agendas are kept secret, and their discussions remain off-the-record. If those supporting world governance want the end result to be democratic, then transparency should be the standard of all the governmental and nongovernmental meetings examined here. The intent to create a one-world government to regulate a one-world economy is easily documented, simply by reporting the many steps being taken by nations including the United States to participate actively in promoting the work of international organizations and to advance the agenda to create regional compacts, including SPP under NAFTA. The call for global governance structures to regulate the world economy has never been as clearly articulated as it is now, as a repeatedly proffered solution to the global Economic Panic of 2009.

Since the 1950s and the election of Dwight D. Eisenhower to be president, David Rockefeller has been identified with the "Rockefeller wing" of the Republican Party, a designation meant to specify the business interests identified in the public mind with the Republican Party. In contrast, the Democratic Party has been the political party of labor unions since the presidency of Franklin D. Roosevelt began during the Great Depression in 1932. When Ronald Reagan first started running for the presidency, conservatives such as Howard Phillips encouraged him to form a conservative party instead of running as a Republican. The argument was that moral and social conservatives such as Reagan would not easily blend with the Rockefeller wing of a Republican Party that was becoming increasingly internationalist, as was David Rockefeller himself. This tension has continued, especially as George H. W. Bush and George W. Bush supported international organizations, including the United Nations, the International Monetary Fund, and the World Bank while they worked hard to advance the interests of multinational companies in a series of free-trade agreements, including NAFTA and CAFTA, and in their support of the World Trade Organization.

PRESIDENT BUSH CREATES THE
TRANSATLANTIC ECONOMIC COUNCIL

Almost as if he were following a script written by Zbigniew Brzezinski, President George W. Bush created the Transatlantic Economic Council with the stroke of a pen, affirming the need to create a regional union between the EU and the United States. Combining the United States and the EU as two democratic regions sharing a common heritage has appeared as a natural move to globalists favoring regional structures as a stepping stone to world government. A considerable amount of history supports the current efforts to integrate the U.S. and the EU even though the American public remains largely unaware of the effort.

In an official ceremony at the White House on April 20, 2007, President Bush signed the "Transatlantic Economic Integration" agreement between the United States and the European Union, along with Chancellor Angela Merkel of Germany, the current president of the European Council, and Jose Manuel Barroso, president of the European Commission. The agreement, which was not ratified by the Senate as a treaty or passed by Congress as a law, committed the United States to "deeper transatlantic economic integration," solely on the signature of President Bush. The document acknowledged that "the transatlantic economy remains at the forefront of globalization" and asserted that the United States and the European Union "seek to strengthen transatlantic economic integration." [65]

The new Transatlantic Economic Council was to be chaired on the U.S. side by a cabinet-level officer in the Executive Office of the President and on the EU side by a member of the European Commission. The council was to be headed by Allan Hubbard, assistant to the president for economic policy and director of the National Economic Council. Gunther Verheugen, vice president of the European Commission in charge of enterprise and industry, was selected as the EU head. The council was tasked with creating regulatory convergence between the United States and the EU on some forty different public policy areas, ranging from creating common U.S.-EU intellectual property rights to establishing a "regular dialogue" to address obstacles to investment. At the joint press conference following the signing ceremony, Bush thanked the other two leaders for signing the "trans-Atlantic economic integration plan," commenting, "It is recognition that the closer that the United States and the EU become, the better off our people will be." Barroso added that the council is meant to be "a permanent body, with senior people on both sides of the Atlantic."

The plan to create the Transatlantic Economic Council has roots in a plan written before World War II by Clarence K. Streit, a world-government advocate whose 1940 book, *Union Now*, called for the creation of a Transatlantic Union to be formed as a step toward world government. Streit's idea was to create a new governmental federation with an international constitution, unifying the democracies of the United States, United Kingdom, France, Australia, Belgium, Canada, Denmark, Finland, Holland, Ireland, New Zealand, Norway, Sweden, Switzerland, and the Union of South Africa.[66] Streit promoted the idea that one-world governance should emerge by democracies coming together to install democratic principles at the core of global governance. Calling world government "public problem number one," Streit proposed to start by organizing the world democracies into a union that would exclude dictatorships.

The Streit Council, formed as a nonprofit educational group headquartered in Washington, D.C., remains committed to advancing Streit's agenda to create a world union of democracies according to a plan that would first create Euro-Atlantic integration, with particular emphasis on NATO and the European Union.[67] The work to create a Transatlantic Common Market can be traced back to the Clinton administration's decision in 1995 to join in the New Transatlantic Agenda with the European Commission.[68] The website of the Transatlantic Economic Council at first openly proclaimed that the council is "a political body to oversee and accelerate government-to-government integration between the European Union and the United States of America." That direct proclamation has since been removed from the site.

Another group advancing the agenda to integrate the United States and the EU is the Transatlantic Policy Network, or TPN, a nongovernmental organization headquartered in Washington, D.C., and Brussels.[69] The honorary president of the TPN is Senator Robert Bennett, Republican of Utah; the TPN is advised by a bipartisan congressional TPN policy group consisting of six U.S. senators and forty-nine U.S. congressmen. The TPN has targeted 2015 as the date by which a Transatlantic Common Market between the United States and the European Union should be formed. Ira Straus, former founder and U.S. coordinator of the Committee on Eastern Europe and Russia in NATO, a group dedicated to including Russia within NATO, credits Bennett as TPN chairperson with reviving Streit's work "seven decades later."[70] A globalist with leftist political leanings, Straus was a Fulbright professor of political science at Moscow State University and the Moscow State Institute of International Relations from 2001 to 2002.

Writing in the fall 2007 issue of the Streit Council journal *Freedom and Union*, Representative Jim Costa, Democrat of California, and the chairman of the U.S. Steering Committee of the TPN, affirmed the TPN target date of 2015 for the creation of a Transatlantic Common Market.[71] Costa also argued that the Transatlantic Economic Council is tasked with the mission to establish a common set of U.S.-EU economic regulations, creating by bureaucratic action the required Transatlantic Common Market regulatory infrastructure without seeking specific congressional approval of a new free-trade agreement. Writing in the same issue of the Streit Council publication, Senator Bennett also confirmed that what has become known as the "Merkel initiative" would allow the Transatlantic Economic Council to integrate and harmonize administrative rules and regulations between the United States and the EU "in a very quiet sort of way," without having to introduce a new U.S.-European free-trade area to Congress for enabling legislation.[72]

The congruity of ideas between Bennett and Streit is clear when Bennett writes passages that precisely echo goals Streit stated in the same terms in 1940. One such example is Bennett's claim in his Streit Council article that creating a Transatlantic Common Market would combine markets that constitute 60 percent of world gross domestic product under a common regulatory standard that would become "the de facto world standard regardless of what any other parties say." Similarly, Streit wrote in *Union Now* that the economic power of the fifteen democracies he sought to combine in a Transatlantic Union would be overwhelming in its economic power and a clear challenge to the authoritarian states then represented by Nazi Germany and the communist Soviet Union. In an article titled "From Atlantic Market to Atlantic Polity?" in the Streit Council journal *Freedom and Union*, World Bank economist Domenec Ruiz Devesa openly acknowledged that "transatlantic economic integration, though important in itself, is not the end." [73] Then he made the key admission. "As understood by Jean Monnet," Devesa continued, "economic integration must and will lead to political integration, since an integrated market requires common institutions producing common rules to govern it."

In February 2007, the Transatlantic Policy Network formed a Transatlantic Market Implementation Group to put in place "a roadmap and framework" to direct the activity of the Transatlantic Economic Council to achieve the creation of the Transatlantic Common Market by 2015. With this move, the Transatlantic Policy Network, a nongovernmental organization (NGO) with a policy advisory board of U.S. congressmen and senators, set about to influence the activities of the Transatlantic Economic Council, an official international governmental body established by executive fiat in the United States and the EU, to create a new common market structure below the radar of public opinion, without official congressional approval or oversight.

So even though U.S. congressmen and senators were involved in the process indirectly as advisers to an influential policy NGO, no new law or treaty was sought by the Bush administration to approve or implement the plan to create a Transatlantic Common Market.

In a February 2007 document titled "Completing the Transatlantic Market," the TPN's Transatlantic Market Implementation Group stated its purpose: "The aim of this roadmap and framework would be to remove barriers to trade and investment across the Atlantic and to reduce regulatory compliance costs." [74]

THE STATE DEPARTMENT GETS ON BOARD

What could easily appear to be separate and unrelated agendas are actually understood by the U.S. government at the highest levels to be combined efforts designed to create regional structures of governance to preside over the global economy. A largely unreported meeting held on March 10, 2008, at the U.S. State Department in Washington, D.C., combined the North American Union agenda to integrate the United States, Mexico, and Canada with a transatlantic agenda to integrate the United States with the European Union into a Transatlantic Union.

The State Department meeting was limited to selected press. Yet attending reporters were required to agree in advance to adhere to what are known as "Chatham House" rules. These rules prohibit reporters from attributing specific comments to individual participants. Chatham House rules, designed to stimulate open discussion, still prevent reporters from crediting the views expressed to the participants expressing those views, giving an otherwise "open meeting" the cover of limited disclosure. World Net Daily agreed to abide by the rules and was cleared by the State Department to receive the credentials needed to attend the meeting.

The meeting was held under the auspices of the Advisory Committee on International Economic Policy, or ACIEP.[75] Membership in ACIEP includes nonelected representatives from business, labor, environmental, academic, legal, and public interest groups. ACIEP meetings take place three times a year. A complete membership list of the sixty-person ACIEP is published on the State Department website. ACIEP members include corporate officers from General Electric; Exxon Mobil Corporation; JPMorgan Chase; Archer Daniels Midland Company; United Parcel Service; Citibank; Procter & Gamble; Hunt Oil; CMS Energy; Boeing; 3M; and Goldman Sachs.[76]

World Net Daily observed about twenty-five ACIEP members attending, including U.S. corporations involved in international trade, prominent U.S. business trade groups, law firms involved with international business law, international investment firms, and other international trade consultants. No members of the U.S. Senate or the House of Representatives were present. The agenda for the ACIEP meeting was not published and State Department officials in attendance refused to grant WND permission to publish the meeting agenda, citing the Chatham House rules.

Knowing that attending reporters could not attribute their comments to a particular speaker, the speakers at the meeting were quite forthright about expressing their thoughts and intentions. Several participants openly said in their presentations to the group that the unstated premise of the SPP was to create a North American business platform. The goal of the SPP, the speakers alleged, was to advantage the multinational corporations based in North America the way the European Union benefits the multinational corporations based in Europe. Other participants noted that a key operating purpose of the Transatlantic Economic Council is to create a convergence in administrative rules and regulations between Europe and North America, anticipating the creation of a Transatlantic Economic Union uniting the European Union with North American markets organized under the SPP.

Participants pointed out that transatlantic trade is currently 40 percent of all world trade, and argued that trade and nontrade barriers need to be further reduced to maintain that market share as a framework is put in place to advance transatlantic economic integration. Still, some participants argued that many corporations in North America have already moved beyond a North American focus to adopt a global perspective that transcends even the transatlantic market. "Supply chains and markets are everywhere," one participant asserted. "What's to stop global corporations from going after the cheapest labor available globally, wherever they can find it, provided the cost of transporting goods globally can be managed economically?" Other participants argued that regional alliances were still important, if only to put in place the institutional bases that would ultimately lead to global governance founded on uniform global administrative regulations favorable to multinational corporations.

"North America should be a premier platform to establish continental institutions," a participant said. "That's why we need to move the security perimeters to include the whole continent, especially as we erase the borders between North American countries to accommodate expanding free trade." The discussion left no doubt that the SPP working groups and the Transatlantic Economic Council were being supported by top-level cabinet officers and the heads of state in both the EU and in North America. "Working groups" is a term of trade in the European Union. The working groups created under the SPP fell within the auspices of the commerce departments in the three governments and consisted of top-level bureaucrats in each country.

A part of the discussion was devoted to concerns that national regulators in North America and Europe were too reluctant to abandon provincial regulatory advantages. "Regulators by nature are advocates and they are hard to move," one participant grumbled. "What we need is more diplomats and negotiators to identify solutions, otherwise the bureaucrats will bog down the progress we need to see coming out of the SPP and TEC."

"North America is already an integrated continental economy and a continental-wide business platform," another said. "What we need now is more regulatory convergence. When we say the regulations should be 'harmonized,' what we mean is that a common set of administrative regulations and procedures, once approved, should be ready to be implemented throughout NAFTA, SPP and the TEC."

GLOBALISTS ENVISION A POST-AMERICAN WORLD

During the 2008 presidential campaign, Democratic candidate Barack Obama was photographed carrying a copy of *Newsweek* magazine editor Fareed Zakaria's book *The Post-American World*.[77] Zakaria's thesis was that globalism had caused an economic rise in much of the rest of the world, thereby reducing the world dominance the United States held economically at the end of World War II. "Look around," he wrote. "The tallest building in the world is now in Taipei, and it will soon be overtaken by one being built in Dubai. The world's richest man is Mexican, and its largest publicly traded corporation is Chinese."[78] Zakaria pointed out that even with shopping, "America's greatest sporting activity," of the world's top ten malls, only one is in the United States, and the world's largest is in Beijing.

The assessment of Parag Khanna was harsher. Khanna, who had worked for both the World Economic Forum and the Council on Foreign Relations, wrote a book titled *The Second World*, in which he argued that the United States is currently on a Toynbee-like decline from historic world dominance and empire at the end of World War II to the possible status of a second-class nation saddled by debt and taxes.[79] Just as the Roman Empire and the British Empire declined, Khanna argued, the United States is also destined to decline. "The United States share of the world economy has fallen from 50 percent to 25 percent since World War II—with Europe and Asia building the other two world-regions," he wrote. Khanna expressed doubt that the United States could long remain on the debt-funded "consumption binge"[80] that had fueled the world economy since the 1990s. The consumer binge of the 1990s was supercharged after the 9/11 attacks by the historically low interest rates and readily available mortgages, even to unqualified buyers, that built the mortgage bubble, and the heavily marketed home-equity loans that buoyed the retail sales boom through 2006. "And because America's debt payments already exceed the investment it receives, it is living beyond the wealth saved for the next generation, actually making the country poorer," Khanna warned.[81]

Perhaps predictably, the world economy so promoted by globalists has resulted in a diminishing of the relative economic position of the United States. Khanna was more harsh, warning that grim economic times await the United States for the foreseeable future. He noted that the United States ranks near the bottom of OECD (Organisation for Economic Co-operation and Development) countries in average-worker income and income inequality. "America's median income is far less impressive than the mean income its individual wealth deceptively inflates," he commented.[82] Arguing that America is becoming a dual country composed of the wealthy and the poor, with a middle class diminishing to the point of extinction, Khanna observed: "For three decades now, America's working class has seen no increase in its wages in real terms, its share of the economy dwindling even as its numbers swell."[83]

Still, globalists continue to see globalism as inevitable, even when they are forced to acknowledge that an inevitable consequence of economic globalism is that the relative economic status of the United States has declined to the point where the United States is at risk of losing not only world economic dominance but a first-class life style for the U.S. middle class. Somehow, most globalists see this evolution as unavoidable, anchored in their belief that a world economy is already an indisputable and irreversible reality. "America is a first-world country in need of a Marshall Plan to stay where it is," Khanna concluded.[84] On the horizon, globalists see more globalism, even if the end result is a post-American world.

MEET THE GLOBALISTS

In a 1997 article in *Foreign Affairs*, Peter Drucker noted that the demise of the nation-state has been predicted for the last two hundred years, "beginning with Immanuel Kant in his 1795 essay 'Perpetual Peace,' and continuing through Karl Marx in 'Withering Away of the State,' to Bertrand Russell's speeches in the 1950s and 1960s."[85] In the last few decades, globalists have persisted to the point where *New York Times* columnist Thomas Friedman could declare in his book *The World Is Flat* that the world has entered Globalization 3.0, an era Friedman defined as "the newfound power for individuals to collaborate and compete globally." [86] Incrementally, the concept of globalization has become conventional wisdom, ever since Kant in his 1795 essay called for a world-governance organization that became the model for the League of Nations and the United Nations itself.

In the age of Kant, internationalists were introducing a new concept. Today, as the majority of people in the world are conditioned to accept globalism as an accomplished fact, a difference in scale has become a difference in phenomenon. Anyone objecting to globalism with a desire to secure a strong economic future for the American worker and the American middle class is increasingly at risk of being demonized as a "protectionist," or as an "isolationist." Yet the fact that the world has become more global in telecommunications and economic markets does not mean the United States must compromise sovereignty in order to participate in world trade. Nor is the exploitation of labor or natural resources a necessary condition of free trade. Workers and the U.S. middle class can and should have as strong a voice in dictating the terms of free trade as do the globalist elite and the multinational corporations. To argue this position is not the same as arguing that the United States should withdraw from global economics or politics and return to a pre–World War I separatism.

Speaking during the 2008 presidential campaign, Barack Obama told a public audience in Berlin that "the 21st [century] has revealed a world more intertwined than at any time in history," articulating a key tenet of globalist conventional wisdom. Obama envisioned a "global citizenship" and called for walls between races and tribes, natives and immigrants, Christians and Muslims and Jews to be torn down. In words that could have been written by Zbigniew Brzezinski, candidate Obama proclaimed, "America has no better partner than Europe." In asking to build "new bridges across the globe as strong as the one that bound us across the Atlantic," Obama included "new institutions" on the list of the required components necessary "to meet the challenges of the 21st century." [87]

A world in which the United Nations, the IMF, World Bank, and the WTO are raised to the level of world-governance organizations is a difference in phenomenon—a world in which U.S. sovereignty will be viewed as an outmoded term of reference, much as strengthening the

U.S. economy is viewed with skepticism by globalists fearing the U.S. economy might be strengthened to the detriment of the world economy. Yet while globalists such as Joseph Stiglitz criticize globalism, in Stiglitz's case for failing to bring prosperity to developing countries, the solution is typically *more* globalism, a veneer of global governance over the global economy to regulate it in pursuit of goals perceived to be more fair to those less fortunate in the global economy.

What is left unchallenged by globalists is the possibility that globalism itself may be inherently flawed. The world economy is necessarily moving to a leveled labor market in which a government and business elite will be the only winners. Successful middle classes in nations such as the United States will be forced to struggle for their very existence.

It should be clear from the Economic Panic of 2009 that globalism has not worked. What the global economy produced in the United States is historically unprecedented deficit spending, such that economic growth itself has become totally dependent on credit-driven bubbles of false economic prosperity that are doomed to be short-lived.

If this is the economic future for which Americans are being asked to sacrifice U.S. sovereignty, a rejection of the very premises of globalism makes sense before the United States becomes a second-rate economic power.

What all Americans must understand is that global governance will end up destroying the very American nation-state our Founding Fathers intended to create for us to pass on to future generations.

SIX

Here Come the Cheap Chinese Goods

For the last 30 years trade has been an ever increasing part of economic activity, with trade growth often outpacing gains in output.

—World Trade Organization Director-General Pascal Lamy, 2009[1]

Free trade was sold to Americans on the promise that reducing tariffs would increase U.S. exports and create U.S. jobs. Americans were told that protectionism was the formula for economic disaster in the global economy, while the road to prosperity could be paved only by expanding U.S. free-trade agreements throughout the Western Hemisphere, across to the European Union, and around the globe, to include China, India, and the rest of the developing world.

Yet the U.S. balance of trade has steadily deteriorated since the early 1990s, when President George H. W. Bush first pushed the idea that the United States should enter the North American Free Trade Agreement with Mexico and Canada. Nothing has changed in the nearly ten years since 2000, when President Bill Clinton signed a landmark bill granting permanent normalized-trade-relations status to China to accommodate the latter's entrance into the World Trade Organization. Currently, the United States leads the world in imports, not exports, and our negative balance of trade has been in the consistent range of $55–60 billion since 2005.[2] As noted above, the U.S. imbalance of trade with China is in the billions and growing every year, from a deficit of approximately a negative $162 billion in 2004 to a negative $266 billion in 2008, a straight line downward.[3]

Even as the U.S. recession that officially began in December 2008 deepened and the global Economic Panic of 2009 developed, U.S. exports did not revive sufficiently to make the U.S. balance of trade go positively, as classical economists would have predicted. Yes, the economic slowdown in the United States did make U.S. exports cheaper for the rest of the world, but by 2007 so many millions of jobs had been outsourced to cheaper labor in foreign countries that cheaper exports were not sufficient to return the jobs to U.S. shores. In January 2009, the United States still had a $36 billion negative balance of trade.[4]

Instead of tooling up the United States to benefit from a renaissance in job creation stimulated by exports and free trade, North America has engaged in a massive reengineering of the entire continental transportation system to make cheaper the transport into the continent of hundreds of millions of containers with cheap goods largely from China. The conclusion was clear: in a world economy, the United States was valued as a consumer country, not as a producer, manufacturer, or exporter. The transformation of America from a producer of goods to a consumer of cheap goods from China makes the nation vulnerable to a never-ending negative balance of trade from which there is no sure plan to reverse the trend.

THE GLOBAL TRANSFORMATION OF
U.S. TRANSPORTATION INFRASTRUCTURE

In the final analysis, multinational corporations are not served by pursuing cheap labor in China unless the transportation of those cheaply produced goods to U.S. markets can also be done cheaply. The solution demands a massive reconfiguration of North American transportation infrastructure. In the United States, the Eisenhower administration began the interstate highway system in the 1950s as a means of improving intercity transportation across the nation. In the nearly six decades of interstate highway construction, the fill-in effort has been to build beltway networks of intracity freeways to facilitate transportation within cities. Now, to meet the robust demands of international trade under the

current rules of free trade, the nation's transportation needs are differ-
ernt. A continental transportation infrastructure must be built to connect to deep-water ports capable of handling post-Panamax ships. This
includes the construction of a new generation of north–south freeways
in the United States that will be designed with separate lanes for passenger automobiles, commercial trucks, and trains. Pipelines built into separate corridors of international trade superhighways will carry oil,
natural gas, and water throughout the United States. Moreover, the railroad network of the continent needs to be reconfigured to interconnect
the United States, Mexico, and Canada so continental ports can be used
as drop-off points, with railroads carrying containers across great distances until truck transport takes over to bring containers to their final
destinations.

The reconfiguration of North American transportation to accommodate millions of containers from China is fundamental to a vision of
free-trade prosperity in which the United States is primarily a consumer
market, not a producer nation. Truthfully, if multinational corporations
are given full license to pursue cheap labor wherever it is available
around the globe, American workers will be undercut in wages and benefits in the vast majority of manufacturing and assembly activities.
Long-term, only giant U.S. agribusinesses will be able to compete with
cheaper food production from China, Mexico, Latin America, and
South America. For the multinational corporations operating in North
America, profits can be maximized only if the costs of transporting
goods are reduced to as close to zero as possible, just as the pursuit of
foreign labor is aimed to reduce the cost of international labor to as
close to zero as possible.

International free trade depends upon the concept of "intermodal"
transportation, a term transportation economists have developed to re-
fer to containers loaded once and transferred to various other modes of
transportation, including trucks and trains, without being unloaded or
reloaded. So, an oceangoing containership picks up the container in a
Chinese port. That container is then carried across the Pacific Ocean to
a West Coast Canadian port in British Columbia, a West Coast U.S.
port, or a Mexican port on the Pacific. After arriving at port, the container can be transferred by a crane, without unloading or reloading the
container, onto a train or a truck that will carry the container to market
in the interior of the United States.

Simply imposing a dramatically increased volume of containers upon
existing ports, highways, and railroad lines is not the solution to the

problem. If the plan is to flood North America with tens of millions of containers over the foreseeable decades, then new deep-water ports will be needed to accommodate the larger post-Panamax ships carrying containers across the oceans with a minimum of workers. New continental superhighways designed with moving international trade as their primary purpose will have to be built. These modern free-trade continental-transport systems will need to be designed to reduce the number of workers required to operate and maintain the transportation system itself. When moving the containers from the ports, Mexican trucks and trains will be utilized whenever possible, once again to reduce labor costs.

As the international free-trade plan progresses, North American workers who manufactured the goods a generation ago will be employed only to move and merchandise the foreign-manufactured goods. Still, the U.S. consumer is expected to remain the engine that drives the international trade, despite the outsourcing of millions of jobs to China and the Far East to produce the goods now arriving in North America by container.

GLOBAL ECONOMIC RECESSION
SLOWS INTERNATIONAL TRADE

The years 1998 through 2007 were an expanding era of international trade, in which economic projections for increasing container traffic began driving a need to reconfigure North American transportation systems. The current economic recession that officially began in December 2008 has slowed down international trade. On March 23, 2009, the World Trade Organization released projections indicating that the volume of international trade, which grew by 6 percent in 2007 and by 2 percent in 2008, would fall a dramatic 9 percent in 2009. The WTO characterized the downturn in international trade as a "collapse in global demand" that has produced the biggest contraction in international trade since Word War II. The contraction in developed countries was projected to be particularly severe, with exports falling by 10 percent in 2009. The WTO also noted that real global output growth slowed in 2008 to 1.7 percent, compared to 3.5 percent in 2007, with a further fall likely in 2009. "This is the first decline in total world production since the 1930s, and its impact is magnified in trade," the WTO commented.[5]

The worldwide economic recession has dealt a severe blow to international trade, further undermining the proposition that a global economy would be sufficiently robust to grow even during a U.S. downturn. The obvious conclusion is that world trade remains driven by the U.S. consumer, despite the rosy expectations of globalists that emerging economies including China and India are sufficiently strong internally to fuel global economic growth on their own. Globalists tragically failed to realize that outsourcing jobs in the millions would inevitably undermine the purchasing power of the U.S. middle class; the recession that officially began in December 2008 has resulted in the elimination of jobs measured in the hundreds of thousands each month, thereby creating unemployment that hit 9.5 percent in June 2009.[6]

THE MOVE AWAY FROM WEST COAST PORTS

As a clear indication of globalism impacting the U.S. economy, international trade has grown from 13 percent of the U.S. gross domestic product in 1990 to 24 percent in 2000, with projections of 30 percent by 2010, according to Andrew Goetz and Sutapa Bandyopadhyay, transportation economists at the University of Denver.[7] Goetz and Bandyopadhyay observe that until now most foreign trade has entered the United States through containers delivered to West Coast ports, including Los Angeles and Long Beach, with the containers "transferred to rail cars and trucks for distribution to inland load centers and eventually to wholesale and retail outlets throughout North America."

With the West Coast ports "sagging from the weight" of the massive increase anticipated in containers coming from China, Goetz and Bandyopadhyay suggest that the transportation infrastructure of North America is being transformed, with a plan to open new international trade "gateways," including deep-water ports in Canada and Mexico, as well as develop advanced truck-train transportation infrastructure, including newly configured north–south transportation corridors connecting the United States with Mexico and Canada. What is envisioned is a fundamental redesign of North American transportation, not to improve interstate or intrastate travel in the United States but to open the U.S. market to a cheap flow of containers from China.

"Supply-chain economics" has also been a catchphrase since 1998, as multinational corporations have geographically diversified manufacturing and assembly globally in search of the cheapest labor available anywhere in the world. The *Economist* eloquently expressed how supply-chain economics have compounded the current meltdown in international trade: "Earlier, a tractor made in America would use American steel and parts: its only contribution to trade would come if the finished item were exported. Now, that tractor may use steel from India that is stamped and pressed in Mexico, before being exported to Tanzania. Global supply chains have increased the amount of international trade involved in getting a product made and delivered to its final user." [8]

CHINA PREPARES TO EXPORT MILLIONS OF CONTAINERS TO NORTH AMERICA

The Chinese deep-water port at Yangshan, near Shanghai, provides ample evidence that North America is about to be hit by a tsunami of containers from China.

Yangshan is a reclaimed island the size of 470 soccer fields that lies offshore Shanghai in the East China Sea Port. The Chinese invested $15 billion to develop Yangshan into a deep-water container port, destined to be the largest in China, capable of surpassing Hong Kong as the world's busiest harbor.[9] Currently handling 20 million containers a year, Yangshan is expected by 2010 to operate up to thirty berths, capable of exporting 30 million containers a year, with the vast majority of the containers destined for North America. Yangshan Port is connected to the mainland by the twenty-mile Donghai Bridge.

The Chinese developed Yangshan to accommodate the largest post-Panamax megaships now being constructed, with a capacity to carry up to 12,500 containers, many times the size of containerships now operating. In the shipping industry, Panamax container ships are defined as those that were able to fit through the Panama Canal, which is one thousand feet long and 110 feet wide. Typically, Panamax containerships were designed to carry 4,500 TEUs, or "twenty-foot units," the length measurement of the standard ocean steel container. The first generation of post-Panamax containerships was built to carry up to 9,800 TEUs. The *Emma Maersk,* one of the largest containerships currently in operation, is over four football fields wide (1,300 feet), capable of handling 12,500 containers, stacked in twenty-two rows across the deck. Post-Panamax ships are being designed to rely upon computer sophistication to monitor the containers while in transport, thereby reducing the crew to fewer than fifteen persons, a surprisingly small crew for the journey thousands of miles across the high seas.

The post-Panamax fleet in service at the end of 2000 consisted of some three hundred containerships. In 2009, containerships with 9,000 to 10,000 TEU capacity still dominated main-arterial shipping, such as between China and the United States. Containerships with 12,000-plus TEU capacity are being phased into operation between 2009 and 2010. Supercontainerships with 12,500 TEU capacity have to be built with twin engines to maintain the twenty-five-knot speed required for a maximum load that will involve at least twenty-one containers stacked across the weather deck.[10] In North America, ports that anticipate playing a major role in international trade are either being developed or re-engineered to the deep-water standards required by post-Panamax ships.

PUBLIC-PRIVATE PARTNERSHIP FINANCING

On April 30, 1992, President George H. Bush signed Executive Order No. 12803, on infrastructure privatization, clearing away federal barriers for cities and states to lease public-works infrastructure to private investors. This action created a new category of finance known as public-private partnerships, or PPPs. The basic idea is that a private investment consortium will put up the funds, typically hundreds of millions or even billions of dollars, to engage with a state government or the federal government to develop an infrastructure project, including the construction of new highways. PPP-infrastructure projects can be far-reaching, extending to almost any public project imaginable, including public schools and even prisons. In return for investing private capital, the investment consortium obtains the right to enter into a long-term lease with the government, so that the investment consortium is able to receive usage fees for operating and maintaining the facility, typically over a twenty-five- to fifty-year period.

As state governments and even the federal government have become strapped by budget deficits, PPP projects have been used primarily to develop new highways or to take over the operation of existing highways. Typically, PPP-infrastructure deals are packaged so that the investment consortium makes a substantial one-time payment to the government for the right to develop, operate, and maintain the infrastructure involved. States have generally invited foreign-investment groups to bid on highway contracts, with the intention of turning the highway into a toll road that the foreign group will manage through an infrastructure subsidiary or partner. The deals have been controversial in that PPP leases allow foreign infrastructure companies to take effective control of major highways, often raising the possibility that what once was a "freeway" constructed initially with taxpayer dollars may end up a toll road operated by a company based outside the United States. Also, critics have questioned why taxpayers and U.S. infrastructure companies are not offered rights of first refusal on PPP infrastructure deals, especially when the deals are obviously favorable enough that foreign interests want to participate.

Under the U.S. Department of Transportation, a Federal Highway Administration website offers a "how-to" guide for state highway administrators to examine PPP case studies and receive instructions on how state laws need to be modified to accommodate the sample "Comprehensive Development Agreements," which are examples of the legal requirements needed to implement PPP highway-development contracts.[11] In 2005, the Texas Department of Transportation signed the agreement with a Spanish investment consortium and infrastructure company to build the Trans-Texas Corridor 35 for automobiles, trucks, trains, and pipelines through the heart of Texas. Ever since then, PPP deals have played a major role in the development of the North American transportation infrastructure designed for a new generation of international trade.

The international experience with PPP highways has not been universally favorable, especially if we turn to a nation such as Australia, which has much more extensive experience with PPP-developed highways than does the United States. In New South Wales, the government responded to public protests over the high tolls imposed by the PPP-funded Cross-City Tunnel, forcing the NSW government to reopen routes that had been closed in order to guarantee the profits of the private operator. Another Australian case involves the Scoresby Freeway in Victoria, where the cost of buying the PPP lease operator out of their high toll rates was estimated at $7 billion, even though the cost of constructing the freeway was estimated at $2.5 billion. The differences were attributed to "compensating private investors for bearing risk that properly belongs with the public." [12]

CANADA OPENS ASIA-PACIFIC GATEWAY CORRIDOR

Canada is developing western ports on the Pacific to compete with the U.S. ports of Long Beach and Los Angeles, as well as with the Mexican ports of Manzanillo and Lázaro Cárdenas on the Pacific Ocean south of Texas, for a substantial market share of the millions of containers expected to flow into North America in the coming decades from China and the Far East. To attract Chinese container traffic, the Canadian government now plans a large infrastructure investment to develop a major ports-rail-truck-airport transportation infrastructure designed to build Canada's version of the emerging NAFTA Superhighway in the continent's northwest. To implement the plan, the Canadian government, under the direction of Conservative Party leader Stephen Harper, launched in October 2006 the Asia-Pacific Gateway and Corridor Initiative, or APGCI, as a key component of Canada's national transportation policy.[13]

A video on the Canadian National Railroad's website billed British Columbia's Prince Rupert Port as "North America's Northwest Gateway," stressing that its location on the 54th parallel offers the closest connection to the Far East and China, "shaving 30 hour shipping time for the shortest quickest route across the Pacific."[14] Prince Rupert is 5,286 miles from Hong Kong, while Los Angeles is 6,380 miles away; Shanghai is 4,642 miles from Port Rupert, but 5,810 miles from Los Angeles. Protected by the Queen Charlotte Islands, Prince Rupert Port is a natural deep-water tidal harbor easily capable of handling the new post-Panamax ships, the same standard being used in constructing the Yangshan island port off the coast of Shanghai.

According to Transport Canada, Canada's equivalent to the U.S. Department of Transportation, rail and road connections to Prince Rupert and Vancouver will carry the Asian containers into Canada through Edmonton and Calgary in Alberta. From there, the planned rail-truck-passenger superhighways will head toward Winnipeg, where cross-border connections south will direct the containers from China and the Far East onto the Interstate 35 corridor in the United States, establishing a major link in the emerging continental NAFTA Superhighway.

The plan is clearly explained in Canada's National Policy Framework for Strategic Gateways and Trade Corridors, and is presented with a graphic that shows Canada on a world map with arrows of trade leading from the Far East and China into the heart of Canada.[15] The Canadian federal government has committed to developing transportation infrastructure around the concept of creating an Asia-Pacific Gateway and Corridor, identified as "a network of transportation infrastructure including British Columbia's Lower Mainland and Prince Rupert ports, their principal road and rail connections stretching across Western Canada and south to the United States, key border crossings, and major Canadian airports."

Transport Canada's vision was driven by the concept of North America and continental trade, not Canada or Canadian trade specifically. "The integrated North American economy provides the 'platform' for Canada's successful global engagement," a brochure on the Transport Canada website proclaims in explaining how Canada's National Policy for Strategic Gateways and Trade Corridors would work.[16]

Between 1997 and 2006, Canada's exports to China more than doubled, from $2.4 billion to $7.7 billion, in Canadian dollars. Yet imports from China dwarfed these numbers. Between 1997 and 2006, Canada's imports from China grew almost 550 percent, jumping from $6.3 billion to $34.5 billion in Canadian dollars.[17] With these numbers, the Canadian pattern of trade with China parallels the experience of the United States. Trade between China and North America has expanded dramatically since the Clinton administration, but the winner is China, not the United States, Canada, or Mexico.

The vast majority of containers from China are destined to be unloaded in the United States, not Canada. The Transport Canada plan is driven by Canada's desire to benefit economically by serving as a conduit for containers entering North America and headed for the United States, not specifically for the goods in Chinese containers to enter the much smaller Canadian market for sale to Canadians.

CANADIAN NAFTA SUPERHIGHWAYS AND NAFTA RAILROADS

In 2007, Transport Canada announced the signing of a Memorandum of Understanding between the governments of Canada and the provinces of Ontario and Quebec to develop the "Continental Gateway and Trade Corridor."[18] A background paper noted that Ontario and Quebec are "vital contributors to the Canadian economy representing approximately 60 percent of Canada's exports and gross domestic product."[19] "The main objective of this MOU," the background document continued, "is to establish this commercial gateway and trade corridor as a strategic, integrated and globally competitive transportation system that supports the movement of international trade." The Canadian government planned to seek PPP partners to develop the gateway and trade corridor project.

On September 12, 2007, Canadian National (CN) railroad used the opening of its new container terminal at the port in Prince Rupert to declare the railroad the "Midwest Express," a reference to the railroad's ambition to move containers of goods manufactured in China into the heartland of North America through the railroad's distribution hubs in Chicago and Memphis. James Foote, CN's vice president of sales and marketing, boasted that Canadian National could move containers from China into the U.S. Midwest more quickly through Prince Rupert than through any other West Coast port, including Los Angeles and Long Beach. "Thanks in part to the focused efforts of governments, CN is now positioned to provide shippers with a seamless door-to-door transportation solution and to ensure the safe and secure flow of goods throughout the North American Continent," Foote said.[20] The completed Phase I development of the Canadian National container terminal at Prince Rupert has a capacity to handle 500,000 twenty-foot containers per year, growing to a 2 million–container capacity in 2010, when Phase II development of the 150-acre facility is completed.

The Canadian National route map can be conceptualized as a giant "T" that stretches across Canada from Prince Rupert and Vancouver in British Columbia to Halifax in Nova Scotia. The Canadian National then crosses into the United States at Winnipeg and at Windsor, Ontario, to complete the T into the United States through Detroit, Chicago, and south through Memphis, ending up at the Louisiana Gulf Coast. The route map roughly parallels the U.S. Department of Transportation's plans to develop Interstate 69, ultimately connecting into the heart of Texas through Houston, on a route through the north–south heart of the United States east of Interstate 35.

The Canadian National railroad also has marketing agreements in place with Kansas City Southern (KCS), a U.S. railroad that has acquired railroads in Mexico, linking to the Mexican ports of Manzanillo and Lázaro Cárdenas on the Pacific. In January 2005, KCS took control of the Texas Mexican Railway Company and the U.S. portion of the International Bridge in Laredo, Texas. In April 2005, KCS purchased the controlling interests in Transportación Ferroviaria Mexicana, or TFM, which KCS promptly renamed the Kansas City Southern de Mexico, or KCSM.

Canada's second national railroad, the Canadian Pacific, or CP, also has continental plans to link to the ports in British Columbia. In 2007, it announced an agreement to acquire the Dakota, Minnesota & Eastern Railroad.[21] Railroad analysts saw the move as a strategic attempt by CP to move into Wyoming's coal-rich Power River Basin, an area where previously the Burlington Northern Santa Fe and Union Pacific have enjoyed exclusive access.[22] Included in the deal was the Iowa, Chicago, & Eastern Railroad (IC&E), a sister railroad. The IC&E runs to Kansas City, where a shared yard with Kansas City Southern allows the Canadian Pacific to reach down to the Mexican ports of Manzanillo and Lázaro Cárdenas.

Before these acquisitions the Canadian Pacific stretched across Canada from Vancouver to Montreal, and south from Montreal to New York. After the acquisitions, the Canadian Pacific was positioned to compete with the Canadian National not only for NAFTA trade, but for a large share of WTO trade.

KANSAS CITY PLANS TO OPEN A MEXICAN CUSTOMS OFFICE

In 2005, Kansas City developed plans to allow the Mexican government to open a Mexican customs office in conjunction with the Kansas City SmartPort. On May 18, 2006, the Council of Kansas City voted to give the Mexican customs facility an innocuous name, the "Kansas City Customs Port," which covered its true identity as an arm of the Mexican government, staffed by Mexican government custom officials. Kansas City was so enthusiastic about the opportunity that the cost of building the $3 million facility for Mexico will be paid for by Kansas City taxpayers, not by the Mexican government.[23]

The Kansas City SmartPort is designed to be a central hub in the planned international trade passing through the heart of the United States. Post-Panamax containerships carrying goods made by cheap labor in the Far East and China could unload in the British Columbian ports of Vancouver and Prince Rupert, as well as in the deep-water Mexican ports at Manzanillo and Lázaro Cárdenas, eliminating the need to use costly union longshoremen in Los Angeles or Long Beach. Rather than transporting the containers by trucks from the West Coast, using Teamster drivers, or on rail, with the assistance of railroad labor in the United Transportation Union, the containers could be loaded onto nonunion Mexican railroads at Lázaro Cárdenas. At Monterrey, Mexico, the containers would be loaded onto nonunion Mexican semitrailer trucks that would cross the border at Laredo, Texas, to begin their journey north along Interstate 35. Alternatively, the containers from China could move into the United States through the Kansas City Southern, the Canadian National, or the Canadian Pacific. Conveniently, the Kansas City SmartPort was designed to be intermodal, tying into highways, rail lines, and Kansas City's municipal airport. In March 2005, Kansas City signed a cooperative pact with representatives from the Mexican state of Michoacán, where Lázaro Cárdenas is located, to increase the cargo volume between Lázaro Cárdenas and Kansas City. A brochure on the Kansas City SmartPort website contained a map very similar to the Asian-routes map printed by Canada Transport on Asia-Pacific Gateway and Corridor Initiative brochures. The map showed red lines connecting ports in the Far East and China to Lázaro Cárdenas, and from there north to Kansas City.[24]

TRANS-TEXAS CORRIDOR 35

In 1998, the Federal Highway Administration warned that increasing NAFTA truck traffic was expected to create a safety concern with bridges in states along the I-35 NAFTA Superhighway, including Minnesota.[25] The study concluded, "The I-35 Corridor's multimodal transportation hubs—where air, rail, river, and truck cargo converge—make I-35 ideally positioned to be a major route for what is expected to be increasing levels of international trade activity." However, "Over the next few decades, about 65 percent of I-35 will require major upgrades . . . the entire route will have a continued need for rehabilitating pavements, resurfacing sections of the highway, and providing replacements of some bridge decks. Bridge substructures and superstructures will also need to be maintained, requiring repairs to maintain the integrity of the bridges."

Rather than reengineer Interstate 35 to the demands of NAFTA and WTO free trade, the state of Texas took the radical step of designing the nation's first free-trade corridor, a NAFTA or WTO Superhighway, in the resolve to build a new highway parallel to I-35 along the standards Texas viewed as required by the demands of free trade in the twenty-first century.

The Texas Department of Transportation, or TxDOT, announced plans for a massive Trans-Texas Corridor project to be completed over a fifty-year period.[26] The cornerstone of the project would be TTC-35, a new toll road to be built parallel to Interstate 35 from Laredo, Texas, through the heart of Texas, passing through Austin and Dallas, on the way to the Texas border with Oklahoma. TTC-35, when completed, could conceivably extend north to Canada, roughly following the Interstate 35 route. TTC-35 was planned as a four-football-fields-wide 1,200-foot car-truck-train pipeline supercorridor, with the land required to be seized through eminent domain authority.

After massive public opposition, Texas governor Rick Perry changed gears in 2009 and engaged in a public-relations effort to distance the state from the project. "The days of the Trans-Texas Corridor are over, it's finished up," Perry said.[27] However, TxDOT can still proceed with the components of the original TTC plan.

Still, nothing in Perry's announcement indicated that the contract with the Spanish company to construct TTC-35 had been canceled.

After the announcement, TxDOT removed the Trans-Texas Corridor section of the TxDOT website, replacing it with a more generic section titled "Texas Corridors."[28] A controversy had developed when TTC-35 was broadly described as a "NAFTA Superhighway." Critics denied any plans existed to create NAFTA Superhighway corridors or that TTC-35 was itself a NAFTA Superhighway.[29] The North American's SuperCorridor Coalition, Inc., or NASCO, a Dallas-based trade group originally named the North American Superhighway Coalition, has changed its website many times to eliminate a map that appeared on the group's website in 2006.[30] That map graphically illustrated I-35 as the spine of a continental North American highway and railway transportation that extended in Canada to Vancouver on the West Coast and to Montreal on the East Coast, as well as south to Manzanillo and Lázaro Cárdenas in Mexico.

Official government reports in Mexico had documented that Mexico had officially entered into discussions with the state of Texas and the U.S. Department of Transportation in 2007 with the goal of extending the Trans-Texas Corridor into Mexico. Mexico's plan was to connect TTC-35 through Monterrey to Manzanillo and Lázaro Cárdenas.

SAN ANTONIO AND DENVER: INLAND PORTS

Kansas City is not the only city in the continental United States that has declared itself an inland port. San Antonio and Denver have both followed suit. The Kansas River, the San Antonio River Walk, or the Platte River in Colorado were not the waterways justifying the designation of these cities as "inland ports." The concept was that Kansas City, San Antonio, and Denver would function as warehouse cities: containers carried primarily by train from deep-water ports on the Pacific could be deposited at these inland-port destinations, used as hubs. The containers could then be picked up by truck to be transported the final miles to their ultimate destination, typically the warehouses of mass-market merchandisers. From there, the containers could be opened and re-packed as needed, for delivery to retail stores, where the goods could be put on the shelves for sale to U.S. consumers.

On August 22, 2007, the Union Pacific railroad announced plans to build a $90 million, state-of-the-art, three-hundred-acre intermodal rail terminal alongside I-35 in San Antonio, advancing San Antonio's goal to establish the city as a NAFTA inland port.[31] In a press release, Union Pacific said the San Antonio terminal will process over 100,000 truck trailers annually when completed in 2008, with the capacity to grow to a potential of 250,000 trailers and containers per year. Kyle Burns, the president and CEO of the Free Trade Alliance San Antonio, told World Net Daily in an email, "The new Union Pacific Intermodal facility located in south San Antonio will be a benefit to San Antonio by further enhancing our world-class logistics and transportation infrastructure, that currently handles interstates and rail lines, running both north–south and east–west. San Antonio is at the cross-roads of U.S.-Mexico-Canadian trade."[32]

With more than 80,000 semitrucks currently traveling to rail yards within the San Antonio city limits to pick up or drop off containers and trailers, the new facility was designed to relieve truck traffic in the city. Additionally, the new terminal was planned to give truckers the option to drop off their containers with easy access from I-10 and I-35, accommodating many trucks that now must go through San Antonio to Houston to drop off containers for trains bound for other destinations. The *San Antonio Business Journal* noted that the Union Pacific terminal was strategically located to ship and receive containers containing household goods both from West Coast ports such as Los Angeles and Long Beach, as well as Mexican ports such as Manzanillo and Lázaro Cárdenas.[33]

MIAMI AND THE PLAN TO EXPAND THE PANAMA CANAL

Panama is currently building a deeper, wider Panama Canal under a "Third Set of Locks Project" that was approved by a national referendum on October 22, 2006. The goal is to allow post-Panamax ships to cross from the Pacific Ocean into the Gulf of Mexico and the Atlantic Ocean, so containers from China and the Far East can reach U.S. ports, including New Orleans, Houston, and Miami. Otherwise, post-Panamax ships containing goods from China and the Far East are forced to reach destinations in the Gulf Coast and on the Atlantic Ocean via the Suez Canal.

In 2003, West Coast ports handled approximately 80 percent of the more than $100 billion imported from China, with Atlantic ports accounting for about 19 percent and Gulf Coast ports picking up the extra 1 percent. As noted by Michael Bomba of the Center for Transportation Research at the University of Texas at Austin, "The volume of Chinese import trade handled by East Coast ports has more than doubled between 2000 and 2003, with the largest jump occurring in 2002, when shippers began to search for alternative routes." [34] In the shipping industry, a West Coast longshoremen's strike is widely cited as a reason importers of goods from China have sought to open up Mexican ports, Canadian ports, and a variety of East Coast ports. Among the East Coast ports are Miami, Newark and New York, and the Port of Virginia, for its access to Norfolk. [35]

In 1998, the state of Florida created FTAA Florida, a nonprofit corporation, primarily to promote Miami's bid to become the headquarters of a planned Free Trade Area of the Americas (FTAA) secretariat. "Florida FTAA's aggressive effort to unite the hemisphere around trade has strengthened the state's economic reputation as the 'Gateway of the Americas,' " the group's website proclaims. "Respected economist J. Antonio Villamil, Ph.D., and Enterprise Florida, Inc., the state's economic development partnership, estimated in 2003 that winning the FTAA headquarters in Florida would mean 89,259 new jobs and a $3.2 billion annual payroll increase for Florida businesses." [36] When he was governor of Florida, Jeb Bush sat on the FTAA Florida Inc. board, helping to administer the organization's annual $1.3 million budget, funded in part by the Florida legislature.

At the Fourth Summit of the Americas, held at Mar del Plata, Argentina, in November 2005, the Bush administration continued to push for reviving an FTAA initiative, a plan to extend the North American Free

Trade Area, NAFTA, and the Central America Free Trade Area, CAFTA, to the tip of Argentina.[37] The Bush plan failed, largely because of the vocal opposition expressed by Venezuela's president, Hugo Chavez. Chavez became a "lightning rod" for the opposition to the Bush administration plan, arguing the FTAA would only represent U.S. domination of the South American economies under a system of capitalism where workers and resources would be exploited to the advantage of U.S.-based multinational corporations.[38]

The FTAA vision is also carried forward on the Port of Miami's website. Describing CAFTA as a "stepping stone toward FTAA," the site continues to proclaim Miami's port as the "Cargo Gateway of the Americas,"[39] keeping alive hopes that the FTAA dream will revive. Perhaps not surprisingly, China already tops the list of twenty-five countries ranked in total tonnage utilizing the Port of Miami.[40]

MEXICO DEVELOPING DEEP-WATER PORT ON BAJA CALIFORNIA

Mexico plans to develop Punta Colonet, today a desolate Mexican bay in Baja California, as a West Coast Mexican alternative to the U.S. ports in Los Angeles and Long Beach. About 150 miles south of Tijuana, Punta Colonet is designed to rival those U.S. cities as a destination for the 30 million containers headed to North America from China and the Far East each year, according to a report published by the *Los Angeles Times* in 2008.[41] The publicly expressed reasons for wanting to develop alternatives to the international ports at Los Angeles and Long Beach involve complaints of congestion and occasional work stoppages by the longshoremen's union. While these arguments have some legitimacy, the lure of Punta Colonet is perhaps more truly understood in the cost reductions available if Mexican transportation labor is used to move Chinese containers into the interior of the United States, replacing more expensive U.S. workers.

The project, which may take as much as $9 billion in private capital to develop, will involve some seven thousand acres at Punta Colonet, about as large as the ports of Los Angeles and Long Beach combined. The goal is to construct a modern port capable of handling annually 8 million containers or twenty-foot equivalent units, or TEUs, according to a report published by the *San Diego Union-Tribune*, based on an interview the newspaper conducted with Eugenio Elorduy Walther, the governor of Baja California in Mexico.[42] Mexico has opened the bidding to foreign investment consortia and infrastructure companies seeking to enter a PPP contract with Mexico to develop the port.

The containers will then move to the interior of the United States on a 180-mile rail line that is expected to connect the port with existing U.S. railroad networks at Yuma, Arizona. Truck transportation could also link up with CANAMEX, another north–south highway corridor that is planned to begin at Mexico City and end in Canada at Edmonton, Alberta, after connecting a string of U.S. cities, including Tucson, Phoenix, Las Vegas, Salt Lake City, Idaho Falls, Idaho, and Great Falls, Montana.[43]

CHINA TO INSTALL RFID SENSORS ON INTERSTATE 35

Communist China, operating through a port-operator subsidiary of Hutchison Whampoa, has been active in developing North American ports for the anticipated volume of international trade planned for future decades.

Hutchison Ports Holdings,[44] a wholly owned subsidiary of China's giant Hutchison Whampoa Limited (HWL),[45] is investing millions to expand the deep-water ports the company manages at Manzanillo and Lázaro Cárdenas and on Mexico's Pacific coast. Now Hutchison Ports is pledging millions more to develop Punta Colonet. Hutchison Ports also operates both ends of the Panama Canal.

As documented by Judicial Watch, "Hutchison Whampoa, Ltd. is the holding company of billionaire Li Ka-shing, a well-known businessman, whose companies make up 15 percent of the market capitalization of the Hong Kong Stock Market." According to a complaint submitted by Judicial Watch in 2002 to various federal officials and agencies, at the time that HWL was purchasing the then-bankrupt Global Crossing, Li Ka-shing's holdings included ports, telecom, and energy assets around the world.[46] According to a declassified U.S. government intelligence report that Judicial Watch obtained in a Freedom of Information Act request, "Li is directly connected to Beijing and is willing to use his business influence to further the aims of the Chinese Government." Judicial Watch had objected that "Li Ka-shing's agency relationship to the Communist Chinese should disqualify him from owning Global Crossing's network, which controls a significant percent of all the fiber optics currently leaving the United States."[47] Global Crossing was closely allied to the Democratic Party during the Clinton administration. Global Crossing's bold move to control the U.S. international fiber-optics network overreached, ending in a corrupt corporate meltdown that was an unfortunate prelude to the Enron debacle. Hutchison Ports was forced to drop the bid to purchase Global Crossing when the Committee on Foreign Investments in the United States, or CFIUS, refused to approve the transaction on national-security grounds.

In 2007, Hutchison Whampoa began working with U.S. defense contractor Lockheed Martin and the Dallas-based trade organization North America's SuperCorridor Coalition, Inc., or NASCO, to place radio frequency identifier (RFID) stations all along Interstate 35. The idea was to utilize RFID chips placed in containers with manufactured goods shipped from China to track the containers as they are transported to final destinations within the United States. Lockheed Martin planned to use RFID tracking technology that it developed for the U.S. Department of Defense to be applied in supplying the U.S. military in combat situations in Iraq and Afghanistan, as well as at U.S. military stations throughout the world. Hutchison Port Holdings has 49 percent ownership of Savi Networks, the Lockheed Martin subsidiary contracted to place the sensors along I-35.

Nathan Hansen, a Minnesota attorney, has archived on his blog a series of NASCO documents obtained under a Minnesota Data Practices Act.[48] Among these documents released by Hansen is the letter of intent between NASCO and Savi Networks that details how NASCO and Lockheed Martin intended to implement the NAFTRACS (North American Facilitation of Transportation, Trade, Reduced Congestion & Security) program.

The letter of intent called for Savi Networks to establish RFID sensors along I-35, with tracking designed to begin at Manzanillo and Lázaro Cárdenas and additional "inland points of data capture" positioned at "inland port" locations in Laredo, Texas, San Antonio, and Dallas, as well as in Kansas City, along its Ambassador Bridge, and in Winnipeg.[49] Data captured by the RFID sensors would be sent to a NASCO data-collection center, "The Center of Excellence," which was to be integrated into Lockheed Martin's militarized GTN (Global Transport Network) Command and Control Center, installed and operating at the Lockheed Martin Center for Innovation or "Lighthouse" facility in Suffolk, Virginia. Lockheed Martin's GTN was developed for the U.S. Department of Defense as an electronic system used to support supply shipments and defense logistics to U.S. armed forces deployed worldwide. GTN is operated by the U.S. Transportation Command at Scott Air Force Base in Illinois. NASCO described Total Domain Awareness as the ability to "automatically gather, correlate, and interpret fragments of multi-source data," including data received from radar, AIS (Automatic Identification System shipboard radar), GPS (Global Positioning System), open-source data including weather reports, military intelligence data, law enforcement data, bioterrorism data, plus video surveillance and security cameras.

NASCO planned to receive 25 cents in revenue for each "revenue-generating intermodal ocean cargo container" registered by the RFID sensors.

DOES CHINA REPRESENT A NATIONAL-SECURITY THREAT?

Advocates of free trade have typically insisted that trading with China would ensure peace with China. Why, free-trade advocates ask, would China be an enemy to the United States when China's economy is so dependent on manufacturing goods for the U.S. market? Why would China take any hostile action toward the United States when China holds 80 percent of its $2 trillion in foreign-exchange reserves in U.S. assets, including Treasury securities?

This perspective ignores fundamental foreign policy differences the United States and China have had for decades. China, for instance, still claims sovereignty over Taiwan, while the United States is pledged to come to the defense of Taiwan if China were to attack Taiwan. After an incident on March 8, 2009, when five Chinese navy ships surrounded and harassed the unarmed USNS *Impeccable* in the South China Sea, the Pentagon released a report claiming China's military power is so much on the rise that China is shifting the military balance in the region and beyond.[50] Should an incident escalate to the point of creating military tension between the United States and China, the United States is at a clear disadvantage, simply because of the extent to which the United States is indebted to China. If China did decide to utilize its holdings of U.S. Treasury securities as a weapon against the United States, $1–2 trillion dollars may end up being a relatively inexpensive price for reducing the international power and influence of the world's once-dominant superpower.

Moreover, for at least a decade, Congressional Research Service reports have warned Congress repeatedly that U.S. ports are vulnerable to a nuclear terror attack. With both ends of the Panama Canal managed and operated by Hutchison Whampoa, as well as Mexican ports including Manzanillo, Lázaro Cárdenas, and soon Punta Colonet, the United States is relying on Chinese security for containers entering the United States. The RFID infrastructure China is installing along Interstate 35 may give Beijing as much or better intelligence on the transport of Chinese containers through the United States than the U.S. government has. Warning that terrorists "might try to smuggle a bomb into a U.S. port in many ways, but containers may offer an attractive route," the Congressional Research Service estimated the potential danger as follows: a terrorist Hiroshima-sized nuclear bomb in the range of 15 kilotons, or the equivalent of 15,000 tons of TNT, detonated in a port "would destroy buildings out a mile or two; start fires, especially in a port that handled petrol and chemicals; spread fallout over many square miles; disrupt commerce; and kill many people." [51]

Still, under World Trade Organization reassurances, the United States is allowing China to build, operate, and maintain key points of entry for foreign containers into the United States.

PPP TOLL ROADS CONCEPT PUSHED IN OKLAHOMA

In 2007, Robert Poole, a mechanical engineer who has advised the administrations of George H. W. Bush, Bill Clinton, and George W. Bush to privatize U.S. highways, estimated that more than $25 billion in public-private-partnership (PPP) highway projects have been planned or approved in the United States. [52] In 2007, the Oklahoma House speaker, Republican Lance Cargill, the founder of a group known as "The 100 Ideas Initiative," invited Poole to give a luncheon speech in Tulsa. Beginning in February 2007, Cargill held a series of town-hall meetings across Oklahoma promoting the development of "100 Ideas of Innovation for Oklahoma's Second Century," with plans to write a book on the theme. Oklahoma activists opposed to the PPP Superhighway toll roads objected that bringing a "heavy hitter" like Poole to Oklahoma signals that state politicians are already lining up with investment bankers in a PPP plan designed to bring the Texas Department of Transportation's TTC-35 into their state.

Republican Oklahoma state senator Randy Brogdon joined with others in the Oklahoma state legislature to propose a bill that would require the Oklahoma Department of Transportation, or ODOT, to withdraw from the NASCO trade organization and to block any moves to build a NAFTA Superhighway like TTC-35 in Oklahoma. Brogdon directly opposed Poole's contention that as the U.S. highway market matures, Americans are certain to see "the emergence of domestic toll road companies." Since 2009, state legislators joining with Brogdon have held the line, proposing a series of resolutions and bills aimed at preventing the Texas Department of Transportation from recruiting states along I-35 into Canada from agreeing to extend TTC-35 into those states.

A critical article in *Mother Jones* noted that Poole's estimate that $25 billion in PPP highway projects are planned or approved in the U.S. was "remarkable," especially given that as of 1991 the total cost of the interstate highway system was estimated at $128.9 billion.[53]

THE "FREE TRADE" PROSPERITY MYTH

The last year the United States had a positive balance of trade was in 1975, during the presidency of Gerald R. Ford. Ever since 1976, when President Jimmy Carter moved into the White House, the U.S. balance of trade has been negative. In 1991, the U.S. negative balance of trade was 0.52 percent of the U.S. gross domestic product. This percentage has grown steadily, and so by 2007 the U.S. negative balance of trade was 5.13 percent of GDP.[54] The United States is gradually shifting to a much greater reliance on imports, a fact China clearly appreciates. As discussed above, the U.S. negative balance of trade with China in 1985 was under $1 billion; in 2008, the U.S. negative trade balance with China had grown more than 250 percent, to a negative $266 billion.

The incremental change in U.S. international trade imbalances has now reached a magnitude where the phenomenon is totally different. During the Carter administration, the idea that the United States would be inundated by containers from China was not a consideration. Right now, in the midst of the global economic recession, 453 containerships, 11 percent of global capacity, float outside the harbors of Hong Kong, Singapore, and other Southeast Asian ports. Those ships are just waiting. Only five years ago, huge demand from China meant all these ships, and more, were desperately needed, as reported by the *Economist*.[55] When the global economy revives, the ships will be needed once again.

When Americans became more aware that north–south world trade or NAFTA Superhighways would mean confiscating tens of thousands of acres of land under eminent domain, protesters forced Texas governor Perry to reconsider the Trans-Texas Corridor plans in Texas. Even the once proud and insistent Texas Department of Transportation was forced to drop the name "Trans-Texas Corridor," as a public relations move designed to reduce opposition. Public-private partnerships continue to be opposed, because the deals involved leasing transportation infrastructure to foreigners for a onetime up-front payment, yet the foreign operators would collect tolls for decades.

In the midst of the economic downturn, however, transportation infrastructure projects have been touted by the Obama administration as a possible way to stimulate the economy back to recovery. Voters are certain to reassess transportation projects designed to reconfigure North America to the demands of international trade if the projects provide badly needed jobs. When middle-class Americans are losing their jobs and homes, the injection of foreign capital into the U.S. economy through PPP deals may suddenly look welcome.

As White House chief of staff Rahm Emanuel and Secretary of State Hillary Clinton suggested, no good crisis should be allowed to go to waste. Ironically, if transportation infrastructure projects take off in earnest as economic stimulus initiatives, a good portion of the resulting construction jobs could end up going to undocumented workers, unless the enabling legislation and contracts demand that all workers employed prove the legitimacy of their immigration status and their authorization to work under current immigration laws.[56]

SEVEN

The Plan to Destroy the Dollar

In order to globalize safely, countries should abandon monetary
nationalism and abolish unwanted currencies, the source of much
of today's instability.

—Benn Steil, Council on Foreign Relations, 2007[1]

In a book sponsored by the Council on Foreign Relations titled *Regional Monetary Integration*, Princeton economist Peter Kenen and American University economist Ellen Meade pointed to the European Monetary Union, or EMU, as "the most ambitious project of its type." Kenen and Meade described the EMU as "a group of highly developed countries with sophisticated monetary systems managed by some of the world's best-known central banks" that agreed "to substitute a single European currency for their own national currencies and to subordinate their own countries' central banks to a new institution—the European Central Bank."[2]

For many economists, nation-states are nothing more than artificial, geographically drawn barriers that do not define how markets work. Seeking to maximize international trade, globalist-thinking economists have raised for decades the question that nation-states are not the natural, efficient, or optimal basis for defining currencies in the global economy.

The naysayers who for years have ridiculed the idea that any serious

plan existed to destroy the dollar were either uninformed or intentionally trying to disguise a plan globalist economists openly discussed. For
decades, economists have argued that international trade will require
redefinitions away from nation-states. Regional currencies like the euro
are merely stepping-stones on the path to the Holy Grail of a one-world
currency. Now that the world is in the throes of an economic panic, every American must take seriously the possibility that a North American
regional currency or even a one-world currency might replace the dollar
as the world's foreign-reserve currency. A regional or one-world currency is today seriously under consideration by top international economists to be a solution to the badly beleaguered dollar.

ECONOMIST ROBERT MUNDELL: THE FATHER OF THE EURO

Columbia University economics professor Robert Mundell, widely regarded as the "Father of the Euro," has argued for decades that nation-
state currencies, including the dollar, need to give way to a new official
world currency. For his work in defining the "optimal currency area" as
regional markets instead of nation-states, Mundell won the Nobel Prize
in economics in 1999.

Mundell's argument was that nation-states are not optimal currency
areas, because nation-state borders are artificial constraints imposed on
the globe to create ethnic or historical divisions that do not necessarily
represent how international markets operate. To understand the concept, Mundell cites former Federal Reserve chairman Paul Volcker's frequently quoted dictum, "A global economy needs a global currency." [3]

For global economists, multinational corporations add currency risk
simply because their companies operate in many different nations. Currency risk is defined as the possibility that holdings in one particular
nation-state currency may depreciate in value against the currency of
the nation-state in which the corporation is based. The result can be a
business loss resulting from the currency fluctuation itself, not from a
downturn in the company's primary business activities. A regional or
one-world currency would eliminate currency risk because prices in all
countries operating in the market area would be denominated in the
same currency unit.

Free-trade advocates see elimination of nation-state currencies as removing yet another barrier to international trade, much as eliminating
tariffs and customs controls removes other international trade barriers.

Furthermore, one-world-currency advocates believe a worldwide monetary policy established by a one-world central bank would be more stable, in that individual nation-states would no longer be free to set interest rates in order to benefit national markets to the detriment of other countries operating in the international marketplace. Advocates of a one-world currency believe abandoning national currencies would facilitate flows of private capital across borders, thereby stimulating economic growth across the globe. Finally, establishing a one-world currency would eliminate the possibilities of speculators attacking nation-state currencies.

In an important paper titled "What the Euro Means for the Dollar and the International Monetary System," Mundell told the Forty-Fifth International Atlantic Conference, assembled in Rome in March 1998, that "the introduction of the euro will be the most important change in the international monetary system since the transition, achieved during World War I, from the pound to the dollar as the dominant international currency."[4] Acknowledging that after World War II the dollar achieved a position in world finance unequaled since the days of the ancient Roman denarius, Mundell said, "There will come a time when the pileup of international indebtedness makes reliance on the dollar as the world's only main currency untenable."[5] Going one step further, Mundell advised that "it is no longer necessary or even healthy for the U.S. or the rest of the world to rely solely on the dollar."[6]

Mundell argued that a two-currency world dominated by the dollar and the euro would be a transitional state before the world began dollar-dumping and euro-buying, marking the end of dollar dominance much as World War I marked the end of the pound as a dominant world currency. He further anticipated that the emergence of an official world currency would begin with the International Monetary Fund accepting deposits of gold, dollars, or euros in exchange for credit balances denominated in credit balances defined by IMF Special Drawing Rights, or SDRs. These IMF credits would then serve as the beginning of a one-world international currency that could be used by all countries to hold their foreign-exchange reserves.

COUNCIL ON FOREIGN RELATIONS FORESEES
THE END OF NATIONAL CURRENCY

Benn Steil, the director of international economics at the Council on Foreign Relations (CFR), launched a scathing attack upon sovereignty and national currencies in *Foreign Affairs* magazine in 2007. In an article titled "The End of National Currency," Steil argued that "the world needs to abandon unwanted currencies, replacing them with dollars, euros, and multinational currencies as yet unborn."[7] Steil expressed his view that the dollar and the euro are temporary currencies because "economic development outside the process of globalization is no longer possible." His inevitable conclusion was that "countries should abandon monetary nationalism."

DIGITAL GOLD

Digital gold is a proposal that globalists are pushing as a private bank solution to the devaluation potential that fiat currencies such as the dollar face in the current worldwide economic downturn. A fiat currency is a currency that has no gold or silver backing; instead, a fiat currency is backed only by the "full faith and credit" of the nation issuing it.

Private gold banks have already made a market in digital gold by creating electronic accounts that allow private clients to make and receive digital gold payments. Digital gold is a form of electronic market that is backed by gold storage; a private client deposits gold with a digital gold bank or buys gold reserves from it. The client then utilizes the digital gold account to make or receive international payments, with the value of the payments determined by the price of the gold backing the transaction.

The growth experienced in the digital gold private banking market reflects increasing concern in international foreign currency markets that the major currencies, including the dollar and the euro, will not be sufficiently strong to survive the current global financial meltdown.

WILL THE AMERO REPLACE THE DOLLAR?

The "amero" as a North American currency was first argued by Canadian economist Herbert Grubel in a 1999 paper published by the Simon

Fraser Institute in Canada and titled "The Case for the Amero: The Economics and Politics of a North American Monetary Union." [8] In introducing the idea of a North American Monetary Union, Grubel took pains to argue that the innovation would not necessarily erode national sovereignty. He suggested printing the new currency with the "amero" symbols on one side and the national emblems on the other side. The amero, however, would have its own value on foreign-exchange markets, after the three countries converted their currencies into the amero "at rates that leave unchanged each country's real income, wealth, and international competitiveness at the time of conversion." [9] While the United States, Canada, and Mexico would retain their national sovereignty under Grubel's analysis, monetary sovereignty would be lost in the creation of a North American Monetary Union, much as the European nations adopting the euro lost their monetary sovereignty in creating the European Monetary Union.

In an analysis derived from Robert Mundell, Grubel argued that the United States, Canada, and Mexico today constitute an "optimal currency area" that economists feel justifies the creation of a common currency across the region. "On the day the North American Monetary Union is created—perhaps on January 1, 2010," he wrote as an example, "Canada, the United States, and Mexico will replace their national currencies with the amero. On that day, all American dollar notes and coins will be exchanged at the rate of one U.S. dollar for one amero. Canadian and Mexican currencies will be exchanged at rates that leave unchanged their nations' competitiveness and wealth. In all three countries, the prices of goods and services, wages, assets, and liabilities will be simultaneously converted into ameros at the rates at which currency notes are exchanged." [10] Grubel also proposed creation of a North American Central Bank, which would replace the national central banks of the three countries and have a board of governors chosen to reflect the economic importance and the population of the three countries.

Grubel argued for the typical benefits globalists envision from creating regional currencies, including a reduction in "the size and risk of foreign-exchange operations engaged in by banks, firms, and travelers as part of their routine economic activities." [11] Grubel believed that by defining North America as the optimal currency area, the increased size of the market will make for more efficient and deeper capital markets. American firms will have even more incentives and opportunity to produce and market their goods and services in the entire continent. At the same time, Canadian and Mexican firms will invest in the United States and bring consumers better and lower-priced goods and services. These and other gains will grow through time as the economies of Canada and Mexico grow absolutely and probably also relatively to the American economy.[12]

To reach the Spanish market, Grubel's argument on the amero has also been published as a book in Spanish: *El Amero: Una Moneda Común para América del Norte*.

In a January 2008 op-ed piece titled "Fix the Loonie," in Canada's *National Post*, Grubel expressed concern about the current relative strength of the Canadian dollar, or "loonie," in comparison to the weakening U.S. dollar.[13] In 1987, the *loonie* became slang for the Canadian dollar when a well-known Canadian bird, the common loon, also known as the great northern diver, appeared on the back of the Canadian dollar coin that replaced the Canadian dollar bill.

In January 2008, the Canadian dollar was trading at U.S. $1.02 to the Canadian dollar, more than "par," or a 1:1 value, a phenomenon that caused Canada's exports to be more expensive in the U.S. market. Approximately 85 percent of all Canadian exports are headed to the United States, and so a more expensive Canadian dollar always threatens to harm that export market. The Canadian dollar began trading at par to the U.S. dollar in September 2008, for the first time in thirty-one years.

Grubel wrote that Canada "has a bad case of the dreaded Dutch disease, which is named after the problems that developed in the 1960s when the Netherlands sold natural gas that had been discovered on its coast." The resulting increase in Dutch exports caused a strong appreciation of exchange rates, which in turn caused the loss of Dutch manufacturers' ability to compete abroad with their imports. Grubel noted that in Europe the problem was solved when the euro eliminated national currencies, forcing all countries to operate under interest rates set by the European Central Bank.

"The analogous creation of the amero is not possible," Grubel lamented, "without the unlikely co-operation of the United States." Instead, Grubel called upon Canada to create a new Canadian dollar to replace the loonie; it could be valued at par with the U.S. dollar, with the possibility that the Bank of Canada might peg the new Canadian dollar at $0.90 on the U.S. dollar. "The public would readily use the new Canadian and the U.S. dollars interchangeably and enjoy savings in the conversion of one currency into the other," he wrote. "The present exchange risk premium on Canadian interest rates would be eliminated completely."

CANADA'S LEADING INVESTOR CALLS FOR A NORTH AMERICAN CURRENCY

Stephen Jarislowsky, a billionaire money manager and investor who is frequently called the "Canadian Warren Buffett,"[14] told a Canadian parliamentary committee that Canada and the United States should abandon their national dollar currencies and move to a regional North American currency as soon as possible. Jarislowsky told the Canadian House of Commons' finance committee in 2007, "I think we have to really seriously start thinking of the model of a continental currency just like Europe."[15] Jarislowsky emphasized that a regional North American currency was needed to reduce the adverse currency-exchange risk being experienced in Canada since the Canadian dollar had risen more than 20 percent against the U.S. dollar as the U.S. economy was entering recession and the dollar was weakening in value.

When Jarislowsky speaks, Canadian investors, markets, and politicians tend to listen, much as Warren Buffett's opinions influence investors, markets, and politicians in the United States. In November 2005, the Canadian business press reported that Jarislowsky had amassed a personal fortune of $12 billion, ranking him as the twenty-fifth-richest person in Canada.[16] *Canadian Business* reported that the average private client at Jarislowsky's investment firm typically has more than $10 million in liquid assets to invest. In 2006, *Forbes* ranked Jarislowsky's net worth at $1.5 billion, ranking him at number 512 on the list of the world's richest people.[17] *Forbes* estimated that Jarislowsky's firm currently manages $50 billion for a select list of institutional clients and high-net-worth individuals. In 2005, Jarislowsky's book *The Investment Zoo: Taming the Bulls and the Bears* was a business bestseller in Canada.[18] Jarislowsky's investment firm, Jarislowsky Fraser Limited, was founded in 1955 and is headquartered in Montreal.[19]

In an interview with World Net Daily, Jarislowsky repeated his call for a currency to be created between Canada and the United States.[20] "The idea would be a European Union–type setup," Jarislowsky said, "with a North American Central Bank that would issue the new currency and sit over the Bank of Canada and the Federal Reserve Bank in the United States." He expressed that an alternative would be to create a peg on the U.S. dollar that would allow the Bank of Canada to adjust the Canadian dollar in a 5 percent plus or minus range, based on the fluctuation in value of the U.S. dollar.

Still, Jarislowsky was less confident that the U.S. dollar peg would work. "The Bank of Canada only pinpoints inflation," he argued. "My idea would be to have the Bank of Canada manage the Canadian dollar with a view both to inflation and the U.S. dollar. The Bank of Canada has never been very receptive to this idea." Jarislowsky insisted Canada was going to be forced to do something because the increased value of the Canadian dollar vis-à-vis the U.S. dollar was likely to depress business activity in Canada and cause a recession. "Two-thirds of the Canadian economy is tied to the U.S. economy," Jarislowsky pointed out. "Some eighty-five percent of our exports are headed for the U.S. market. Our economy is tied to the U.S. dollar, whether we like it or not."

In an interview with the *Globe and Mail*, Jarislowsky emphasized the likely adverse impact on the Canadian economy the rise in the value of the Canadian dollar was likely to have. "We don't have a single mill in Canada which isn't losing cash at the current exchange rate despite the fact we invested hundreds of millions in dollars into new equipment when we had the money," Jarislowsky said. "I believe that if we stay at the present levels, the entire forest products industry practically is going to be in liquidation-bankruptcy and there's going to be an enormous loss of employment."

World Net Daily reminded Jarislowsky that the Canadian Finance Department had come out against creating a North American currency. The *Globe and Mail* had reported that documents obtained from the department revealed that officials had advised Finance Minister Jim Flaherty against a common North American currency, arguing it would mean an erosion of sovereignty for Canada. Jarislowsky brushed aside these objections. "I know Finance Minister Flaherty quite well," Jarislowsky responded. "Sure, first he will have to deny he is taking seriously the idea of a new currency, then later he will come out and say he was forced to create one anyway."

Jarislowsky insisted he made the suggestion to create a euro-style currency for North America very seriously. "Pretty soon, the Finance Ministry will have no choice but to create a new currency," he argued. "In the provinces we are already seeing economic activity slow down because of the rise in value of the Canadian dollar. If our automobile and lumber industries begin to decline, we will have a serious recession as a result. The Finance Ministry knows how closely our economy in Canada is tied to the U.S. market. A common currency would avoid the problems we are now facing with currency exchange risk added to the normal risks of doing business."

Grubel's and Jarislowski's arguments belied an article published in the *Boston Globe* in November 2007 arguing that the call for the amero to become the new North American regional currency was "purely theoretical." [21]

MEXICO'S VICENTE FOX CONFIRMS PLAN TO CREATE A NORTH AMERICAN CURRENCY

As noted in the introduction to this book, in October 2007, on CNN's *Larry King Live*, former Mexican president Vicente Fox confirmed the existence of a government plan to create the amero as a new regional currency to replace the U.S. dollar, the Canadian dollar, and the Mexican peso. On the program to promote his book *Revolution of Hope*,[22] Fox admitted that he and President Bush had together developed a plan to create a regional currency by evolving regional trade agreements already in place, such as NAFTA and CAFTA, into an advanced form of North American integration that would include introducing a regional currency.

According to the CNN transcript,[23] near the end of the broadcast King relayed to Fox a question posed by a Ms. Gonzalez by email from Elizabeth, New Jersey: "Mr. Fox, I would like to know how you feel about the possibility of having a Latin America united with one currency?" Fox responded by admitting he and President George W. Bush had agreed to pursue the Free Trade Agreement of the Americas, or FTAA, a free-trade zone extending throughout the Western Hemisphere, and that part of the plan was to institute a regional FTAA currency from Canada to the tip of South America in Argentina. Fox answered in the affirmative: "Long term, very long term. What we propose together, President Bush and myself, it's ALCA, which is a trade union for all the Americas." ALCA is the acronym for the Área de Libre Comercio de las Américas, the FTAA counterpart in Spanish.

Ironically, Fox correctly noted that the FTAA plan had been thwarted by Hugo Chavez, the radical socialist president of Venezuela. "Everything was running fluently until Hugo Chavez came," Fox commented. "He decided to combat the idea and destroy the idea." King, evidently startled by this revelation, asked pointedly, "It's going to be like the euro dollar, you mean?" Again, Fox responded affirmatively. "Well, that would be long, long term," Fox repeated.

Then Fox proceeded to explain that he and President Bush intended to proceed incrementally, establishing FTAA as an economic agreement first and waiting to create an amero-type currency later, a plan Fox also suggested was in place for NAFTA itself. "I think the process to go, first step is trading agreement," Fox argued. "And then further on, a new vision, like we are trying to do with NAFTA."

In March 2009, in a speech to the University of Texas at San Antonio's College of Business, Fox repeated his hope that someday Canada, the United States, and Mexico, as well as the rest of Latin and South America, would function like the European Union. "It's an extremely successful model," Fox told the university audience. "My vision is to speed up the process of further integration." While acknowledging the resistance to establishing a European Union–like structure in the Americas, Fox expressed his confidence that President Obama would continue the dream of creating a North American Union. "Hope is back again," Fox said, referring to President Obama's election and the capacity of the United States "to fight for ideals." [24]

ECONOMIST ROBERT MUNDELL
OPENLY BACKS ONE-WORLD CURRENCY

In March 2009, economist Robert Mundell openly endorsed an idea from Kazakhstan president Nursultan Nazarbayev to create the "acmetal" as a world currency, according to *The Australian*.[25] Nazarbayev explained that his coining of the word *acmetal* comes from the Greek *acme,* meaning "peak" or "best," and *capital.*

"I must say that I agree with President Nazarbayev on his statement and many of the things he said in his plan, the project he made for the world currency, and I believe I'm right on track with what he is saying," Mundell said. Nazarbayev and Mundell urged the G20, scheduled to meet in London only a few weeks later, to form a working group to study the proposal.

This endorsement from the prominent Nobel Prize–winning economist who introduced the concept of "optimal currency areas" and who is credited with being the "Father of the Euro" was another indication that globalists have become more open about advancing the idea of global governance and structures, including the idea of a global currency, as solutions to the worldwide economic recession.

Within days of this announcement, China proposed dropping the dollar as the world's foreign-exchange currency, in a proposal that came directly out of Mundell's suggestion that Special Drawing Rights at the International Monetary Fund were available to establish the basis for a new one-world foreign-exchange currency. The coincidence was not unanticipated. Over many years, Mundell has been a frequent visitor to China, invited to advise the government and top Chinese economists on how best to deal with the threat to the dollar caused by worsening problems in the negative balance of trade maintained by the United States with China and with the trillions of dollars of debt the U.S. Treasury has planned to issue in order to finance Obama administration–planned deficit spending.[26]

MOSCOW AND BEIJING PROPOSE DROPPING THE DOLLAR

Increasingly, the International Monetary Fund, or IMF, with the support of the United States and Russia, appears positioned to launch a one-world currency.

On March 17, 2009, the *Moscow Times* published an article revealing that the Kremlin intended to use the April meeting of the G20 in London to push for the IMF to utilize Special Drawing Rights, or SDRs, as "a super-reserve currency widely accepted by the whole of the international community."[27] A few days later, the *Financial Times* reported that China's central bank governor, Zhou Xiaochuan, proposed to utilize SDRs, issued by the International Monetary Fund as a world reserve currency.[28] The proximity of the two announcements gave the impression that Moscow and Beijing had coordinated their efforts to undermine the dollar.

On March 25, Zhou Xiaochuan took center stage for the proposal and Treasury Secretary Timothy Geithner suggested the United States would not reject the idea without serious consideration. In answering a question from the audience after delivering a speech at the Council on Foreign Relations in New York, Geithner responded to Zhou Xiaochuan's plan. "I haven't read the governor's proposal," Geithner said. "He [Zhou Xiaochuan] is a very careful distinguished central banker. I generally find him sensible on every issue." Then Geithner added, "We're actually quite open to that suggestion—you should see it as rather evolutionary, rather building on the current architecture, rather than moving us to global monetary union." [29]

Within ten minutes of Geithner's remarks, the dollar plummeted by as much as 1.3 percent against the euro and the Obama administration was backtracking to clarify that Geithner was not seriously recommending the dollar could or should be dropped as the world's foreign-exchange reserve currency in favor of IMF-created SDRs. Later in the day, White House spokesman Robert Gibbs attempted to reassure world currency exchanges by insisting that the Obama administration expects the dollar to be the world's reserve currency for "a long, long time." [30] Still, White House economic adviser Austan Goolsbee seconded Geithner. [31] Appearing on CNN, Goolsbee told Wolf Blitzer that, while he too had not seen the details of what China was proposing, "the dollar is the dollar. If people don't want to buy it, they don't buy it," suggesting he as well might be open to the Chinese proposal.

China's proposal called for the IMF to issue at least $250 billion in SDRs to IMF member states as a way of placing a safety net under developing countries that might otherwise have to declare bankruptcy. SDRs are international reserve assets that are calculated by the IMF in a basket of major currencies that are allocated to the 185 IMF member nation-states in relation to the capital, largely in gold or widely accepted foreign currencies, that the members have on deposit with the IMF. China's proposal would require the IMF to issue SDRs to central banks of IMF member states far in excess of any gold or currency reserves the members had on deposit.

China was clearly worried that its massive holdings of U.S. dollars are at risk of devaluation because of the enormous deficit financing required by the Obama administration's proposed $3.6 trillion budget, on top of the administration's deficit-financed $787 billion economic stimulus plan and $410 billion omnibus funding bill passed by Congress. In 2009, China held approximately $2 trillion in foreign-exchange reserves, the most any nation has ever held in the history of the world, gained largely by the positive balance of trade China has enjoyed exporting cheap goods to the United States since 2000, when President Bill Clinton signed a landmark bill granting permanent normalized-trade-relations status to China to accommodate the latter's entrance into the World Trade Organization.

On March 27, 2009, bowing to political pressure from the United States, IMF managing director Dominique Strauss-Kahn said the dollar was not under any threat but that he understood China's questioning of the future of the U.S. currency.[32] Yet the question, once raised, affirmed that Robert Mundell's influence is still being felt and that the dollar is under attack as the world's reserve currency, much as Mundell predicted. In June 2008, Mundell said a major dollar crisis would come within five years and that China was discussing with him proposals to reform the global monetary system. "There's no doubt about it that inside the Chinese government there's a lot of discussion going on," Mundell told Reuters. "I'm not sure how they're doing it, but I know they're going to get input from me." Mundell went so far as to speculate that the Chinese-recommended solution would involve the IMF. "What you need to have is an International Monetary Fund that's going to take some of these excess dollars [such as those held by China in foreign-exchange reserves], put them into a substitution account inside the IMF or some other institution and then use that to create what is a new international currency." Mundell stressed that such a proposal would be "very acceptable" to China.[33]

The United Nations also weighed in when an advisory committee to the 192-member world organization endorsed China's proposal. The *Financial Times* quoted Andrei Denisov, Russia's deputy foreign minister, as telling a U.N. General Assembly meeting on the global financial crisis, "The current situation requires new collective solutions agreed at the international level." Separately, Denisov told reporters that China's proposal "is aimed at a practical realization of the idea about a new global accounting unit or a new global currency. It is a question which should be discussed to create a consensus."[34]

THE FEDERAL RESERVE BEGINS
BUYING U.S. TREASURY DEBT

On March 25, 2009, the Federal Reserve began to buy longer-term U.S. Treasury securities in a move several economists believed would end up "monetizing the dollar," a process that could easily inflate the amount of currency in circulation and cause serious devaluation of the dollar on world currency markets. A Federal Reserve Bank of New York press release specified that the Federal Open Market Trading Desk within the Fed would purchase $1 trillion of government and quasi-government debt, including up to $300 billion of longer-term U.S. Treasury securities over six months, in what amounts to the government-subsidized purchase of U.S. government debt.[35] The announced Fed purchases also included $750 billion of Freddie Mac and Fannie Mae debt and up to $100 billion of debt issued by various other government agencies.[36]

To many Americans, the move appears equivalent to a retail consumer in debt using a MasterCard to pay the Visa bill. "The Fed is monetizing U.S. Treasury debt in order to debase the dollar—to create inflation—in hopes of avoiding deflation," economist John Williams told World Net Daily. "This move also sets the precedent for the Fed acting as lender of last resort to the U.S. Treasury, if foreign and other investors in U.S. Treasuries balk at upcoming auctions or look to dump existing holdings. The record federal deficits ahead mean record Treasury borrowings. Fed monetization of the debt eventually means surging money supply growth and much higher inflation."

As documented at the start of this book, the U.S. Treasury's GAAP accounting of the federal budget deficit, which indicated the negative net worth of the U.S. government in 2008, was $65.5 trillion in total obligations, a sum that exceeds the gross domestic product of the world. "Because of the U.S. government's effective insolvency with $65 trillion in obligations, even before the Obama administration deficits, the higher inflation caused by the Fed buying Treasury debt has the early potential of evolving into an uncontrolled hyperinflation, in which the U.S. dollar becomes totally worthless," Williams said.

Williams's comments were especially pertinent after Great Britain announced that on March 25, 2009, for the first time in almost seven years, the country had failed to find enough buyers of £1.75 billion ($2.55 billion) of bonds as debt investors rejected Prime Minister Gordon Brown's plan to stimulate England's economy with deficit-financed government spending.[37] The looming risk was that the U.S. Treasury would also have increasing difficulty in raising trillions of U.S. debt on world bond markets, unless interest rates were raised dramatically. Even with the Fed entering the market to buy U.S. long-term Treasury bonds, professional bond traders were uncertain how much of a depressing effect on interest rates the Fed's actions could exert on the bond market. In the final analysis, if the Fed is the buyer of long-term debt issued by the Treasury, we are borrowing from ourselves to finance unprecedented trillions in Obama administration deficit spending, a phenomenon that few professional bond traders would consider sustainable for long without ruinous consequences.

PUBLIC-PRIVATE PARTNERSHIPS TO BUY
TOXIC BANK ASSETS

On March 23, 2009, U.S. Treasury Secretary Timothy Geithner caused nearly a 500-point stock-market rally by announcing the Obama administration had decided to fund a public-private partnership structure to buy toxic assets off bank balance sheets. The idea was that banks, once their balance sheets were relieved of toxic assets largely resulting from the meltdown in mortgage-backed securities, would begin lending once again. The Obama administration was betting that inducing the banks to begin vigorous lending was the key to bringing the economy out of recession. Geithner's plan envisioned a series of PPP investments designed to purchase at least $500 billion and possibly as much as $1 trillion in troubled bank loans and asset-backed securities that were threatening bank insolvencies as long as the assets remained on bank balance sheets.[38]

Geithner's plan involved utilizing financial guarantees provided by the Federal Reserve and the Federal Deposit Insurance Corporation, or FDIC, along with government loans provided on favorable terms to private investors to induce private capital to enter the market to buy up to $1 trillion in toxic bank assets. The Treasury was attempting to create a market in which private investors would put their capital at risk to create a market in which the toxic assets could be removed from bank balance sheets to be worked out in the private market. In other words, not all mortgages in a particular mortgage-backed security were necessarily nonperforming or in default. Picking through the mortgages that make up a particular mortgage-backed security purchased in a PPP deal, the private investors could hope to recover some cents on the dollar by selling off the bad mortgages at a deep discount and retaining the good mortgages as long-term investments.

Within a few days of the initial market euphoria that the Obama administration had launched a plan to remove toxic assets from bank balance sheets, the market retreated, less confident that an idea that initially appeared good in broad outline would prove to be nearly as good in the details required for implementation.

For starters, the government faced a high hurdle to induce private capital to enter the PPP marketplace. If the government guarantees and loans were structured correctly, the private-capital firms deciding to participate could possibly obtain "no lose" investments, such that the government and the taxpayer absorbed most, if not all, of the losses, while the private investors enjoyed most, if not all, of the gains. To the extent that the government loans and guarantees were not sufficiently strong to reassure PPP investors, the plan would not work. In the final analysis, while the government was attempting to induce private capital to share in the risk created by working out bank-held toxic assets, the government and the taxpayer would have to remain on the hook for the vast majority of losses; otherwise private capital would not be induced to enter the fray.

Another hurdle was that banks holding toxic assets must try to avoid taking massive losses in selling their toxic assets to PPP investors. Deep discounts taken in selling toxic assets would have to be booked as losses on bank balance sheets. Depending upon the magnitude of the losses banks would be required to book, the sale of the toxic assets could have the immediate effect of worsening the financial condition of the banks selling the assets. Yet if PPP investors paid too much for the toxic assets, their chance to make a profit in the asset workouts required could be significantly diminished. This pricing dilemma was the inevitable hang-up in making the plan work. Put simply, an inevitable gap between the "bid" and "asked" in the bank toxic assets was the fatal flaw in the Treasury proposal.

Geithner's proposal also involved an implicit admission that bank management was not properly equipped with the expertise needed to maximize returns in the asset workout situation. Yet PPP investors willing to take the risk would have to have the expertise to give them the confidence a profit could be made buying assets that were admittedly toxic. After studying the plan, PPP investors demanded that their position in the deal needed to be structured to minimize their downside risk, even if that meant the government needed to virtually guarantee them a profit. If the government wanted to allow the banks to sell toxic assets at more than deeply discounted fair-market value, PPP investors would demand that the government take 100 percent of the resulting market risk. The only risk that PPP investors were likely to take on was that they might not get as much value as initially anticipated after they had purchased bank toxic assets at the deeply discounted values those investors were willing to pay.

Very quietly the Obama administration allowed the accounting rules to be relaxed so banks were not forced so severely to mark to market their toxic assets. In the short run, this allowed financial institutions to continue booking assets they knew were toxic at a value above their true worth. In the long run, the accounting scheme just papered over the problem, hoping the market for the toxic assets would recover.

HOW MANY LOSSES WILL DUBAI TAKE?

In the economic downturn, investors from the United Arab Emirates were continuing to take losses that discouraged further investment.

In March 2009, Abu Dhabi bought 9.1 percent of Daimler, the maker of Mercedes-Benz, while Dubai, one of the other emirates composing the United Arab Emirates, or U.A.E., launched a lawsuit against MGM Mirage charging that it mismanaged an investment by Dubai World, a conglomerate owned by the Dubai government, in the $8.6 billion City-Center project on the Las Vegas Strip. These developments illustrate that, while Middle Eastern oil-producing states have capital badly needed to reinvest in the United States and the world economy, no one is ever happy when investments turn into losses. As noted previously, Middle Eastern oil-producing countries and China have established extensive sovereign-wealth funds with trillions of dollars available to invest in the global economy right now, including buying key assets in the United States. Yet, increasingly, these Middle Eastern funds have become cautious about making investments in a world economy that remains deeply mired in recession.

According to the *Wall Street Journal*, as a result of the Dubai investment in Daimler, Aabar Investments PJSC became the largest single stakeholder in the Stuttgart, Germany–based automaker, topping Kuwait's 7.6 percent stake. Now, between Dubai and Kuwait, 16.7 percent of Daimler is in Middle Eastern hands. "The best time to invest is when people panic," Khadem Al Qubaisi, the chairman of Aabar Investments, told the *Wall Street Journal*. "We are buying a high-quality asset here." Daimler suffered a loss in the fourth quarter of 2008, due largely to a slump in Mercedes-Benz car sales worldwide and a loss on Daimler's stake in Chrysler LLC. The largest shareholder of Aabar Investments, according to the *Journal*, is the International Petroleum Investment Company, which is wholly owned by the government of Abu Dhabi.[39]

The *Wall Street Journal* also reported that Dubai World was suing MGM Mirage for massive cost overruns on CityCenter, a resort and residential complex being built on nearly 67 acres in the heart of Las

Vegas.[40] Dubai World threw the entire CityCenter project into jeopardy by suggesting in its lawsuit that Dubai might default on a $100 million payment due imminently on the CityCenter project. A failure by Dubai to make the payment could jeopardize CityCenter's ability to make scheduled debt payments, with the risk that the construction on the project might stop while bankruptcy proceedings began. MGM Mirage was saddled with $13 billion in debt and negotiating with lenders to receive a reprieve on payments to prevent a loan default that could threaten the solvency of MGM Mirage itself.

At the time the MGM Mirage deal was done, Dubai World invested $5 billion for half of the CityCenter project, plus a 9.5 percent stake in MGM Mirage. Then, Ahmed bin Sulayem, Dubai World's chairman, characterized the deal as part of Dubai's effort to expand internationally, and the investment in MGM Mirage as the beginning of what he hoped would be a long-term relationship. The CityCenter complex, which is scheduled to include five thousand hotel rooms in three hotels, a casino, and two condo towers, was initially projected to cost $7.48 billion, but overruns have raised estimates to $8.6 billion.

The global economic downturn has also hurt the economy in the United Arab Emirates. In February 2009, the U.A.E. central bank lent Dubai $10 billion as an economic stimulus measure. The following month, the government of Dubai itself outlined a plan to provide government-owned or government-managed businesses with $10 billion in loans on favorable terms. Corporations in the United Arab Emirates were laboring to meet loan payments on the $75 billion in debt the corporations already had in place, according to the *Financial Times*.[41] The global recession also hit emirates such as Dubai by depressing real estate values, including values on commercial real estate in the massive world-class skyscrapers Dubai constructed in boom times, anticipating the possibility of becoming a Middle Eastern commercial hub to supplement the banking hub Dubai has already become in the Middle East. To compound problems, tourism to Dubai has slowed dramatically and expatriates are leaving; as much as 17 percent of Dubai's population could leave the country by the end of 2009.

As many countries in the world do, Dubai blames the United States for causing the global economic recession, arguing that Federal Reserve policies keeping interest rates artificially low at 1 percent in 2003 and 2004 caused credit to be so readily available that a mortgage bubble was inevitable. Middle Eastern countries, including those in OPEC, of which the United Arab Emirates is a member, have suffered as oil prices retreated to under $50 a barrel from the record high of $147 a barrel in July 2008. With the dollar under duress as the Economic Panic of 2009 progressed, OPEC nations curtailed supply in an attempt to elevate prices. From the perspective of the Middle East, countries like the United Arab Emirates are questioning whether their oil sales at reduced prices now amount to a subsidy to the United States.

Inevitably, the end result will be to increase foreign ownership of key U.S. corporate structures, including banks and investment firms, as the plan to place "America for sale" continues apace. Globalists, seeking to avoid seeing tariffs and other international trade restrictions put in place to protect U.S. workers and U.S. jobs, undoubtedly are examining ways to position badly needed foreign capital into the United States. Middle Eastern oil producers and foreign trade partners such as China are likely to pull back from making these investments unless the U.S. government can figure out some way to protect downside risk.

The U.S. government has already tried to induce more foreign investment in U.S. corporations and financial institutions. In June 2008, the Department of Commerce made a decision to stop publishing data on foreign investment in the United States,[42] a step that can be expected to promise a massive future foreign investment in the U.S. that the Commerce Department wants to hide, in order to defuse criticism. Interestingly, the report announcing the decision to stop publishing these data indicated that outlays by foreign direct investors to acquire or establish U.S. businesses increased sharply in 2007, after also increasing strongly in 2006. According to the report, outlays reached $276.8 billion in 2007, the second-largest recorded and the highest since 2000, when new direct investment by foreigners peaked at $335.6 billion. Now all that may be required for direct foreign investment in the United States to hit new highs is for the Treasury Department and the Federal Reserve to find a way to guarantee the foreign investors against the possibility of loss. They could adapt the plan developed to buy toxic assets off bank balance sheets, and provide PPP guarantees for foreign sovereign-wealth funds willing to invest in the United States.

CHINA'S PLAN TO CONVERT U.S. DEBT INTO EQUITY

Writing in the *Financial Times* of London, Yu Qiao, a professor of economics at Tsinghua University in Beijing, has proposed a way for the U.S. government to guarantee foreign investments in the United States.[43]

Under the plan, the Obama administration would grant a financial guarantee as an inducement for China to convert U.S. debt into Chinese direct equity investment to establish Chinese ownership in successful U.S. corporations and potentially profitable infrastructure projects. Is the Obama administration willing to put the United States up for sale to China to induce them to keep financing U.S. government deficit spending?

The U.S. Treasury is preparing to borrow $2.5 trillion in 2009 and another $4 trillion in 2010, an amount that would increase by 65 percent in two years the $10 trillion in national debt accumulated since George Washington was president. The U.S. government also faces more than $65 trillion in unfunded Social Security and Medicare benefits scheduled to be paid out largely to baby-boomer retirees in the coming decades. Yu Qiao observed that foreign nations now hold $1.6 trillion of U.S. government debt, with Asian nations including China and Japan holding half of the outstanding publicly owned U.S. Treasury bonds. He also noted that China directly or indirectly holds more than $1.2 billion of U.S. Treasury bonds.

If the U.S. dollar collapsed under the weight of proposed Obama administration trillion-dollar budget deficits in the foreseeable future, holders of U.S. debt would face substantial losses that the *Financial Times* estimated "would devastate Asians' hard-earned wealth and terminate economic globalization."

"The basic idea is to turn Asian savings, China's in particular, into real business interests rather than let them be used to support U.S. overconsumption," Yu Qiao wrote, reflecting themes commonly suggested by Chinese government officials. "While fixed-income securities are vulnerable to any fall in the value of the dollar, equity claims on sound corporations and infrastructure projects are at less risk from a currency default."

The problem is that China does not want to trade Chinese investment in U.S. Treasury debt securities, with their inherent risk of dollar devaluation, for equally risky investments in U.S. corporations and infrastructure projects, where a struggling U.S. economy could risk the depreciation of those assets.

"But Asians do not want to bear the risk of this investment because of market turbulence and a lack of knowledge of cultural, legal and regulatory issues in U.S. businesses," Yu Qiao stressed. "However, if a guarantee scheme were created, Asian savers could be willing to invest directly in capital-hungry U.S. industries."

Yu Qiao's plan included four components:

1. Asian countries would negotiate with the U.S. government to create a "crisis relief facility," or CRF. The CRF "would be used alongside U.S. federal efforts to stabilize the banking system and to invest in capital-intensive infrastructure projects such as high-speed railroad from Boston to Washington, D.C."

2. Asian nations and especially China would pool a portion of their holdings of Treasury bonds under the CFR umbrella to convert sovereign debt into equity. Any CFR funds that were designated for investment in U.S. corporations would still be owned and managed by U.S. equity holders, with the Asians holding minority equity shares "that would, like preferred stock, be convertible."

3. The U.S. government would act as a guarantor, "providing a sovereign guarantee scheme to assure the investment principal of the CRF against possible default of targeted companies or projects."

4. The Federal Reserve would set up a special account to supply the liquidity the CRF would require to swap Chinese-held U.S. debt into industrial investment in the United States.

"The CRF would lessen Asians' concern about implicit default of sovereign debts caused by a collapsing dollar," Yu Qiao concluded. "It would cost little and help the U.S. by channeling funds to business investment."

This plan to convert Chinese debt into equity investments in the United States could easily add another $1 trillion to outstanding Obama administration guarantees issued in the current economic crisis.

THE PLAN TO DESTROY THE DOLLAR

The government response to the Economic Panic of 2009 has pushed the U.S. economy from a private-enterprise-managed model to a government-managed model. The process began with the Bush administration creating the Troubled Asset Relief Program, or TARP, to bail out troubled banks. The Obama administration moved government intervention into high gear, proposing in the first days in office a $787 billion economic stimulus plan that involved a massive growth in the federal government and an expansion of social-welfare programs unseen since Franklin Roosevelt's New Deal and Lyndon Johnson's Great Society. The Obama administration quickly announced that any private corporation accepting government funds also accepted government regulations, including caps on the salaries and bonuses top executives in companies accepting bailouts could be paid.

The Obama administration did not announce its plans to intervene massively in the private economy. That result developed as, step-by-step, the Obama administration advanced Bush-administration bailout efforts. Almost imperceptibly, the bailouts became not just a way for private companies to survive, but also a way for the government to take over increasing management of the private economy. As the Obama administration took shape in its first months in office, what was becoming increasingly clear was that President Obama was comfortable with the type of government central management of a hybrid government-private model of a social welfare state that increasingly looked like the European model. While the administrations of George H. W. Bush and George W. Bush had pioneered in public-private partnerships, the PPP model looked as if it could become a predominant motif for the Obama administration, with heavy emphasis on the "public," or government, control part of the formula.

Skeptics have doubted that North American integration could advance toward forming a North American Union along the model of the European Union, or to the creation of a North American currency, such as the amero, to replace the dollar. Yet once again, the incremental process is already in play. Globalist-thinking economists such as Robert Mundell have received academic support from economists such as Benn Steil at the Council on Foreign Relations. Now China has advocated a proposal to replace the dollar as the world's foreign-exchange reserve, to be replaced by the International Monetary Fund's use of Special Drawing Rights as an international foreign-exchange reserve alternative. A serious review of economists writing about the status of the dollar in international currency reveals decades of academic work in which the demise of the dollar has been anticipated and predicted. In Canada, top investors such as Stephen Jarislowsky have openly called for the Canadian dollar to be pegged to the U.S. dollar, to prevent a strengthening Canadian dollar from hurting Canadian exports and, in turn, the export companies that investors such as Jarislowsky finance.

With the Federal Reserve already buying U.S. Treasury securities, the Obama administration has advanced the unavoidable: that the U.S.

dollar is already being "monetized." The U.S. government buying its own debt is calculated to reduce interest rates. The result could boomerang, however, if the government continues running massive deficits that require massive deficit financing through debt creation. The danger with a fiat currency like the dollar is that the U.S. government faces no limit on how much money can be printed, except the possibility of a dollar devaluation that could well induce hyperinflation. Sooner or later, the Obama administration will have to face a dollar that foreign currency markets deeply devaluate, with or without the cooperation of the U.S. government. The resultant prospect is that hyperinflation could occur in the United States on a magnitude not seen since the Weimar Republic.

As U.S. assets are sold to foreign interests, the U.S. government will most likely be motivated to encourage foreign capital investment to return to the United States, regardless of what national-security concerns the investment may create. With the U.S. government under both President Bush and President Obama supporting free-trade agreements, a free flow of foreign capital back into the United States will most likely be seen as business as usual, even if the nation investing the capital is not necessarily a friend of the United States. The end result is that foreign interests will end up owning increasingly important segments of U.S. private corporations and public infrastructure.

Part III

FIGHTING THE NEW WORLD ORDER, SURVIVING A GLOBAL DEPRESSION, AND PRESERVING U.S.A. SOVEREIGNTY

The first key to understanding the global Economic Panic of 2009 is to understand that it could well precede a Great Depression of 2010.

Like the Great Depression of the 1930s, the stock market decline beginning at the end of 2007 did not immediately lead to any dramatic economic downturn.

The stock market crashed over a series of days, highlighted by October 29, 1929, known as Black Thursday, when a record 16.3 million shares were sold so fast that people panicked and prices collapsed. Still, the stock market low was not reached until nearly three years later, when, on July 8, 1932, the Dow Jones Industrial Average bottomed out at 41.22.

Nor was the stock market crash of 1929 viewed at the time as a sign of imminent economic downturn. On Black Thursday, Treasury Secretary Andrew W. Mellon went to the White House to attend a cabinet meeting with President Herbert Hoover. The stock market situation was discussed at the cabinet meeting, but President Hoover didn't feel that immediate action by the White House was required. The Federal Reserve Board, which was holding a regularly scheduled meeting at 10 A.M. on Black Thursday, continued discussions through lunch, but ultimately also decided no special action was required, except to remain in frequent contact with the New York Federal Reserve Bank to monitor the situation as the trading day on Wall Street continued.[1]

While the nation's gross national product began declining in 1930 and unemployment began rising, the real impact of the economic downturn did not become fully evident until 1931. That year, the GNP declined 8.4 percent and unemployment rose to 15.9 percent. In 1932, the GNP fell 13.4 percent and unemployment rose to 23.6 percent. Franklin D. Roosevelt was elected president in November 1932 and the Great Depression of the 1930s had fully begun.

Similarly, the DJIA reached a height of 14,164.53 on October 9, 2007, only to hit a subsequent low of 6,594.44 less than two years later, on March 5, 2009. Nor is there any certainty yet that this will be the bottom of a stock market, even though the DJIA lost half its value. The recession did not officially begin until December 2008, after government statistics reported two consecutive down quarters of negative growth in the gross domestic product. The full dimensions of the subprime-mortgage meltdown were not apparent to the U.S. public until the end of the Bush administration, when the president signed off on TARP on October 3, 2008. The point is that deep recessions take time to develop and government policies may have the unintended consequence of deepening a recession rather than ending it.

Instead of cutting taxes, as he had promised to do when campaigning, President Roosevelt launched a massive expansion of government and deficit-financed social-welfare spending that marked the beginning of the New Deal. President Barack Obama may be headed on the same course, likely with the same result, namely that an economic downturn that might have lasted months, or possibly one or two years at most, becomes another decade-long depression.

The second key to understanding the global Economic Panic of 2009 is recognizing that the economic downturn was caused by globalism. Still, the only solution the globalists have offered to recover from the worldwide economic downturn is more globalism.

On March 30, 2009, when President Obama ordered General Motors chairman and chief executive Rick Wagoner fired, a new chapter in U.S. economic history began. That day the United States moved into a more clearly government-managed economy, since the White House had assumed the right to intervene in internal corporate decision making because GM had taken federal bailout money.

In a fundamental sense, the demise of the Big Three automakers represented the revenge of free trade. In 1955, during President Eisenhower's first term in office, GM's chairman and chief executive boldly but truthfully proclaimed to Congress that what was good for General Motors was good for America. Yet in January 2009, China surpassed the United States in vehicle sales for the first time ever, putting China on track to be the world's largest automaker.[2] Truly, with the decline of the Detroit automakers, the United States has taken second place to China in yet another manufacturing arena the United States had dominated since the end of World War II.

U.S. auto sales dropped precipitously in 2008, with many experts predicting 2009 would be even more difficult. Full-year 2008 vehicle sales, including heavy and medium trucks, dropped in 2008 to approximately 13.5 million vehicles, compared with 16.5 million in 2007, and U.S. auto production could fall to as low as 10.7 million vehicles in 2009.[3] With production figures this low, GM and Chrysler were bankrupt, given the legacy costs of paying retirement and health benefits to generations of no-longer-working UAW workers who weigh down the automakers beyond any point of economic recovery.

The U.S. auto industry is in collapse. Across the country, car dealerships that had been in business for decades are now closed. Grant Thornton, a top industry consultant specializing in corporate restructuring, predicted that 3,800 U.S. dealerships, the majority of them Big Three, would need to close in 2009 to keep the industry profitable.[4] Overall, 2008 was the worst year for U.S. auto industry sales since 1992.

Ironically, the United States may be approaching an era where it will be impossible to buy a U.S.-manufactured auto, or an era marked by a global economy in which the only manufacturers that survive will be the multinational corporations with car-manufacturing capacity in China, aimed at taking advantage of China's low-cost labor markets.

Yet when President Obama traveled to London to attend the G20 meeting on April 2, 2009, he proclaimed a "declaration of interdependence" in which he insisted global solutions were required to bring the industrialized nations out of recession.

Americans today are well advised to plan for how families can survive economically if one or more wage earners in the family are unemployed for six months or longer.

If Americans concerned about preserving U.S. sovereignty, as well as U.S. jobs, begin fighting back right now, the First Amendment and the ballot box are the only tools such patriots will need to reverse the globalist agenda.

Here we will explore specific strategies for peacefully resisting the globalist agenda and for preparing families to survive what could well develop into a prolonged global depression.

EIGHT

Say "No!" to the Global New Deal

We need a global New Deal. We need a grand bargain between the countries and continents of this world, so that the world economy can not only recover but, as [German chancellor] Angela Merkel said, the economic system of the future can be based on the soundest and best principles of all.

—Prime Minister Gordon Brown, 2009[1]

The April 2009 meeting of the G20 in London marked the end of the "Washington Consensus" that had shaped international economics since the end of World War II. This amounted to a declaration that the United States was no longer the most dominant world economy and U.S. economic policy making would no longer shape international economics unilaterally through decisions made in Washington. Moreover, the heavily overleveraged and indebted U.S. consumer could no longer be relied upon to drive world economic growth. "A new world order is emerging and with it the foundations of a new and progressive era of international cooperation," British prime minister Gordon Brown proclaimed at the end of the meeting. "We have resolved that from today we will together manage the process of globalization to secure responsibility from all and fairness to all."

A FIVE-POINT PLAN TO SAY "NO!"
TO THE "GLOBAL NEW DEAL"

A global New Deal does not have to be a reality simply because progressives like Prime Minister Gordon Brown and President Barack Obama proclaim their intentions to make it so. "We the People" are the sovereign in the United States, not the president. If Congress passes a presidential agenda that the people of the United States oppose, the ballot box remains an option. Right now the Democratic Party has control of the presidency and Congress. In the midterm 2010 elections, an American electorate unhappy with the direction of the Democratic Party can vote Democrats out. If the incoming Republicans do not get the message, the electorate can vote the Republicans out next. Politicians targeted for electoral defeat will soon realize that an angered electorate is not the ticket to a permanent career in public service.

Globalism is not inevitable simply because intellectual and political elites on both the Right and the Left have embraced the concept. Modern telecommunications technologies, including satellite TV and the Internet, may create a global village in which we can instantaneously communicate around the world. Still, the president of the United States continues to take an oath of office in which the president swears to preserve, protect, and defend the Constitution of the United States. The president does not swear to preserve, protect, and defend the Federal Reserve, or the United Nations, or the World Trade Organization—at least not yet. Just because telecommunications erases the impact of distances around the globe does not mean nation-states must inevitably give way to international one-world governance.

Proposed here are five specific points of a plan to reverse the global New Deal:

1. Close Down the Federal Reserve

There is no function the Federal Reserve performs that could not also be performed by the U.S. Treasury, including the creation of money. Instead of going into debt to print dollars, the U.S. Treasury could simply print the dollars on its own authority. That this fiat creation of money would be inflationary might well be a curb on the federal government's continued irresponsibility in running now trillions of dollars of budget deficits. The Treasury could still issue debt securities, if it decided to reduce the inflationary impact of printing money. Right now, a private bank—the Federal Reserve—owns the U.S. currency, not "We the People." Closing down the Federal Reserve is the necessary first step to the people of the United States gaining control of the dollar.

Today, the Federal Reserve's Open Market Committee sets key interest rates, including the fed-funds rate, specifying the rate at which banks can lend and borrow from one another via overnight facilities. Fed-funds rates could be set by a Treasury committee equally well. Perhaps even better, all interest rates in the United States could be set by the market, much as LIBOR, the international interbank lending rate, currently is.

Congressman Ron Paul's call for a public audit of the Federal Reserve should become a legal requirement for an annual public audit of the Treasury, after the Federal Reserve is abolished. All minutes of Treasury committee meetings should be published. Complete documentation should be published on any and all market manipulations in which the Treasury engages, including repurchase agreements or any other buying and selling of Treasury-owned securities. U.S. monetary policy should no longer be in the hands of private bankers operating behind closed doors.

2. Pull Out of NAFTA, CAFTA, and the WTO

Free-trade agreements including NAFTA, CAFTA, and the WTO have not proved to support the creation of U.S. jobs. What the United States has experienced is the loss of millions of blue-collar and white-collar jobs to outsourcing. The only winners in this free-trade scenario have been the multinational corporations. The principle of NAFTA, CAFTA, and the WTO is that U.S.-based multinational corporations are free to pursue cheap labor wherever in the world it can be found. If the guiding principle of free trade is that multinational corporations can find, somewhere in the world, someone who will do the job cheaper than a U.S. worker, then all workers lose.

Wages and benefits race for the bottom worldwide as U.S. workers are unemployed in favor of foreign workers who are given no option but to sell their labor at slave or near-slave prices. The end result is that only the owners, managers, and senior executives in the multinational corporations win as profit margins are increased because labor costs are reduced to the minimum possible levels. Income gaps between the 5 percent of the population serving multinational corporations at the top and the rest of the population increase dramatically, as the possibility of creating an economically strong middle class is wiped out in the United

States, as well as the foreign lands where the multinational corporations go in order to exploit foreign labor.

Trade agreements such as NAFTA, CAFTA, and the WTO need to be eliminated, because labor was never properly included in the capital equation from the beginning. In the first part of the twentieth century, the labor movement arguably kept the United States from going through a communist revolution. In what were often bloody battles, labor-union leaders calling strikes forced management to include labor in the capital equation. By agreeing to pay union workers a living wage plus the benefits needed to maintain health and prepare for retirement, the United States built the greatest middle class ever seen in the history of the world.

By allowing multinational corporations to set the rules of free-trade agreements, the United States is at risk of losing that middle class within this generation or the next generation.

International trade agreements used to include "antidumping" requirements, meaning that goods made by labor that undercut U.S. labor in cost were not permitted to be imported into the United States. Including and enforcing antidumping requirements in all U.S. international trade agreements would support U.S. workers while encouraging foreign countries to compensate their workers with living wages and benefits that make health services available and retirement savings possible.

Put simply, the United States should not engage in international trade with any nation where the creation of a labor union is a crime. Right now, the United States is so at the mercy of China to buy U.S. debt that U.S. official delegations to China no longer dare challenge China on that country's abundant human-rights and environmental violations. The United States should also not engage in international trade with any country, including China, where belief in God or participation in organized religion is a crime. If religious rights must be sacrificed on the altar of free trade, the profits gained by the globalists are gained for naught.

Granted, labor unions may abuse their power over time. The remedy in industries where labor unions have raised costs unduly should be a market remedy. Bankruptcy and reorganization, even in industries as large as the Big Three automakers, may be a necessary solution from time to time. Still, the ability to form a labor union is a fundamental freedom the United States should demand from all international trade partners.

As the United States renegotiates a new set of international trade agreements, each agreement must specify that U.S. laws apply exclusively regarding all goods entering or leaving the U.S. market. International laws must no longer apply within the boundaries of the United States.

3. Close Down the United Nations, the International Monetary Fund, and the World Bank

There is no requirement in the U.S. Constitution that the United States be a member of any international organization.

Through a series of treaties, the United States could agree with those U.N. declarations that two-thirds of the U.S. Senate voted to ratify. In all instances, the United States must insist that U.S. law remain sovereign over U.S. citizens, even when the Senate ratifies narrowly defined treaties with other nations.

Similarly, the U.S. Treasury could agree to contribute to the IMF or World Bank ventures when a treaty specifying the obligation is submitted to the Senate for a two-thirds vote.

Right now, the United States does not control the voting or decision making in any international organization of which the United States is a member. To the contrary, the U.N., IMF, and World Bank feel free to make international rules obligating the United States to compliance simply because the United States is a member. U.S. sovereignty demands that the United States maintain an arm's-length relationship with all international organizations.

Still, the United States pays a disproportionate share of the operating expenses of these international organizations and is a major contributor of the capital that the U.N., the IMF and World Bank require to function. Yet when it comes time for decision-making, the United States is typically outvoted by countries that may have national-security interests diametrically opposed to those of the United States.

Contrary to what Democratic presidents such as Jimmy Carter or Barack Obama may think, the national-security interests of the United States do not involve a world-popularity contest. Regardless of whether the decisions of the president are popular in Europe or in Russia and China, the president swears an oath to preserve, protect, and defend the United States, not the United Nations or the European Union.

Nor is there any certainty that the national-security interests of the United States will be advanced simply because we feel compelled to accept decisions made by these international organizations to avoid the risk of being expelled.

In truth, the United States would be better off being expelled from groups such as the United Nations.

4. Cut Taxes and Close the IRS

The United States must cut taxes across the board, including corporate and individual taxes, or else risk becoming one of the most expensive countries in the world in which to operate a business or to earn an income.

There is no provision in the Constitution that authorizes the United States to establish an Internal Revenue Service to impose taxes on income. Increasingly, the United States is creating a punitive income-tax system in which the majority of wage earners will soon be exempted from paying income tax altogether, simply because they earn too little. An income-tax system in which a minority of higher-income wage earners can be taxed heavily by the majority of the electorate that pay no taxes is a formula for creating confiscatory income taxes and reducing all incentives to working for personal or family economic gain.

Social-welfare benefits must be reexamined so that safety-net benefits are made available but the possibility of living on social-welfare benefits is eliminated as a lifestyle choice. The massive social-welfare system created in the United States since the 1930s has bankrupted our country. Under the Ninth and Tenth Amendments of the Constitution, social-welfare obligations should be returned to the states, since those responsibilities are not specifically delegated to the federal government under the Constitution.

Corporate-tax reductions, especially to small businesses, have been proven to create jobs. If tax rates make the United States one of the most expensive places in the world to do business, U.S.-based multinational corporations will have a strong incentive to relocate and operate as foreign corporations doing business in the United States. Thousands of small businesses today are simply shutting their doors and closing up shop.

Many baby boomers facing retirement who yet pay taxes would gladly forgo all government-paid social-welfare benefits, in exchange for income-tax relief on what they currently earn. When those who are paying taxes end up paying half of all they earn in state and federal income taxes, an income-tax revolt is beginning to build. When tax burdens on those who work productively in the private economy reach what appear to be punitive levels, "Why bother to work at all?" becomes a reasonable question.

Instead of pouring countless billions into endless government bailouts, a better strategy may be to let the banks and corporations fail and go into bankruptcy. Under bankruptcy, the banks could take the losses now on toxic assets rather than pass these losses off to the public in the form of a government bailout. Corporations such as Chrysler and General Motors could renegotiate legacy union contracts the company can no longer afford to honor. While in bankruptcy and being reorganized, the banks and other corporations could continue operations. Right now, those corporations accepting Obama administration bailout funds are also accepting Obama administration intervention into company operations, including but not limited to setting executive compensation. If the government begins running private corporations, we will see the end of the private enterprise system itself.

The economy will not truly be stimulated until new jobs are created, and there is no more effective way to do that than to cut taxes. Tax reduction, not trillions of dollars in government bailouts and guarantees, is the way to return the United States to economic prosperity.

5. Create a Gold-Backed U.S. Dollar for International Trade

Point 19 of the final communiqué from the G20 summit in London in April 2009 specified, "We have agreed to support a general SDR which will inject $250 billion into the world economy and increase global liquidity," taking the first steps forward to implement China's proposal that Special Drawing Rights at the International Monetary Fund should be created as a foreign-exchange currency to replace the dollar.[2] "There is now a world currency in waiting," declared columnist Ambrose Evans-Pritchard in the *Telegraph* in London.[3]

The U.S. Treasury should create an international dollar backed by gold, in an effort to preserve the dollar as the world's foreign-exchange currency of choice.

In a two-step process, the U.S. Treasury should consider reestablishing gold backing for the domestic dollar as well.

This is not just a question of status. By removing any gold or silver backing from the dollar, the U.S. government has created a fiat currency the nation is now inflating, with no end in sight to the trillions of dollars being added to the national debt each year.

Not only is the U.S. Treasury bankrupt when the federal budget is analyzed on a GAAP accounting basis, the negative net worth of the United States can only get worse as the baby boomers retire and obligations in Social Security and Medicare continue to mount.

Congress should also mandate that the Treasury conduct a publicly disclosed audit of all U.S. gold reserves. This would involve not just a physical inventory of the gold in depositories such as Fort Knox, but also a full investigation into the ownership status of the gold on deposit. "We the People" should demand a complete accounting of all gold transactions the Fed and Treasury have conducted though the IMF as well as on gold exchanges around the world.

The aim of a gold-based international dollar would be to establish a reliable standard so that U.S. international trade partners, as well as foreign purchasers of U.S. debt, could once again hold dollar-denominated foreign-exchange reserves in a fixed-standard, international-trade U.S. dollar.

If a gold standard were reinstituted for the domestic dollar, a limit would be placed on the ability of the federal government to continue running budget deficits that necessitate either printing money or borrowing from foreigners to cover the shortfall.

Today's collapsing U.S. fiat dollar not only threatens international trade, it also affects the life savings and investment of every U.S. citizen. Protecting the dollar should be high on the agenda of any presidential administration that is serious about economic recovery. The White House must stop using the Economic Panic of 2009 as an excuse to advance an ideological agenda embracing globalism, regardless of whether the globalism favored is from the political Left or the political Right.

SAY "NO!" TO THE GLOBAL NEW DEAL

In his book *The Revolution: A Manifesto*, Congressman Ron Paul makes clear that belonging to international organizations necessarily compromises our sovereignty. In arguing that an "outrageous affront to our national sovereignty" was predictable once the United States joined the World Trade Organization, Paul pointed to a Congressional Research Service report that was clear about the consequences of membership: "As a member of the WTO, the United States does commit to act in accordance with the rules of the multi-lateral body. It is legally obligated to insure that national laws do not conflict with WTO rules."[4]

The generation of Americans that fought World War I refused to join the League of Nations. In less than a century, cosmopolitan Americans graduated from our prestige universities are trained to be "transnational" in their thinking. As foreign policy expert Frank Gaffney has argued, Harold Koh, the former dean of Yale Law School chosen by President Obama to be the State Department's top lawyer, favors U.S. Supreme Court decisions that recognize law established by international courts, including the U.N.'s International Court of Justice at the Hague. "Transnationalism," as Gaffney explains, involves a form of "law-fare" that, like warfare, seeks to subjugate U.S. law to international law, under the principle that international law is somehow derived from higher principles than is U.S. law, derived from our sovereignty as a nation-state.[5]

Like the frog boiling to death in the pot of water on the stove top, Americans since World War II have been conditioned to accept international organizations as somehow beneficial to U.S. national interests. Today, the change in thinking has reached such a magnitude that those wanting to pull out of the U.N. or WTO are regarded as either ignorant "isolationists" or backward "protectionists."

During economic boom times, free-trade agreements have gone largely unquestioned by a mainstream media that has also been conditioned and educated since World War II to believe transnational post-American thinking is natural or correct. But internationalism has placed the United States in a world economy that has bankrupted the U.S. middle class and destroyed the dollar. Now a peaceful revolution is brewing to reject internationalism in favor of U.S. partiotism.

AMERICAN PATRIOTS

American patriots need to reject an Obama-administration-promoted global New Deal precisely because that concept is anti-American at its core. U.S. citizens faced with the loss of their homes, their jobs, their incomes, and their retirement will be hard-pressed to conclude that a European-style expansion of the social-welfare state is the solution. With the global Economic Panic of 2009 threatening to transition into the Great Depression of the 2010s, the Obama administration would be well advised to consider seriously the reforms proposed here.

A difference in scale remains a difference in phenomenon, and thus even a proposed global New Deal is a phenomenon so grandiose in its dimensions that European socialists find it overreaching, beyond the ability of the taxpayers of the world to afford. At some point, even socialists realize that the world cannot afford all the social welfare programs socialists can imagine.

When the obvious result of globalism is a recession that could turn into a global depression, American patriots can be expected to begin rereading the U.S. Constitution very carefully. Politicians wishing to remain in office should carefully consider first how their economic policies and programs are affecting life in Des Moines, before they travel to Paris to hold town-hall meetings with Europeans.

NINE

Strategies for Middle-Class Survival in Economic Hard Times

The world economy has turned out to be a much more dangerous place than we imagined.

—Paul Krugman, *The Return of Depression Economics and the Crisis of 2008*[1]

SEVEN STRATEGIES FOR ECONOMIC SURVIVAL

The following seven strategies are recommended for survival in the economic hard times occasioned by the Economic Panic of 2009 and the possibility that the U.S. economy may enter a depression in the 2010s. The strategies are addressed to the millions of middle-class Americans concerned about losing their jobs and homes in the economic downturn.

Becoming increasingly dependent on social-welfare programs is not a recommended strategy, although use of unemployment-insurance benefits or even food-stamp programs may assist some families in their readjustment after losing employment. The strategies recommended here are premised on the continuing belief that a free-enterprise system remains the best economic system for generating real wealth. The strategies are designed to position Americans in more economically secure settings from which new opportunities for business development and productive work can be identified and pursued. Free enterprise offers individuals unlimited upward gain, while socialism resents personal wealth or individual economic security. The excessive taxes imposed by socialists to maintain a high level of government-provided social-welfare benefits inevitably undermine economic activity. Excessive taxes destroy the economic base that the government depends upon for robust tax revenue. Socialist systems ultimately all go broke. While free-enterprise systems suffer business downturns, no business-cycle recession has yet remained permanent in a capitalist system.

1. Bring Extended Families Back Together

Economics present a strong argument for families to stay together and for extended families to join forces. Divorces are often economically ruinous, frequently for both partners in the marriage. In divorce settlements, even when the division of property approaches fifty-fifty, the family's primary residence may end up being sold, possibly with the result that neither marriage partner has the resources immediately to make a down payment on another primary residence. In good economic times, both partners in a divorce face better prospects of continued employment and recovery of resources. Still, the loss of half the resources available in the marriage will make economic recovery more difficult, especially in an economy where few are confident about continued job security.

Children who postpone a marriage decision into their thirties or beyond can continue to live at home with parents. Even after completing college, the decision to move back home can add another wage earner to the primary family. In another variation, children who establish their own families and buy their own homes may consider moving aging parents into their home, rather than plan for expensive nursing-home or other medical treatment outside the home. The point is that consolidating extended families into one home reduces mortgage-payment or rental expenses while offering the possibility of adding wage earners to the household.

Families planning to consolidate may want to consider adding space to their homes. Adult children living with parents or parents moving in with adult children should consider whether separate living quarters can be added to the extended family's primary residence. While banks today are reluctant to give home-equity loans for frivolous spending purposes, home-equity loans designed to develop a family's primary residence can still be obtained. Adding rooms to an existing home will usually improve the resale and equity value of the home.

Bringing extended families back together requires mature adults able to accept the independent decision making of adult children. Yet in prior generations, extended families were much more common; children were generally born into homes where the grandparents still lived. Family consolidation, maturely planned, can be an important strategy to survive economic hard times.

In 2007, more than 5.7 million U.S. households reported having a grandparent living with grandchildren under eighteen, a 30 percent increase over findings from the 1990 census.[2] While the rise of grandparents living in families with grandchildren may be due to the economic downturn, psychologists have found evidence that spending time with a grandparent is linked with better social skills and fewer behavior problems among adolescents, especially for those living in single-parent or stepfamily households.[3] The Economic Panic of 2009 presents an exellent opportunity to reconsider the value of extended families living together.

2. Relocate in Small Towns and Communities to Develop Local Economies

A move has begun in the United States to focus on redeveloping small towns and communities, reversing the migration to large cities that has been going on for decades in America.

One indication of this trend is seen in an effort to revive a Depression-era idea for communities across America to print their own local currencies, in an effort to stimulate businesses for local merchants in an increasingly difficult economy. As of the beginning of 2009, there were more than seventy-five local currency systems being issued across America.[4] Typically, a group of businesses come up with the idea to print a new local currency, which shoppers can then buy at a discount, such that one dollar of the local currency is sold for 90 or 95 cents.

The revival of local currencies also reflects a backlash against globalism and free trade, which have outsourced local jobs to foreigners and flooded local communities with cheap goods manufactured in China. With the Obama administration planning a $3.6 trillion budget that involves creating trillions of dollars of federal debt to finance the expected revenue shortfall, local currencies appear small in comparison. Still, proponents of local currency argue that the U.S. dollar is a fiat currency that is backed by no gold or silver, so why can't local communities make up their own money? The idea is to make sure that money earned in local communities is spent there, too, at businesses that have agreed to accept at face value the local currency used as legal tender.

With names such as Detroit Cheer, Bay Bucks, and BerkShares, the local currencies bear colorful designs of local scenes and are issued in common denominations, everything from a One Bay Back to a Twenty BerkShare. Moreover, printing local currencies turns out to be legal, much as when airlines issue bonus miles that function as a form of currency that frequent fliers can use to purchase upgrades or free trips. According to the BerkShare website, approximately $2 million of Berk-Shares are currently circulating in the Berkshires, a mountainous rural area of western Massachusetts, and a group of local banks exchange BerkShares, with 350 businesses signed up to accept the currency.[5] Berk-Share's future plans include BerkShare checking accounts, electronic funds transfer, ATM machines, and even a loan program to stimulate the creation of local businesses, including hopefully a revival of manufacturing in the region. BerkShares are typically kept in circulation, to act as a multiplier in promoting local businesses, instead of being cashed in at local banks, where BerkShares are discounted on deposit 10 percent from their stated face value.

Forbes magazine, in an article titled "Funny Money," reported, not surprisingly, that Wal-Mart does not accept Bay Bucks, a local currency created for use in Traverse City, Michigan.[6] In 2002, the Traverse Area Community Currency Corporation began Bay Bucks humbly by issuing $99,000 worth of the local currency, and has since expanded to include fifty-six local businesses.[7]

The move by local communities to direct business away from mass merchandisers such as Wal-Mart to local merchants reflects a reversal of trend, with consumers now motivated less by the lowest possible prices that unfettered free trade offers and more by a desire to develop profitable local businesses, even if the prices paid are somewhat higher. Although Wal-Mart remains the largest mass merchandiser in the United States, a backlash has developed among those consumers who see it as exploiting labor both in the United States and around the world, all in the name of the lowest possible prices.[8] Supporting local communities despite paying somewhat more to purchase goods suggests a growing awareness among Americans of the need to support U.S. businesses and U.S.-made goods in order to preserve the U.S. middle class.

Ithaca, New York, issues Ithaca HOURS. Some $100,000 of it has been issued, facilitating millions of dollars of transactions in some nine hundred local merchants that have agreed to participate.[9] Ithaca HOURS allows participating merchants to decide what percent of a purchase they will accept in Ithaca HOURS, anywhere from 100 percent of the purchase to a much smaller fraction of the purchase price. Participating Ithaca HOURS merchants pay a ten-dollar annual fee to become members. Membership benefits include publishing the merchant's business listing in the Ithaca HOURS directory, of which 10,000 copies are distributed countywide, among a county population of approximately 50,000.

The E. F. Schumacher Society, founded in 1980 to promote the building of strong local economies, publishes on the Internet a directory of local currencies that are printed in the United States, Canada, Mexico, and Europe.[10]

3. Plan for Second and Third Careers

Workers are well advised to assume in advance that their current employment is only temporary. Job dislocations are inevitable in a global free-trade environment, simply because corporations, whether they are organized as multinational corporations or not, will have a tendency to think as if they were multinational. In other words, whenever the impulse to cut costs comes around, management, even of small companies, will begin thinking about what functions can be outsourced—whether that involves legal services, accounting, or customer support. Outsourcing companies that utilize foreign labor will certainly compete for the business. When looking to cut labor costs, many U.S. corporations that are not multinational in structure will still consider using immigrant labor if it is legally possible to do so. These trends will continue as long as free-trade advocates and presidential administrations, whether Republican or Democratic, continue to press to provide a "pathway to citizenship" for the millions of illegal immigrants already in the country.

Losing a job does not have to be the end of a career, especially if workers foresee the need to plan new careers. For many, self-employment is an option. Workers should consider in advance if their skills, training, and experience will qualify them to become consultants doing exactly what they do now as employees. For millions of Americans, the Internet has already created opportunities for self-employment. What may have started as a hobby selling items on an Internet auction site could transition into a career. One strategy to consider is to shift from full-time employment to temporary employment, just to explore a range of occupations a person may never before have considered. For millions of Americans, temporary jobs have developed into more permanent jobs.

Another strategy may be to reduce pay or hours, simply to assist employers in getting through tough economic times. Employers may even be open to creating a class of stock so employees willing to make sacrifices end up with some equity should the company manage to survive the hard times.

The key is that preparing to have multiple careers requires a person to think differently. Anyone who concludes their life is at an end because they have lost a job will not adapt easily to the global free-trade economy the United States has decided to enter. Rather than regret the loss of a job, a person must see the next chapter of their life opening before them. With retirement savings at risk in this down economy, those approaching sixty-five years old can no longer think of themselves as retired. Granted, opportunities for physical labor reduce with age. But opportunities in the service economy, including working in restaurants or in security services, may remain open. So too, those in their retirement years may consider using their prior experience to start up new ventures that draw upon the years they have spent learning a particular business. Those able to imagine a new mountain to climb will continue to have a reason to keep working, even into their advanced years. For those in retirement years who want to continue being productive, working at home to maintain an extended family may free others to be wage earners; services provided to the family may include child care, shopping, cooking, or cleaning and maintenance of the home.

4. Avoid Investing in Stocks and Bonds

Millions of middle-class Americans had their first experience investing when they purchased mutual funds or enrolled in retirement plans, such as 401(k) plans, which in turn invested in mutual funds.

What middle-class investors have learned is that investments, in either stocks or bonds, will typically suffer losses in down markets. Investors receive no guarantees that their investments will only increase in value. Strategies of diversifying investments, in which a person, for instance, buys into several mutual funds, can help cushion losses. Thus, for example, in certain economic situations, bond investments may be up in value when stock investments are down in value. So too, mutual funds with international-investment strategies may cushion mutual-fund losses in U.S. bond or equity strategies. Still, in the final analysis, there is no investment strategy that can guarantee there will never be losses. Investment is inherently risky, which is why investors expect to be able to get returns above guaranteed bank certificates of deposit or savings-account interest rates when they invest their money.

Moreover, sophisticated investment strategies require expertise and time. Most successful investors in individual stocks and bonds either have advanced experience in their area of investment or have the training to analyze financial fundamentals to sort out winners from losers. The typical middle-class investor lacks the experience, training, or time to be a professional investor. More sophisticated investment strategies such as currency or commodity investing require specialized understanding of markets in which futures and options contracts can swing prices. Unsophisticated investors are best advised to ignore financial-services marketing pitches that promise to teach easy-to-learn strategies to make quick money. Reading financial charts is a technical exercise that few can master without study and effort. Stockbrokers promising quick returns should be scrutinized to identify the commissions they make on investments they recommend, even when the recommended investment loses money. Professional advice is essential for most inexperienced investors; even then, track records and references of professional financial advisors must be examined carefully before deciding to invest.

Middle-class investors are advised to place in stock and bond investments, including mutual funds, only money they can afford to lose. Those investing in more risky stock or bond investments to get higher yield are taking even more risk than safer strategies promising lower returns. Even when mutual funds promise to diversify risk by including foreign investments along with U.S. investments, or blending investment in emerging companies or markets with a mix of investment in highly capitalized companies or developed markets, risk factors may not be fully appreciated until it is too late.

Life-insurance investments, including annuities, have tended to be safer, largely because life-insurance companies are still regulated by state governments that tend to be more conservative than federal government regulators. The insolvency of insurance company giant AIG came from billions of dollars in losses experienced by their derivatives unit, not from the company's life-insurance or annuities businesses. So far, no bankruptcy of a life-insurance company in the history of the industry has caused life-insurance or annuity policyholders to lose benefits.

Life-insurance companies have tended to avoid the type of investments in asset-backed securities that got banks and investment firms in trouble. Life-insurance-company investments generally are weighted heavily in municipal and corporate bonds. Still, life-insurance-company asset portfolios have lost value, as nearly all investments have lost value in a market down as deeply as the recession that began in December 2008. Today, municipalities are defaulting on bonds, just as corporations are. China is even concerned that U.S. Treasury securities may not hold their value if the dollar depreciates as the Obama administration incurs multitrillion-dollar federal budget deficits. Life-insurance payouts are also dollar denominated and will lose purchasing power as the dollar loses purchasing power. Still, fixed annuities and life insurance remain relatively safe investments.

Remember, variable-life-insurance contracts are investment contracts. The owner of a variable-life-insurance or annuity contract bears the investment risk, not the insurance company; the cash value or payout of a variable life-insurance contract or annuity can decrease if the underlying investment portfolio decreases in value. Only sophisticated investors should purchase variable-life-insurance or annuity contracts, as the same rules that apply for mutual funds also apply for variable insurance contracts backed by investment portfolios that operate much as mutual funds operate. Fundamentally, variable-life-insurance and annuity contracts amount to not much more than placing a life-insurance contract over a mutual fund, with the result that the investment earnings, if any, in the variable-contract investment portfolio are income-tax deferred until withdrawn from the contract.

5. Invest in Primary Residential Real Estate

For most Americans, the most important investment they will make in a lifetime is their primary residence. Here the recommended strategy is straightforward: homebuyers should seek to purchase a home that is within their ability to make a minimum 10 percent down payment at the time of purchase. If homebuyers can afford down payments larger than 10 percent, the investment is typically made even safer. If at all possible, homebuyers should shop to find fifteen-year or thirty-year fixed-rate mortgages, so as to avoid complex mortgage structures that may have unanticipated costs after the first year.

Homeowners and homebuyers should make sure that their mortgage is one the family can afford even if a principal wage earner loses a job for some significant period of time. To prepare for this eventuality, homeowners are advised to keep in liquid savings up to six months of future mortgage payments, just to have a cushion available for unanticipated hard times. If a family is living in a home with a mortgage that is more than 25 percent of their monthly income, the family is pushing the limit. A family living in a home where the mortgage is 33 percent or more of their monthly income should consider selling the home and moving into a smaller home with a less burdensome mortgage. Financial planners should be consulted to make sure a family has considered monthly expenses and monthly income ratios, so adjustments can be made to reduce expenses where needed.

Particularly troubling are homes purchased at the height of the mortgage bubble. Homeowners must assess whether their current outstanding mortgage exceeds the current resale value of their home. In such situations, where the outstanding mortgage is "underwater," homeowners may not have the option to sell the home without taking a substantial equity loss. In such situations, homeowners should get professional advice to see if one or more of the existing mortgage-refinancing options made available with government mortgage-modification assistance might help reduce the liability. In cases where the homeowner is at risk of default, reducing the current monthly mortgage payment may be possible and reducing the outstanding mortgage should be explored.

Even the most distressed homeowners, including those who have lost jobs, should not abandon the house, despairing that there are no other options. Foreclosure notices can and should be challenged legally. In many instances, especially in this age where mortgages have been sold into mortgage securities, those seeking to foreclose the home may not have legal title to do so. Homeowners facing foreclosure should network with others in similar circumstances to see if legal assistance at a reasonable price can be found to fight the battles in court.

Those purchasing homes should make sure the house is priced at 25 to 50 percent of the home's peak market value in 2006. Before falling in love with a house, prospective homebuyers must make sure the economics of the deal make sense in a market that most likely will continue to decline for the foreseeable future. More experienced buyers can look to foreclosure auctions to see if distressed properties can be acquired at deep discount. In certain instances, banks or other mortgage lenders may be willing to work with prospective buyers to intervene before properties are foreclosed. Experienced real estate agents may also be able to advise prospective buyers regarding how best to negotiate to pick up distressed properties at well below even current market values. Many homeowners facing foreclosure will accept sizable losses of equity simply to prevent foreclosure.

If a home has depreciated in value but is not underwater, property owners might consider selling the home and taking a loss, as long as the mortgage can be paid off at the closing on the house sale. Homeowners in expensive markets might be well advised to consider selling the house and moving to a smaller community or a region of the country where home values are less inflated. The main calculation is to own a home where the family can afford to pay the mortgage and the resale value exceeds the outstanding mortgage amount.

The advantage of investing in primary residential real estate is obvious: you can live in the investment, and everybody needs a place to live. Investing in rental properties is much more difficult. Purchases of investment rental properties are more difficult to finance, simply because mortgage lenders tend to be much more demanding on the down payments required. Managing rental properties also requires expertise to find qualified renters who will maintain the properties. Moreover, all real estate requires maintenance and renters do not have the same incentive owners have to maintain or improve the property. Also, laws protecting renters can make evicting renters difficult, even when they lose the ability to continue paying the rent. Successfully buying and maintaining rental properties at a profit can easily become a full-time business, especially if more than one rental property is purchased.

6. Reduce Debt

In all cases, reducing debt is essential, even if it means cutting up and throwing away credit cards. Excessive credit-card balances can trap a person with hidden costs; interest-rate escalations can easily skyrocket into double-digit numbers. Many credit-card holders with large balances end up in situations where the credit-card balance becomes hard to reduce, especially if the person is able to keep up only with the minimum monthly payments. For those trapped in credit-card debt, a strategy may be to seek professional advice to see if credit-card balances may be negotiated down by talking with credit-card issuers. The ability to make a large payment on outstanding credit-card balances typically makes negotiating down credit-card balances more likely to be successful.

Reducing debt even applies to mortgages. A key strategy for financial success in difficult economic times is to reduce or pay off completely the mortgage on your primary residence. For most Americans, mortgage payments are the largest single monthly payment required in their budget. Once mortgages are completely paid off, the family can be reasonably assured they will have a place to live, regardless of how difficult the economics of employment may become. As long as property taxes can be paid, a family can keep their home once the mortgage is paid off. Once the house is paid off, fluctuations in market value have less impact on the family's finances. Any appreciation in the value of the home adds to the family's net worth, without incurring any capital-gains taxes until the home is sold. Even if the home loses value in a depreciating real estate market, once there is no mortgage to be paid the loss of value is a paper loss of value, as long as the house does not need to be sold.

Being debt free provides additional latitude should a person lose a job or have to relocate for other reasons. Debt obligations do not go away in hard economic times, and those who fall behind in monthly payments, especially on credit cards, may find themselves hounded unmercifully by debt collectors.

7. Buy Gold

For those with sufficient savings to make investments, gold remains a good buy, even as gold prices have topped $1,000 an ounce. As recently as 2000, gold was trading in the range of $285 an ounce. Gold has always been accepted as money. In this age of fiat currencies, gold hedges against a loss in value of dollar investments because the purchasing power of the dollar has declined.

Gold investors are advised against buying gold stocks, since these investments have additional risks the investor may not fully understand. Gold stocks will trade up or down based on the fundamental value of the gold company issuing the stock, not simply as a function of how gold itself is traded on world commodity markets. Owning gold coins or bullion is a way of making sure you are actually investing in gold itself. Numismatic-quality gold coins are an option for investors wanting to own gold in a form where the rareness of the coins has a chance to enhance the value of the investment.[11] All gold investing should be done with reputable firms that have years of experience in the business and readily available references that can be independently verified.

Investing in silver is also an option. The problem with silver is that it is a more available commodity than gold. As a result, professional manipulations of the silver market have led to price fluctuations unrelated to the intrinsic value of the commodity. Gold is scarcer and more likely to continue appreciating in a world where fiat currencies such as the dollar are certain to remain under stress.

STRATEGIES FOR MIDDLE-CLASS SURVIVAL IN ECONOMIC HARD TIMES

Despite the promises of free-trade globalism, the reality of international trade as currently practiced has resulted in a gradual reduction in employment possibilities that has decreased real earnings for most middle-class American families.

Those forced to take a $10-an-hour job in the service economy may find themselves sweeping floors or flipping hamburgers, instead of earning $35 an hour in a manufacturing company where the jobs have been outsourced to foreign labor. Nor are white-collar workers safe, not when technical services ranging from legal research to accounting services to customer-call centers can be operated from India at a fraction of the cost. Since the enthusiasm of President George H. W. Bush to push the United States into the North American Free Trade Agreement with Mexico and Canada, every subsequent president, including President Obama, has gotten aboard the free-trade bandwagon to preach the benefits of globalism.

Today, most universities teach that the world has entered a post-American world in which the United States no longer dominates, either economically or in military power. For the middle-class American, the reality is that families able to advance on the salary of one wage earner in the 1950s and 1960s are today hard-pressed to survive even when both parents enter the workforce.

Now, in the midst of the global Economic Panic of 2009, the magnitude of the problem has produced a different phenomenon. No longer is the middle class simply squeezed to educate children and prepare for retirement; today the middle class is largely one or two paychecks away from bankruptcy.

With unemployment approaching 10 percent in the United States, millions of middle-class families face real fears of losing their jobs and their homes, at a time when their investments, including their retirement plans, have largely evaporated. The strategies for survival recommended here contemplate a fundamental change of lifestyle that will be needed for middle-class families to survive the economic hard times that inevitably will come as long as our leaders persist with global free-trade thinking. Until we insist that free-trade agreements protect labor as part of the capital equation, workers worldwide will be offered less-than-living wages and few if any benefits to maintain jobs that someone else would still do cheaper.

A return to fundamental family planning is necessary if middle-class families are to survive economic hard times.

TEN

The Rise of Twenty-First-Century American Patriots

When, in the course of human events, it becomes necessary for one people to dissolve the political bands which have connected them with another, and to assume among the powers of the earth, the separate and equal station to which the laws of nature and of nature's God entitle them, a decent respect to the opinions of mankind requires that they should declare the causes which impel them to the separation.

—Declaration of Independence, July 4, 1776

A movement of American patriots has begun developing in the United States in reaction to globalism, open borders, and free trade. One example has been the rise of the Minutemen groups that have sought to go to the border with Mexico on their own initiative in an attempt to stem the tide of illegal immigration into the United States.[1]

In response to the global Economic Panic of 2009, American patriots organized Tea Parties throughout the United States to protest what appeared to be out-of-control government spending and budget deficits running into the trillions of dollars. Much like the pre–Revolutionary War patriots who held the original Boston Tea Party, today's twenty-first-century American patriots are again protesting a form of perceived "taxation without representation." While spending bills are currently passed by elected representatives in Congress, millions of Americans to-day do not feel Washington is listening to an increasingly vocal message: middle-class Americans do not want to continue paying trillions of dollars for bailouts of Wall Street firms or for an unprecedented expansion of the social-welfare state designed to provide government-paid benefits even to illegal immigrants.

A growing movement of American patriots in the United States will mount an increasing challenge to the coalition that brought Barack Obama to the White House on promises of "hope" and "change." If the Obama administration fails to stimulate the economy to recovery, patriot-led protest movements are certain to gain momentum.

Nor are the patriots organizing Tea Party protests necessarily aligned with the Republican Party. Conservatives have come to realize, and did so especially during the second term of President George W. Bush, that Republicans are not always conservatives. President Bush ran budget deficits that were unacceptable to conservatives, increased social-welfare spending by passing a prescription-drug plan, and expanded the power and authority of the executive office of the president beyond the limits most conservatives consider appropriate.

Now, thanks to President Bush, expanded emergency powers reside in the office of the presidency, ready for President Obama to exercise.

The United States has not seen an outbreak of political protests or violence since the race riots and Vietnam War protests of the 1960s and 1970s. Hopefully, the coming wave of economic protests will remain peaceful and constructive. Still, when economic protests loom as possibilities, the United States must be sure to avoid unduly militarizing a government response to what may all too easily be declared national-emergency situations. A robust First Amendment demands that the Obama administration temper its ideological fervor with a willingness to tolerate aggressive criticism, even if that criticism extends to peaceful protests and demonstrations in the streets.

PRESIDENTIAL POWER GRABS

On May 9, 2007, without even a press statement, President Bush signed an executive order that granted near-dictatorial powers to the office of the president in the event of a national emergency declared by the president. The executive order was titled "National Security and Homeland Security Presidential Directive," with the dual designation of NSPD-51, as a National Security Presidential Directive, and HSPD-20, as a Homeland Security Presidential Directive.[2]

In a one-paragraph purpose statement, the executive order established under the president a new national continuity coordinator, whose job is to make plans so that "National Essential Functions" of all federal, state, local, territorial, and tribal governments as well as private-sector organizations continue in the event of a national emergency. The executive order loosely defined "catastrophic emergency" as "any incident, regardless of location, that results in extraordinary levels of mass casualties, damage, or disruption severely affecting the U.S. population, infrastructure, environment, economy, or government functions." When the president determines a catastrophic emergency has occurred, he can take over all government functions and direct all private-sector activities to ensure we will emerge from the emergency with an "enduring Constitutional government."

Translated into layman's terms, when the president determines that a national emergency has occurred, the president can declare for the office of the presidency powers usually assumed by dictators to direct any and all government and business activities until the emergency is declared over. Ironically, the executive order sees no contradiction in the assumption of dictatorial powers by the president with the goal of maintaining constitutional continuity through an emergency.

The executive order specifies that the assistant to the president for homeland security and counterterrorism will be designated as the national continuity coordinator. Also established was a Continuity Policy Coordination Committee, chaired by a senior director from the Homeland Security Council staff and designated by the national continuity coordinator to be "the main day-to-day forum for such policy coordination."

The executive order made no attempt to reconcile the powers created there for the national continuity coordinator with the National Emergency Act, which allows that the president may declare a national emergency, but requires that such proclamation "shall immediately be transmitted to the Congress and published in the Federal Register."[3] A Congressional Research Service study in 2007 on emergency powers noted that under the National Emergency Act, the president "may seize property, organize and control the means of production, seize commodities, assign military forces abroad, institute martial law, seize and control all transportation and communication, regulate the operation of private enterprise, restrict travel, and, in a variety of ways, control the lives of United States citizens."[4] The CRS study noted that the National Emergency Act sets up Congress as a counterweight empowered to "modify, rescind, or render dormant such delegated emergency authority" if Congress believes the president has acted inappropriately.

The executive order appears to supersede the National Emergency Act by creating the new position of national continuity coordinator without any specific act of Congress authorizing the position. It also makes no reference whatsoever to the U.S. Congress. The language of the presidential executive order appears to negate any requirement that the president submit to Congress a determination that a national emergency exists.

Under these directives, the president could declare a national health emergency under his own authority and direct USNORTHCOM through the Department of Defense to work with the United Nations to implement the North American Plan for Avian & Pandemic Influenza signed under the SPP.

Those Republican Party voters who did not object to President George W. Bush holding these powers might have second thoughts now that President Barack Obama is in the White House. Our Founding Fathers warned not to judge executive grabs of power by the personality or the political party of the current occupant of the White House. Instead, the American people are best advised to be suspicious of any and all power grabs that assert the authority of the president to be supreme over the constitutionally specified coequal legislative branches of government, namely, Congress and the Supreme Court.

THE STATE-SOVEREIGNTY MOVEMENT

As the Obama administration in its first months in office pushed through Congress a $787 billion economic stimulus plan and a budget initially proposed at $3.6 trillion, a patriot rebellion developed at the state level, opposing the growing dominance of the federal government and the massive expansion of social-welfare programs proposed in Obama administration spending plans.

Resolutions were introduced in nearly half of the state legislatures across the country, declaring state sovereignty under the Ninth and Tenth Amendments to the Constitution. Both amendments were aimed at defining the federal government as one with limited powers:

- The Ninth Amendment reads "The enumeration in the Constitution, of certain rights, shall not be construed to deny or disparage others retained by the people."

- The Tenth Amendment specifically provides that "The powers not delegated to the United States by the Constitution, nor prohibited by it to the States, are reserved to the States respectively, or to the people."

Particularly disturbing to many state legislatures are the increasing number of "unfunded mandates" that have proliferated in social-welfare programs such as Medicare and Medicaid, in which bills passed by Congress have dictated policy to the states and mandated program implementation without providing funding.

"What we are trying to do is to get the U.S. Congress out of the state's business," Oklahoma Republican state senator Randy Brogdon told World Net Daily in a telephone interview.[5] Brogdon sponsored a state-sovereignty resolution in the Oklahoma legislature.

"Congress is completely out of line spending trillions of dollars over the last ten years putting the nation into a debt crisis like we've never seen before," he said. "This particular 111th Congress is the biggest bunch of over-reachers and underachievers we've ever had in Congress. A sixth-grader should realize you can't borrow money to pay off your debt, and that is the Obama administration's answer for a stimulus package."

"We are trying to send a message to the federal government that the states are trying to reclaim their sovereignty," Republican state representative Matt Shea, the lead sponsor of Washington state's sovereignty resolution, told World Net Daily. "State sovereignty has been eroded in so many areas it's hard to know where to start," he said. "There are a ton of federal mandates imposed on states, for instance, on education spending and welfare spending."

"The Obama administration economic stimulus package moving through Congress is a perfect example," Shea continued. "In the state of Washington, we have increased state spending thirty-three percent in the last three years and hired six thousand new state employees, often using federal mandates as an excuse to grow state government.

"We need to return government back down to the people, to keep government as close to the local people as possible," he said.

Shea is a private attorney also allied with the Alliance Defense Fund, a nationwide network of about one thousand attorneys who work pro bono, often to counter efforts of the American Civil Liberties Union and to protect and defend religious liberty, the sanctity of life, and traditional family values.

"The federal government has been trouncing on our constitutional rights," Republican state representative Judy Burges, the primary sponsor of the sovereignty resolution in the Arizona house, told World Net Daily. "The real turning point for me was the Real ID Act, which involved both a violation of the Fourth Amendment's rights against illegal searches and seizures and the Tenth Amendment."

Burges said she is concerned that the overreaching of federal powers could lead to new legislation aimed at confiscating weapons from citizens or encoding ammunition. "The Real ID Act was so broadly written that we are afraid that it involves the potential for 'mission creep,' that could easily involve confiscation of firearms and violations of the Second Amendment," she said.

Burges said she has been surprised at the number of emails she has received in support of the sovereignty measure. "We are a sovereign state in Arizona, not a branch of the federal government, and we need to be treated as such," she insisted.

If the state-sovereignty movement continues to gain momentum, one or more of the states passing such resolutions will demand that the state attorney general or governor inform the federal government that the state does not wish to accept federal funding in a particular program or public policy area. An early sign of this resistance involved the governors who rejected funding in various program areas under the $787 billion economic stimulus package.

A constitutional crisis could easily develop should one or more states take an extreme measure and tell the federal government the state wants no more federal funding in major program areas, such as unemployment insurance or welfare. A state could possibly assert that control of the public schools is a state responsibility under the Constitution, as is the operation of public hospitals. There might even be a competitive advantage for a state that seeks to reject federal control and limit state spending in various social-welfare areas. Conservative voters and American patriots, regardless of their political orientation, might be drawn to live and work in states that reject the expansion of government into a "Nanny State" dedicated to providing government-paid social-welfare programs from crib to grave. A constitutional crisis will develop if the federal government seeks to force the states to stand down and accept federal dictates and funding, whether the state government votes to do so or not.

A state seeking to eliminate income taxes for both individuals and corporations, as well as aiming to have the lowest state property and sales taxes, might end up being a magnet for individuals and businesses looking for a state that provides reduced social-welfare benefits and reduced control over institutions such as the public schools.

The state-sovereignty movement is not just a tax rebellion; it is also a reaction to the insertion of government control into private lives and private enterprise. A state pursuing the state-sovereignty strategy may simply invite citizens who want government-paid welfare benefits to move to other states. At the extreme, the state-sovereignty movement could engage state law enforcement agencies in efforts to help enforce federal immigration laws, with a determination to invite illegal immigrants to join welfare recipients in relocating to states more in agreement with federal government policies.

STATE BUDGET DEFICITS

The *Wall Street Journal* described state tax receipts as being in "free fall" during the fourth quarter of 2008.[6] Approximately half the states, including some of the largest—California, Texas, New York, and Florida—have experienced a budgetary crisis in the recession as revenues have declined from income taxes, sales taxes, and property taxes.

The California budget deficit for 2008–2009 was projected to be approximately $11 billion. The deficit for 2009–2010 could range anywhere from $17 billion to around $40 billion, depending on how severe the economic downturn continues to be.[7] Illegal immigration adds to California's budget crisis. The nonpartisan Public Policy Institute of California estimated there were 2.8 million illegal immigrants living in California in 2006, representing about 8 percent of the state's population and roughly a quarter of the nation's illegal immigrants.[8] While illegal immigrants do pay state taxes, experts estimate shortfalls in the billions of dollars occur when expenses for illegal immigrants are counted among state prisons, public schools, and welfare. According to Reuters, a study conducted by the Federation for American Immigration Reform estimated that the current fiscal outlays for the illegal-alien population in California approached $13 billion annually, amounting to a significant proportion of the state's budgetary shortfall.[9] New York City lost more than 75,000 jobs from August 2008 to March 2009. The Census Bureau reported that over the last decade 1.97 million New Yorkers left the state.

The $787 billion stimulus package passed by the Obama administration was not enough to stem the tide in state-budget shortfalls. Even after receiving assistance from the federal stimulus package, New York's $132 billion 2009 budget was $17.7 billion in deficit. The state's decision to hike income taxes to the highest in the nation has fueled an exodus. The American Legislative Exchange Council declared that New York has the worst economic outlook of all fifty states, including Michigan, a state facing huge job losses because of the bankruptcy problems of the Big Three automakers.[10] During severe economic downturns, raising taxes is an especially unreliable strategy for states determined to maintain social-welfare programs at current levels.

At some point, various state governments will realize that raising taxes is counterproductive. Higher taxes merely give those able to pay taxes, including corporations and wealthy individuals, an incentive to relocate. States with low taxes and minimal social-welfare benefits will be positioned to take the lead in a growing state-sovereignty movement.

THE TEA PARTY MOVEMENT

On February 19, 2009, when CNBC reporter Rick Santelli ranted on live television that he was organizing a Chicago Tea Party to protest Obama administration mortgage modification proposals, he inadvertently launched a national grassroots movement. "We're thinking about having a Chicago Tea Party in July," Santelli proclaimed. "All you capitalists that want to show up at Lake Michigan, I'm going to start organizing."[11] Traders seen in the background on the Chicago Mercantile Exchange greeted Santelli's proclamation with whistles and applause.

This is not 1773, and the modern Tea Party participants are not dressing up like American Indians and dumping British tea into Boston Harbor to protest the Tea Act enacted by the British Parliament. Still, the sentiment is the same—opposition to increased taxes, in this case resulting from continued bailouts and federal budget deficits. Moreover, the organizers of the modern-day Tea Parties are not revolutionaries, although they are clearly angry and frustrated that Congress and the White House are not hearing their concerns. The tax protest has not been endorsed or supported by the Republican Party. The participants appear to be middle-class Americans who were not necessarily supporters of Senator John McCain's 2008 presidential campaign. The video of Santelli's rant went viral on the Internet and was viewed on YouTube more than one million times within a few days of being posted.

On tax day, April 15, 2009, well over one hundred Tea Parties were organized across the United States, marking the development of a movement that the mainstream media could no longer ignore. Local protests drew thousands of people who came out peacefully to carry placards proclaiming their discontent and to listen to speeches given by local politicians, radio-talk-show hosts, and various celebrities who supported the public expression of their grievances.

ACORN ORGANIZES ACTIVIST PROTESTS AGAINST AIG BONUSES

In March 2009, the Association of Community Organizations for Reform Now, or ACORN, paid for the buses needed to transport protesters to the homes of AIG executives who had received millions of dollars in bonuses after AIG received billions in federal bailout funds. The *Connecticut Post* reported that activists, including members of the Working Families Party, rode on the ACORN buses to Fairfield County mansions of what the Leftist protesters termed the "filthy rich and most recently infamous." According to the *Post*, a slow moving caravan of news media from as far away as the Netherlands outnumbered the demonstrators by 3 to 1. The first stop in Fairfield was near the Greenfield Hills estate of an AIG executive who had received a $6.4 million bonus. The demonstrators also "played to the boom mics, clicking camera shutters and whirling videotapes with a noisy but well-mannered demonstration outside AIG's Financial Products headquarters at 50 Danbury Road in Wilton." [12]

ACORN activists subsequently announced plans to protest Tea Parties whenever they occurred across the country.

The radical political Left has been emboldened by President Obama's election to declare, "We won!" With this announcement, they assert that a majority of the country supports their agenda to redistribute income on a scale never before seen in the United States. This determination puts the radical political Left at odds with what Richard Nixon termed the "silent majority" of center-right voters, who today oppose

Obama administration policies because of concerns about excessive taxation and the expansion of government in general.

Should activists on the political Left decide to confront Tea Party street protests or to disrupt official government proceedings with more than silent unfurling of banners, the potential for political violence escalates.

MILLIONS OF ECONOMIC PROTESTERS MARCH IN EUROPE

In what may be a prelude to demonstrations that could occur on a massive scale in the United States, in March 2009 France's trade unions staged a national strike protesting the economic downturn. Strikers caused a one-day stoppage in rail, air, and local transport throughout the country.[13] The *Economist* reported that more than a million people took to the streets throughout France on Thursday, as a national poll showed 74 percent of the French supported the protest.[14] This followed a one-day national strike in January 2009 that sent hundreds of thousands of French workers to the streets, protesting job cuts and demanding higher welfare payments to cushion the impact of the economic crisis.[15] The January protests pressured French president Nicolas Sarkozy to produce an extra €2.6 billion ($3.38 billion) in welfare payments and tax cuts for low-income families.

The mass strikes in France are a particularly French way of protesting the increasing economic distress being felt in the EU from the global economic downturn. In France's socialist political system, leftist workers expect corporations to continue employing workers and providing benefits, often even if the company is not making a profit. The French socialist government, for instance, made a €3 billion ($3.9 billion) low-interest bailout loan to automaker Renault on the condition that it pledge not to close any French factories for the duration of the loan nor resort to any mass layoffs in France for a year, according to the *Wall Street Journal*.[16] The Renault plants in question were not profitable operations. Still, in the French socialist formula, corporations are evil if plants are closed or workers are laid off or fired; in their economy the French assume they have a "right" to a job for life at a pay the French unions determine is acceptable.

In France, angry employees feel justified to hold corporate executives hostage, in events known as "boss-napping," until workplace demands are met. In March 2009, Serge Foucher, chief executive of Sony France, was held hostage overnight in his office by workers protesting the imminent closing of a videotape plant in the southwest of France. Dozens of staff took Foucher hostage and barricaded the entry to the plant with tree trunks. A representative of the communist-leaning CGT union told the press that Foucher had spent the night shut in a meeting room because "he won't listen to us, we didn't find any other solution." [17]

Antiglobalism protestors turned violent in London during the G20 meeting on April 2, 2009. Demonstrators clashed with police in riot gear and smashed windows at a branch of the Royal Bank of Scotland in London's financial district. Mounted police and police in riot gear surrounded the bank building as protesters hurled paint bombs and bottles, chanting, "These streets, our streets! These banks, our banks!" [18]

THE FAILURE OF MORTGAGE-MODIFICATION PROGRAMS

Despite the enthusiasm of the Obama administration that mortgage-modification programs would prevent foreclosures, the experience has been disappointing. A group of state attorneys and state banking agencies operating as the State Foreclosure Prevention Working Group have filed a series of analytic reports on the website of the Conference of State Bank Supervisors. [19] The group's September 2008 report estimated that 20 percent of loan modifications made in the past year were currently delinquent. The report expressed concern that unrealistic or "Band-Aid" modifications have only exacerbated and prolonged the crisis. Many of the modifications ended up not reducing monthly payments enough for the homes to be truly affordable. On February 2, 2009, a letter from the group addressed to U.S. Comptroller of the Currency John Dugan and Director of the Office of Thrift Supervision John Reich stated, "there is a growing body of research that suggests the majority of loan modifications in the past year have not led to meaningful payment relief to homeowners."

Concerned that mortgage modifications were merely "kicking the can down the road," the group argued that principal balances and monthly mortgage payments needed to be aggressively adjusted downward if mortgage modifications were to have any chance of long-term success. The problem here is that aggressive downward adjustments of the type suggested mean mortgage lenders will have to take real losses.

Ultimately, these losses will need to be reflected in mortgage-backed securities, in which the original defaulted loans were included, a process that will inevitably deepen the losses on bank balance sheets.

In the final analysis, the issue returns to jobs. Regardless of how much the mortgage balance or monthly payments are reduced, unemployed homeowners will ultimately face default and foreclosure.

TENT CITIES

In 1932, Washington, D.C., was under siege as more than forty thousand World War I veterans came to the capital to demand the immediate payment bonuses that had been granted in 1924. Medal of Honor recipient U.S. Marine Corps Major General Smedley Butler addressed what became known as the "Bonus Army," calling their protest "the greatest demonstration of Americanism we've ever had, pure Americanism." The marchers camped out in tent cities and were ultimately dispersed by army troops commanded by General Douglas MacArthur. The army's sweep through the Bonus Army's tent cities turned violent, with tear gas being used to disperse the veterans and tent city structures being put to flame.

Tent cities for the homeless, another Depression-era phenomenon, are springing up in dozens of U.S. cities. As in the "Hoovervilles" of the 1930s, many residents of tent cities today were all-too-recently middle-class Americans who owned their own homes.

- In Las Vegas, the city council is considering a proposal to designate a piece of vacant land for the homeless, as an alternative to an impromptu tent city that has persisted on Foremaster Lane despite repeated attempts by city officials to sweep the area clean.[20]

- In Sacramento, California, Mayor Kevin Johnson unveiled plans to make alternative shelter space available for the estimated 150 homeless men and women living in a tent encampment near the American River, at the edge of the city's downtown.[21]

- In Madison, Wisconsin, homeless have begun spending their days in the state capitol for warmth.[22]

Census Bureau statistics show that 1 in 9 homes were vacant in the United States in the first quarter of 2009, totaling more than 14 million housing units.[23] The *New York Times* reported that advocacy groups were placing homeless in vacant residences, exerting squatter rights.[24]

At the height of the Great Depression, in November 1934, unemployment had reached 23.2 percent. In 2009, unemployment hit 9.5 percent in June, with the possibility of hitting 10 percent before the end of the year. Today, the unemployment numbers are intensified once the following groups are added to the total: 1) the chronic unemployed who have given up looking for work altogether; 2) the underemployed who have accepted reduced hours or wages to remain employed; and 3) the working poor who have accepted employment at compensation levels that fall below poverty levels or barely meet the economic requirements needed to sustain a family's standard of living. If unemployment numbers begin exceeding 10 percent, economic protests are more likely to occur.

While economic protests have remained peaceful so far, history demonstrates that should the recession deepen into a depression, economic anger among the U.S. population can be expected to rise. In recent years, the presidency has gained new emergency powers and the U.S. military has been reconfigured to intervene in domestic emergency situations—two developments that give pause to advocates of the First Amendment. Free-speech rights are especially important to protect when protests are aimed at policies advocated by the president and enacted by Congress.

A FIVE-POINT PLAN FOR TWENTY-FIRST-CENTURY AMERICAN PATRIOTS

The famous Newt Gingrich–inspired Contract with America began at a conference of House Republicans in Salisbury, Maryland, in February 1994.[25] Meeting two years into the first term of President Bill Clinton, the House Republicans talked about governing the country with the will of the people in the House of Representatives. From their discussions, the House Republicans articulated a clear vision of what they stood for and they agreed upon five principles to describe their basic philosophy of American civilization:

- Individual liberty

- Economic opportunity

- Limited government

- Personal responsibility

- Security at home and abroad

Based on these principles, the House Republicans writing the 1994 Contract with America articulated a vision "to renew the American Dream by promoting individual liberty, economic opportunity, and personal responsibility, through limited and effective government, high standards of performance and an America strong enough to defend all her citizens against violence at home or abroad." [26] These five principles bear a close relationship to the arguments advanced by the supporters of the state sovereignty movement and by the promoters of Tea Parties today across the nation.

American patriots need to proclaim a new Contract with America for the coming 2010s. Much of the language of the 1994 document could almost be taken verbatim into a new version of the Contract with America.

Most twenty-first-century patriots concerned with preserving, protecting, and defending the Constitution of the United States and the limited government defined by that document would agree with the following five-point action plan:

1. Secure the Borders and Enforce Immigration Laws

No nation can claim national sovereignty if the nation's borders are open to an invasion of illegal immigrants from another nation. In 2006, Republican congressman Duncan Hunter of California sponsored the Secure Fence Act, which required that some seven hundred miles of double-layer fence be built along the border with Mexico. The law was gutted when Texas Republican senator Kay Bailey Hutchison introduced a resolution into the Department of Homeland Security funding bill for fiscal 2008 that left building any fence at all up to the discretion of the director of homeland security.[27] As a result, much of the few miles of fence that were built under the Secure Fence Act ended up being "pedestrian fence" or "virtual fence," stopping virtually no illegal immigrants whatsoever.

Many border activists would be willing to see aggressive quotas set to allow millions of Hispanic immigrants to enter the United States, as long as they entered legally. But an open border is an invitation to criminal gangs, drug cartels, and terrorists to enter the United States with impunity. Those supporting illegal immigration today challenge even the use of any term that suggests "illegal aliens," charging that "no human is illegal." Granted, no human is illegal, but those immigrants who enter the United States in contravention of immigration laws are nonetheless illegal aliens. Tolerance of illegal immigrants by American citizens grows short when economic distress threatens jobs and homes. Acceptance of millions of illegal immigrants in cities throughout America becomes more difficult when state budgets are already in deficit and illegal immigrants demand more social-welfare benefits than are compensated for by the taxes they pay.

Those promoting illegal immigration on both the political Left and the political Right fully understand that open borders lead to a North American integration that ultimately is irreversible.

2. Involve Congress in All National-Emergency Declarations

In general, constitutionalists have difficulty accepting presidential executive orders as law. When presidential executive orders grab power in presidentially declared emergency situations, constitutionalists have legitimate concerns that the type of dictatorial power the Founding Fathers found offensive with the monarchy in Great Britain may well be in the process of being established in the United States of America.

Even if the limited involvement of the military or the creation of temporary camps to house citizens are required in narrowly defined emergencies, such as natural disasters on the magnitude of a Hurricane Katrina, the president should be required to get the concurrence of Congress on the emergency declaration. To do otherwise raises the possibility that the president might use the declaration of a natural emergency as a pretext to suppress political protest the president finds offensive or otherwise objectionable. No president should be above the law. The Founding Fathers designed a system of limited government with checks and balances, such that the powers of the executive, legislative, and judicial were created to be coequals. Executive orders established by the president to assert the power of the presidency over either Congress or the Supreme Court are especially troubling. They vitiate the principles of limited government by negating all checks and balances from the other branches.

The president should not be able to declare a national emergency in order to evoke special powers, including employing the military in domestic events, without the explicit concurrence of Congress. Otherwise, the president could well usurp the power to invoke martial law on what amounts to little more than serving a particular political purpose. At stake is the First Amendment and the ability to protest publicly and petition for the redress of grievances in a robust manner that directly confronts policies the president may cherish.

3. Declare State Sovereignty Under the Ninth and Tenth Amendments

Gradually, in another incremental development over decades, the presidency has assumed an imperial power. Now Congress is enacting laws that the president demands be enacted immediately, when Congress does not even have time to read the legislation before voting. The Founding Fathers knew well that the tendency of power is to grab more power. That is why the Ninth and Tenth Amendments specified that powers not specifically defined for the federal government were to be reserved for the states and the people. That the president and Congress presume the ability to define new powers unto themselves violates the spirit of limited government articulated by the Ninth and Tenth Amendments.

The state-sovereignty movement gains momentum as state governments react against obligations defined for the states by the federal government, often with a requirement that "unfunded obligations" defined by the federal government be paid for from state tax revenue. Unlike the federal government, states do not have the ability to print money to fund budget deficits. So too, there is a limit to the bonds a state can issue before its credit rating sinks to junk-bond levels. States that learn to "just say no!" to the federal government by asserting states' rights under the Ninth and Tenth Amendments have a strong argument for voters who themselves feel pressed by taxes. What begins as a tax revolt could well end up challenging the assumed authority of the federal government to dictate to the states with an ever-growing range of federal legislation.

Short of seceding from the union, states may yet define a scope of limited government that makes it attractive to voters desiring to live in a state defined by the principles of limited government, economic opportunity, personal responsibility, and secure borders. The migration already evident out of high-tax states such as California and New York will soon leave these states with a diminished tax base. The Obama administration has made clear to financial institutions and other corporations such as GM that accepting bailout money means the corporation comes under the direct and active management of government. Should the federal government have to bail out states such as California and New York, the very principle of federalism itself will certainly come under attack. If the federal government covers state budget deficits on a large or continuing basis, the federal government will most likely move to assume increasing federal management of the recipient states. In the process, the states' sovereignty will certainly be compromised.

4. End Bailouts and Balance the Federal Budget

The alternative for government bailouts is to allow insolvent corporations to declare bankruptcy and reorganize. Bankruptcy is not the end of the world. Many corporations emerge from bankruptcy in a financially strengthened position. There may be no better way to eliminate toxic assets on bank balance sheets or to terminate legacy benefits to retired union workers than to declare bankruptcy and reorganize. As difficult as these losses are, bailouts only postpone the inevitable. The losses on toxic assets sooner or later must be taken. If corporations do not have the revenue to pay legacy union benefits, the taxpayer is the only alternative. Once the nation agrees that there are corporations "too big to fail," the nation has accepted the principle of a government-controlled economy. In the history of the world, there are no central-government-managed states that have thrived economically, regardless of whether the central-government control came from the fascist Right or the socialist Left.

A federal government determined to run trillions of dollars in budget deficits must eventually repeat the history of the Weimar Republic. Sooner or later, the inevitable result is hyperinflation and the devaluation of the currency. If the U.S. federal government continues down this path, the United States will soon lose economic sovereignty and become dependent upon foreign governments, such as China and the Middle Eastern oil-producing nations, to buy the debt needed to keep the U.S. federal government in operation. As foreign nations increasingly own trillions of dollars of U.S. Treasury–issued debt, the United States no longer has the freedom of independent action. China and the Middle Eastern oil-producing nations not only hold U.S. debt, they hold the ability to determine U.S. foreign policy as a result. By selling U.S. debt to foreign nations, the U.S. government has sold American sovereignty itself.

The only solution is to balance the federal budget now, no matter how much pain is involved.

5. Eliminate Federal Social-Welfare Programs

The federal budget burden from social-welfare programs, though well intentioned they may be, has created a negative net worth for the United States from which the nation has no possibility of emerging as a solvent nation. The federal government has no way to pay the coming generations of Social Security and Medicare benefits already due, unless it monetizes the dollar. In other words, a Social Security beneficiary may be entitled to receive a monthly check for several thousands of dollars, but the purchasing power of that money will be negligible when the benefits are received.

Social-welfare benefits have ceased being a safety net when millions of people plan to live on those benefits for the foreseeable future. As the United States approaches becoming a nation where more than half the population is too poor to pay income taxes, the ability to generate the social-welfare benefits required breaks down. Even confiscating all the income that individuals and corporations make will soon not be enough to pay the social-welfare burden the nation has voted into effect. Today, politicians want to postpone any discussion of fixing Social Security or Medicare out of fear that the large voting block of seniors will be offended. Yet as long as social-welfare benefits remain entitlement programs guaranteed to be paid by the federal government, the insolvency of the federal government is a certainty just waiting to happen. The bankruptcy of the United States will be unavoidable once foreign nations refuse to buy more trillions of U.S. Treasury–issued debt. As demonstrated above, the Chinese and Russians already are forcing the International Monetary Fund to use Special Drawing Rights as a new form of foreign reserve currency to replace the dollar ultimately.

As a nation, the United States cannot reasonably expect to pay for universal health insurance, or any other form of universal health care, when there is no plan to fund the Social Security and Medicare benefits already booked as liabilities. The only solution to reducing the federal unfunded liabilities is to reduce government-guaranteed entitlement programs by putting a stop to the growth of the social-welfare state the United States seems determined not to curtail, but rather to expand. Economic growth will not solve the problem, especially not when the burdensome taxes needed to fund out-of-control social-welfare programs stifle economic growth itself.

THE RISE OF TWENTY-FIRST-CENTURY AMERICAN PATRIOTS

In 1776, when Congress adopted the Declaration of Independence, the grievances experienced by the colonists against Great Britain had built for decades. The grievances experienced by twenty-first-century patriots have also developed over decades; open borders, the growth of federal entitlement programs, and federal budget deficits are not new crises.

Yet, as a difference in scale is a difference in phenomenon, what is new is that the prospect of one-fifth of Mexico's population living in the United States and the reality of trillion-dollar federal budget deficits create not just bigger problems, but problems different in nature. Today, the very sovereignty of the United States is at stake.

Globalists see the Economic Panic of 2009 as a crisis that presents an opportunity to expand globalism, but twenty-first-century patriots see it as a crisis that demands taking America back to original principles. Twenty-first-century American patriots want a return to the limited government the Founding Fathers intended when they defined the United States as a constitutional republic.

How the great battle between globalists and twenty-first-century patriots will play out remains to be seen. Yet the stakes have never been higher. Globalists want to put America up for sale, believing the United States as a nation-state is an anachronism that long ago served its purpose in today's global village. In sharp contrast, twenty-first-century patriots want to preserve, protect, and defend what they believe is an exceptional form of government the United States must retain if the freedoms defined in the Declaration of Independence and the Bill of Rights are to be passed down to future generations.

This is the great battle the global Economic Panic of 2009 has occasioned.

If the economic panic had never happened, globalists might simply have won incrementally, by the same stealth methodology with which the European Union was created. But now that the Economic Panic of 2009 has occurred, the battle is engaged much more directly, especially as globalist plans are exposed and twenty-first-century patriots organize to fight for U.S. sovereignty.

The only hope these patriots have of winning is the same hope that patriots had in 1776. Pressed by grievances from a dominating monarch, the patriots of 1776 resisted and fought back. Today's patriots have no alternative but to do the same. Thankfully, today's twenty-first-century American patriots have the tools our Founding Fathers provided in the First Amendment and the ballot box to achieve their goals peacefully.

Still, the time is short and the need for action is immediate.

CONCLUSION

Taking America Back

The federal government in Washington no longer feels bound to
the Constitution, nor to the limits explicitly placed on it.

—Joseph Farah, *Taking America Back*, 2003 [1]

With the global Economic Panic of 2009, globalists have decided to
sprint to the finish line in the open, doing everything possible to
undermine American sovereignty while the crisis presents an opportunity to do so. Globalists have calculated that American citizens are sufficiently afraid of losing their jobs and homes that voters will acquiesce
to any solution offered. So the solutions the globalists have offered are
unlimited federal deficit spending and higher taxes, bailouts that permit
a central government takeover of the private economy, and the creation
of a new International Monetary Fund one-world currency to replace
the dollar as the world's foreign-reserve currency of choice for settlement of international trade.

Next, the globalists are planning to reintroduce comprehensive immigration reform, as a way of keeping the border with Mexico open and
permitting 20 percent of Mexico's population to live in the United States
as Mexican national citizens. Threats to Second Amendment gun rights
are intensifying as the Mexican drug war is being offered as a pretext to
take weapons away from U.S. citizens. Barack Obama's campaign promises to renegotiate free-trade agreements such as the North American

Free Trade Agreement to be fairer to U.S. workers and to restore U.S. jobs have been abandoned as the Obama administration is drafting new legislation to allow Mexican trucks to operate freely throughout the United States.

But Americans are not powerless. As long as First Amendment rights and the ballot box remain viable, U.S. citizens can organize Tea Parties to protest peacefully against unreasonably high taxes. State-sovereignty movements are gaining momentum, with the states demanding a roll-back of federal government assumptions of powers not specifically granted to the central government, as determined by the Ninth and Tenth Amendments to the Constitution. A new generation of twenty-first-century American patriots are realizing that the future of the United States of America as a sovereign nation demands redress of grievances right now, since the federal government has become every bit as much a usurper of power as the monarchy in Great Britain had become at the time of the American Revolutionary War.

Key to winning the peaceful effort under way to take back America is the recognition that globalists can readily be found in both the Republican and Democratic parties. As demonstrated in this book, the globalists of the political Left and political Right have differences. Globalists of the political Left, such as President Barack Obama, want to create a massive social-welfare state—on a magnitude even the European socialist states of France and Germany have considered dangerous—financed with deficit spending. On the political Right, globalists such as Senator John McCain support an expansion of multinational corporate authority to outsource jobs at will under ever-expanding free-trade agreements. But behind the political curtain, the same globalist power brokers fund candidates of both parties.

JOHN MCCAIN FUNDED BY SOROS SINCE 2001

In 2001, John McCain founded the Alexandria, Virginia–based Reform Institute[2] as a vehicle to receive funding from George Soros's Open Society Institute, as well as several other prominent leftist nonprofit organizations. Evidence from the public record suggests that McCain used the Reform Institute to promote his political agenda and provide compensation to his key campaign-staff operatives between elections.[3]

In 2006, McCain was forced to sever his formal ties with the Reform

Institute, after a controversy brought to light the $200,000 contribution McCain solicited for the institute from Cablevision, while using his membership on the Senate Committee on Commerce, Science, and Transportation to write a letter to the FCC supporting Cablevision's push to introduce the more profitable "a la carte" pricing, rather than packages of TV programming.[4] That both John McCain and Barack Obama were supported by George Soros in the 2008 presidential campaign meant Soros would win regardless of whether Obama or McCain won.

SOROS PROFITS FROM GLOBAL ECONOMIC PANIC OF 2009

By betting against the U.S. economy and the dollar, investor George Soros has made billions from the economic downturn.

"I'm having a very good crisis," Soros told London's *Daily Mail* in March 2009.[5] Soros, who came out of retirement in 2007 to manage his Quantum Investment Fund, has made $2.9 billion in doing so, including $1 billion made in 2008.

Had Senator McCain won the 2008 presidential campaign, George Soros would have had influence at the White House, exactly as Soros has now, after promoting and funding candidate Barack Obama since the latter first came on the national political scene with his speech at the 2004 Democratic National Convention. No one should be confused into thinking that backing both presidential candidates in 2008 makes Soros a patriot. To the contrary, Soros was concerned only that whoever won, he would be sure to benefit. Globalists like Soros are concerned about money, first and foremost, possibly to the exclusion of all else. Soros appears to make his political bets primarily to ensure that he preserves his ability to make and keep money.

Soros has been outspoken about his views. He began his 2008 book, subtitled *The Credit Crisis of 2008 and What It Means*, by proclaiming, "We are in the midst of the worst financial crisis since the 1930s." Soros went on to explain that the 2008 credit crisis "marks the end of an era of credit expansion based on the dollar as the international reserve currency." He insisted the current crisis was "the culmination of a superboom that has lasted for more than twenty-five years."[6] Soros has consistently proclaimed that the dollar is under selling pressure and "may eventually be replaced as a world reserve currency, possibly by the International Monetary Fund's Special Drawing Rights."[7] Soros told

Reuters that the U.S. economy is in for a "lasting showdown" and could face a Japan-style period of a decade or more of relatively low growth, coupled with high inflation.

Whether Senator Obama or Senator McCain won in 2008, Soros would still have been betting against America, selling short U.S. stocks and buying futures contracts betting the dollar would fall in value.

WALL STREET FUNDED OBAMA'S
2008 PRESIDENTIAL CAMPAIGN

As shocking as it is to conservative Republicans that Senator John McCain was funded by George Soros, it should be equally shocking to progressive Democrats that the Obama administration has top-dollar connections to Wall Street, which included major contributions from Wall Street firms and banks to Senator Barack Obama's 2008 presidential campaign.

OpenSecrets.org reported that of the top twenty campaign contributors to the 2008 Obama campaign, five were Wall Street firms and banks, including Goldman Sachs, Citigroup, JPMorgan Chase, UBS AG, and Morgan Stanley. Through bundling individual contributions from employees and others affiliated with the firm, these Wall Street firms and banks contributed approximately $500,000 or more to the Obama presidential campaign. Goldman Sachs was Obama's second-largest campaign contributor, right behind the University of California at the top of the list; Goldman Sachs contributed nearly $1 million to the campaign.[8]

Once again, Senator John McCain's 2008 presidential campaign top-contributor list included Citigroup, Morgan Stanley, Goldman Sachs, JPMorgan Chase, plus Merrill Lynch, Credit Suisse Group, Bank of America, and the now-defunct Lehman Brothers and Bear Stearns.[9] As was the case with George Soros, the Wall Street firms and banks contributing to the 2008 presidential campaign generally hedged their bets, funding both candidates.

Whichever candidate won the presidency in 2008, Citigroup, Morgan Stanley, Goldman Sachs, and JPMorgan Chase could claim they helped fund the victor.

TOP OBAMA WHITE HOUSE ADVISERS
WITH FINANCIAL TIES TO WALL STREET EXPOSED

In the first months of the Obama administration, investigative reporters also discovered financial ties between financial institutions, including Wall Street firms, and top Obama administration economic advisors.

Larry Summers, director of the National Economic Council in the Obama administration, was paid more than $2.7 million in speaking fees from firms at the heart of the financial crisis, including Citigroup, Goldman Sachs, JPMorgan Chase, Merrill Lynch, Bank of America, and Lehman Brothers, according to a report published by Politico.[10] In 2008, Summers also received $5.2 million from D. E. Shaw, a hedge fund for which Summers served as a managing director from October 2006 until he joined the Obama administration.

Thomas E. Donilon, deputy national security advisor in the Obama administration, was paid $3.9 million in 2008 by the law firm O'Melveny & Meyers to represent clients, including two firms that received federal bailout funds: Citibank and Goldman Sachs. In filling out financial-disclosure forms required by the White House, Donilon also disclosed he was a member of the Trilateral Commission, that he sits on the steering committee of the Bilderberg Group, and that he is a member of the Council on Foreign Relations.[11]

Donilon was also a former top official at Fannie Mae from 1995 to 2005, at a time when its officers and lobbyists were insisting that finances were sound. According to the *Washington Times*, the Office of Federal Housing Enterprise Oversight in a 2006 report said Fannie Mae lobbyists, whose office was overseen by Donilon, had tried to use their ties to members of Congress in an attempt to discredit federal regulators.[12] The newspaper also reported Donilon was paid more than $1 million in salary and cash bonuses in 2002 and 2003 from Fannie Mae. He registered as a lobbyist for Fannie Mae as recently as 2005, according to regulatory filings and court records examined by the *Washington Times*.

Robert Scheer, a contributing editor to the leftist publication the *Nation*, attacked Gary Gensler, President Obama's choice to head the Commodity Futures Trading Commission.[13] When Gensler was an official at the Treasury Department he worked to exempt credit-default swaps from regulation, which, Scheer charged, "led to the collapse of AIG and has resulted in the largest taxpayer bailout in U.S. history." Scheer noted that Gensler worked at Goldman Sachs when Robert Rubin was a partner there, before Rubin left to become Treasury secretary under President Clinton.

Scheer wrote, "Lawrence Summers, his protégé and replacement at Treasury, elevated Gensler to be an undersecretary." Directly contradicting the Obama administration charge that Bush-era deregulation was responsible for the financial-services meltdown, Scheer accused Gensler of acting "as Summers's point man in advocating for deregulation legislation that enabled the current debacle." After analyzing the public record, Scheer charged Summers, Gensler, Treasury Secretary Geithner, and their "*über* mentor" Robert Rubin with being instrumental in preventing credit-swap derivatives from being regulated.

Scheer's scathing conclusion was clear in his heated criticism of the Obama administration inner circle: "We taxpayers are being asked to buy back from the banks the very toxic assets that the members of Obama's economic team once celebrated as an unmitigated blessing." [14]

The *Wall Street Journal* quoted Julian Zelizer, a history and public affairs professor at Princeton University, as defending President Obama by claiming that in the midst of a financial crisis, the administration wants an inner circle of policy advisers "who can think and talk like Wall Street." [15]

PRESIDENT OBAMA AND VICE PRESIDENT BIDEN KEEP THEIR SIX-FIGURE SALARIES

The salaries of President Obama and Vice President Biden were exempted from a presidential executive order Obama signed in his first full day in office that capped compensation for White House aides at $100,000 a year.

At his first White House press briefing, Press Secretary Robert Gibbs dodged a question about whether Obama and Biden intended to "lead by example," by volunteering to reduce their own salaries to the $100,000 cap being demanded for White House senior aides.

Gibbs, in response to the question, said that the president's $400,000 salary and vice president's $227,300 pay are set by law and cannot be modified by a presidential executive order.

The U.S. Constitution, in Article II, Section 1, stipulates that the president's salary cannot be increased or decreased during the president's term in office. Yet nothing prevents a president from voluntarily forgoing compensation. John F. Kennedy, an heir to his father's massive fortune, and Herbert Hoover chose not to receive a presidential salary during their terms.

World Net Daily placed repeated phone calls to the White House regarding President Obama's compensation and was told the press office would have to receive a determination of the question from White House legal counsel.[16]

World Net Daily also asked if the White House could provide a list of those who would be affected by the executive order and, specifically, whether the executive order would apply to White House chief of staff Rahm Emanuel. The press office said it was not likely White House counsel would have an answer available anytime soon.

The White House press office also acknowledged that the executive order issuing the pay cap had not yet been posted on the White House website and that they had no plans to publish the names or titles of the approximately one hundred senior White House staff members to whom the executive order applies.

THE OBAMA BUBBLE

When France and Germany refused to go along with President Obama's plan at the G20 meeting in London on April 2, 2009, to pump up the global economy with trillions of dollars in deficit spending to build a social-welfare state on an unprecedented scale globally, an important message was being communicated: namely, that creating another credit bubble was not the solution to the global economic recession.

The global Economic Panic of 2009 was caused by too much leverage that involved a host of excesses, including excessive borrowing by subprime homeowners, businesses with inflated credit ratings, commercial real estate developers building expensive properties with prospects of continued high rentals, hedge-fund managers borrowing billions to bet on the stock market, and derivative-contract writers speculating on a series of complex bets few experts completely understood. The credit bubble caused by Federal Reserve Board Chairman Alan Greenspan's decision to keep interest rates at historically low 1 percent rates in 2003 and 2004 was being repeated by Ben Bernanke's decision to push interest rates to zero once the Economic Panic of 2009 was beginning to take hold. From there, the Obama administration printed money as if there were no tomorrow, engaging in trillions of dollars of deficit spending to finance the following: a $787 billion economic stimulus package; a

TARP bank bailout compounded by bailouts of GM, Chrysler, and insurance giant AIG; and a proposed $3.6 trillion 2009 federal budget.

The decision of the Federal Reserve to go into the bond market to buy U.S. Treasury securities, plus bonds issued by Freddie Mac and Fannie Mae, was calculated to lower interest rates. The Obama administration's idea was that if mortgage rates could be lowered, then homeowners facing foreclosure might engage in mortgage modifications that would lower their monthly payments enough to prevent mortgage defaults. Besides, lower interest rates would make mortgages more affordable, hopefully stopping the downward adjustment in home prices occurring throughout the nation. All these moves shared the common characteristics of being leverage-driven attempts to ease credit once again, repeating the very cause of the economic downturn in the first place.

Simply put, the Obama administration was trying to stimulate the economy by credit, in the hope that pumping deficit spending into the economy would generate economic activity. Even the determination to pump up the social-welfare state was justified by the Obama administration on arguments that welfare, food stamps, and unemployment dollars would somehow create jobs. As an end result, the U.S. taxpayer has been forced to assume the burden of yet-uncounted trillions of dollars in losses that must be taken in the toxic assets held by banks. Even though millions of private investors have lost as much as half their 401(k) investments, the taxpayer is being asked by the Obama administration to absorb losses from insolvent government pension funds. In the bankruptcy of companies such as GM and Chrysler, union leaders expect the Obama administration to pay campaign debts by putting the taxpayer on the hook to pay the retirement benefits of now-retired UAW workers, absolving GM, Chrysler, and their shareholders of the responsibility to make good on these legacy retirement benefits as part of their bankruptcy obligations.

Unfortunately, losses in the real estate market will not subside until home prices around the country decline by as much as one-half of their peak bubble market value in 2006. Similarly, just removing toxic assets from bank balance sheets will not solve the problem. Even if the assets are purchased by public-private partnerships, the losses must be realized and it's most likely that the taxpayer will once again be asked to absorb the losses. Instead of bailouts, the economic pain in all instances could have been endured much more quickly by letting failed banks and other corporations declare bankruptcy without any government guarantee to absorb losses.

The one move the Obama administration refused to make on ideological grounds was the one move that has been proven to create jobs since President Kennedy was in office, namely, cutting taxes. Instead of cutting taxes, the Obama administration proposed to increase taxes on the "rich," defined as anyone making over $250,000 a year. Moreover, by fanning anger against bonuses to executives in companies receiving federal bailouts, the Obama administration suggested executive compensation itself was under attack. At a time when the Obama administration should have been fostering private-enterprise activity aimed at job creation, the administration seemed hostile to business, especially struggling businesses, such as GM, where the Obama administration insisted chairman and CEO Rick Wagoner be fired, as a condition of continued government assistance for GM in bankruptcy proceedings.

By failing to cut taxes dramatically, especially on small business and the entrepreneurs capable of creating small-business growth, the Obama administration was repeating a key error of the Roosevelt administration in 1932. By engaging in deficit spending to grow government and build the social-welfare state, the Obama administration was repeating Roosevelt administration errors that ended up prolonging the Great Depression of the 1930s for a decade. By cutting taxes, the Roosevelt administration arguably could have ended the Great Depression within a year or two. The same argument today is being made over the Obama administration's management of the economy.

Yet the fundamental changes globalists are requiring could not be made if the global Economic Panic of 2009 were to end within a year or two. A prolonged depression lasting through the decade of the 2010s could easily reduce the American middle class to a point of submission where steps taken to compromise U.S. sovereignty will be accepted, when otherwise those same steps would be rejected outright.

THE FAILURE OF THE DEMOCRATIC AND REPUBLICAN PARTIES

That President Obama himself and top advisers within the administration have close ties to Wall Street should surprise no one who has looked past the Obama rhetoric to see that if "hope" and "change" mean anything at all, what they mean is more Wall Street and more globalism.

With President Obama in the White House, the nation will get globalism from the political Left, creating more of a welfare state than would have been created had Senator McCain won the 2008 presidential election. Yet, in truth, it is difficult to tell President Obama apart from President George W. Bush. Both presidents engaged in deficit spending and increased the national debt by trillions of dollars. Both presidents increased federal welfare spending, with George W. Bush getting the nation's first prescription-drug government-payment scheme passed in Congress. Both presidents have continued the war in Iraq, with President Obama even expanding the war in Afghanistan. In the final analysis, both presidents are more easily understood as globalists than as traditional liberal Democratic or conservative Republican presidents.

In the spirit that no good crisis should go to waste, globalists in both the Democratic and Republican parties have moved to offer more globalism as the solution to the global economic downturn. A global economy managed by international regulatory organizations with a new one-world currency is predictably the formula America and the world are being offered to emerge from the global Economic Panic of 2009. Nowhere in the political lexicon of either major party is there any consideration of closing down the Federal Reserve or the IRS, pulling out of the United Nations, canceling free-trade agreements such as NAFTA and CAFTA, or withdrawing from the World Trade Organization, the International Monetary Fund, or the World Bank.

No matter which party is in the White House, the American people are certain to get more globalism offered as a solution, more reasons why our border with Mexico must remain open, more arguments that comprehensive immigration reform should be passed, and more insistence that North American economic integration needs to proceed full speed ahead.

The G20 meeting in London in April 2009 represents a major victory for the globalists. The decision to fund $250 billion for the International Monetary Fund to develop Special Drawing Rights as an international foreign-exchange currency marks the beginning of the end for the dollar. The decision to create a Financial Stability Board empowers an international group controlled largely by Europeans to make fundamental decisions about how U.S. corporations operate. These decisions include limits that the Financial Stability Board may decide to place on executive compensation. Moreover, the Financial Stability Board on its own judgment might decide that U.S. business operations should be outlawed because the board has determined the operations are too risky because the businesses involved have a "systematic risk" simply by being "too big to fail."

AMERICA FOR SALE

China and the Middle Eastern oil-producing nations will not be willing to hold trillions of dollars of depreciating U.S. dollar–denominated government debt forever.

Nor can the United States pump up a failed economy by deficit spending forever.

The Economic Panic of 2009 was caused not by a credit crisis, but by a capital crisis. America is being put up for sale right now because no economy can operate for long without generating capital. A social-welfare state generates debt, not capital.

At some point, foreign nations holding U.S. debt will refuse to stand for the Federal Reserve entering the market to monetize another trillion dollars of Treasury securities by serving as the buyer of last resort. Creditor nations eventually reach a point where they have had enough debt and begin to demand assets. When the U.S. federal government has no choice but to deliver the assets as collateral against mounting government debt with no end in sight, the U.S. taxpayer will be guaranteeing the final selling of America, without a single shot having to be fired by any enemy nation.

When capital returns to the United States from China and the Middle Eastern oil-producing nations, public-private partnerships will be created so foreign investments in U.S. corporations and infrastructure can be made without risk of loss. The U.S. taxpayer will be asked to make this last guarantee, namely, that the foreign capital returning to own America will be insured against loss by a U.S. government guarantee.

Still, the global Economic Panic of 2009 will not be solved by globalism, precisely because the panic was caused by globalism in the first place. The U.S. economy cannot quickly recover, because manufacturing and white-collar jobs outsourced to foreigners by multinational corporations will not quickly return. Federal-government tax rebates and economic stimulus programs ironically create more jobs in China and India than they do in the United States, even when those measures do successfully stimulate consumer spending.

With typical shortsightedness, multinational corporations that improved quarterly profits by outsourcing U.S. labor to slaves or near-slaves in foreign countries destroyed the middle class on which their quarterly sales depended. While Americans cannot send their lawns to China or India to be mowed, an immigrant underclass imported across the Mexican border will gladly do the job at wages and benefits no middle-class American could afford to accept. With the income gap increasing in the United States under globalism, the U.S. middle class that was the engine of global economic growth is now damaged, perhaps beyond repair. Nor have foreign countries built deep or lasting middle classes, not when the premise of U.S. outsourcing was that foreign labor would remain cheap.

Yet as long as billionaire investors can make more billions by selling economic recovery short, more globalism will be the prescribed remedy.

As long as Wall Street bankers can either make money from bailouts, or bail themselves out with White House advisory positions, Wall Street will continue to make more billions from the economic downturn itself.

TAKING AMERICA BACK

The only barrier between America today and the final sellout of America is the U.S. taxpayer. The only chance that globalism may fail is if the U.S. taxpayer says a resounding "No!" to Democrats and Republicans alike.

The state-sovereignty movement is neither a Democratic Party nor a Republican Party phenomenon.

Tea Parties held in the streets across America are neither a Democratic Party nor a Republican Party phenomenon.

When millions of middle-class Americans see through the globalist lie, there is a strong chance America will be taken back peacefully. The politicians in Washington and the state capitals are hired to do a job; when the politicians in office fail to listen to "We the People," they must be voted out. If voting Democrats out of office is not sufficient to end globalism, then the twenty-first-century American patriots need to vote out next the Republicans who replace them in Congress, the White House, and in state capitals across the land.

Either that, or twenty-first-century American patriots need to create a third party that will listen to "We the People," the ultimate sovereign in the United States.

When the U.S. taxpayer finally refuses to pay, there can be no more federal government deficits, no more federal government bailouts, and no more international organizations.

Now, all that is required is for the twenty-first-century American patriots to do what our Founding Fathers did in establishing the United States of America in the first place.

- We, the patriots, cannot lose provided we insist upon returning to the limited government specified in our founding documents.

- We, the patriots, are a force the globalists of today cannot defeat, just as Great Britain, the most powerful nation on the globe in 1776, could not defeat the American patriots of that time.

- The inalienable freedoms defined in our founding documents are worth fighting to preserve.

- The generations of patriots who fought and died for the United States of America did not fight and die for an America we allow the globalists to put up for sale.

In the final analysis, the Economic Panic of 2009 is worth all the pain if, as a result, we American patriots just say "No!" to the globalists who are doing their best to put America up for sale.

NOTES

Preface: A "Transformational Crisis"

1. "A 40-Year Wish List," *Wall Street Journal*, January 28, 2009, http://online
   .wsj.com/article/SB123310466514522309.html.
2. Pete Harrison, "Never waste a good crisis, Clinton says on climate," Reuters, March 7, 2009, http://in.reuters.com/article/environmentNews/idIN
   TRE5251VN20090306.
3. "Davos delegates gather to 'shape new world,' " CNN.com International/
   World Business, January 27, 2009, http://edition.cnn.com/2009/BUSINESS/
   01/27/davos.tuesday.crisis/. A video of Schwab's interview was archived
   by CNN.com at http://edition.cnn.com/2009/BUSINESS/01/27/davos
   .tuesday.crisis/#cnnSTCVideo.
4. Christopher Wood, "Insight: Swedish model for western banks," *Financial Times*, February 8, 2009, http://www.ft.com/cms/s/4f777b38-c642
   -11dd-8e4f-0000779fd2ac.Authorised=false.html?_i_location=http%3A
   %2F%2Fwww.ft.com%2Fcms%2Fs%2F0%2F4f777b38-e642-11dd-8e
   4f-0000779fd2ac.html%3Fnclick_check%3D1&_i_referer=&nclick_
   check=1.
5. Henry A. Kissinger, "The chance for a new world order," *International
   Herald Tribune*, January 12, 2009, http://www.iht.com/articles/2009/01/
   12/opinion/edkissinger.php.
6. Jean Monnet, *Memoirs* (New York: Doubleday, 1978), p. 524.
7. Ben Feller, "Obama caps executive pay tied to bailout money," Associated
   Press, February 4, 2009, http://www.google.com/hostednews/ap/article/
   ALeqM5iYX—wRrv7CQhjxb9FFjidsIvjLQD9653GGO0.

Introduction: The New World Order

1. President George H. W. Bush, "War in the Gulf: The President; Transcript
   of the Comments by Bush on the Air Strikes Against the Iraqis," *New
   York Times*, January 17, 1991, http://query.nytimes.com/gst/fullpage.html
   ?res=9D0CE2DF1F3AF934A25752C0A967958260.

2. Jerome R. Corsi, *The Late Great USA: The Coming Merger with Mexico and Canada* (Los Angeles: WND, 2007). The book was issued as a paperback with a revised title and an updated epilogue. See Jerome R. Corsi, *The Late Great USA: NAFTA, the North American Union, and the Threat of a Coming Merger with Mexico and Canada* (New York: Threshold Editions, 2009).

3. Organisation for Economic Co-Operation and Development (OECD) Data on Balance of Payments available on the OECD website at http://stats.oecd.org/wbos/Index.aspx?datasetcode=MEI_BOP.

4. Oil consumption data comes from the U.S. Department of Energy, Energy Information Administration reports titled "Summary of Weekly Petroleum Data," such as the report for the week ending January 23, 2009, http://www.eia.doe.gov/pub/oil_gas/petroleum/data_publications/weekly _petroleum_status_report/current/txt/wpsr.txt.

5. "Gross Domestic Product: Fourth Quarter 2008 (Final)," U.S. Department of Commerce, Bureau of Economic Analysis, March 26, 2009, http://www.bea.gov/newsreleases/national/gdp/gdpnewsrelease.htm.

6. Jean Monnet, *Memoirs* (New York: Doubleday, 1978), p. 524.

7. Walter Hallstein, *Europe in the Making* (New York: Norton, 1972), p. 28.

8. "Interview with Vicente Fox," Transcript, *Larry King Live*, October 8, 2007, http://transcripts.cnn.com/TRANSCRIPTS/0710/08/1kl.01.html.

9. For description of Vicente Fox's "20/20 vision" plan, see the North American Forum on Integration, "NAFTA Timetable: North American Agenda," at http://www.fina-nafi.org/eng/integ/chronologie.asp?langue= eng&menu=integ.

10. Jerome R. Corsi, "It's Official: Mexican Trucks Coming," World Net Daily, February 23, 2007, http://www.wnd.com/news/article.asp?ARTICLE _ID=54411.

11. Richard N. Gardner, "The Hard Road to World Order," *Foreign Affairs,* April 1974, http://www.foreignaffairs.org/19740401faessay10106/ Richard-n-gardner/the-hard-road-to-world-order.html.

12. J. B. S. Haldane, "On Being the Right Size," in James R. Newman, ed., *The World of Mathematics* (New York: Simon and Schuster, 1956), vol. 1, p. 950 ff.

13. Jerome R. Corsi, *The Obama Nation: Leftist Politics and the Cult of Personality* (New York: Threshold Editions, 2008).

Part 1: The Global Economic Panic of 2009

1. Jonathan R. Laing, "Are You Ready for Dow 20,000?" *Barron's*, March 24, 2008, http://online.barrons.com/article/SB120615098415256845 .html?mod=9_0031_b_this_weeks_magazine_main.

2. Council of Economic Advisors, *Economic Report of the President—2007*, p. 3, http://www.gpoaccess.gov/eop/download.html.

3. Emily Kaiser, "U.S. household wealth falls $11.2 trillion in 2008," Reuters, March 12, 2009, http://www.reuters.com/article/domesticNews/

idUSTRE52B58720090312?feedType=RSS&feedName=domesticNews
&rpc=22&sp=true.

4. "Gross Domestic Product: Fourth Quarter 2008 (Final)," Bureau of Economic Analysis, U.S. Department of Commerce, Press Release, March 26, 2009, http://www.bea.gov/newsreleases/national/gdp/gdpnewsrelease.htm.

Chapter 1: The U.S.A. Bankrupt

1. James Dale Davidson and Lord William Rees-Mogg, *The Great Reckoning: How the World Will Change in the Depression of the 1990s* (New York: Summit, 1991), p. 12.

2. World Development Indicators Database, World Bank, revised September 10, 2008.

3. Congressional Budget Office, "The Budget and Economic Outlook: An Update," September 2008, http://www.cbo.gov/doc.cfm?index=9706; and Congressional Budget Office, "The Budget and Economic Outlook: Fiscal Years 2009 to 2019," http://www.cbo.gov/doc.cfm?index=9957.

4. Financial Management Service, U.S. Department of the Treasury, "2008 Financial Report of the United States Government," December 17, 2008, http://www.fms.treas.gov/fr/.

5. John Williams, "December 2008—GAAP-Based 2008 Federal Deficit Hits $5.1 Trillion: Government Bankruptcy/Hyperinflation Just a Matter of Time," Shadow Government Statistics, no. 48, "Section 4: Reporting/Market Focus," January 3, 2009, http://www.shadowstats.com/article/401.

6. Jerome R. Corsi, "Federal obligations exceed world GDP," World Net Daily, February 13, 2009, http://www.worldnetdaily.com/index.php?fa=PAGE.view&pageId=88851.

7. Daniel Schorn, "U.S. Heading for Financial Trouble," *60 Minutes*, CBS News.com, July 8, 2007, http://www.cbsnews.com/stories/2007/03/01/60minutes/main2528226.shtml.

8. David Walker's 2007 appearance on the CBS News's *60 Minutes* television show can be viewed on YouTube at http://video.google.com/videoplay?docid=7461407498377956300.

9. Chairman Ben S. Bernanke, "Long-term fiscal challenges facing the United States," Testimony before the Committee on the Budget, U.S. Senate, January 18, 2007, http://www.federalreserve.gov/newsevents/testimony/bernanke20070118a.htm.

10. Ibid.

11. U.S. Treasury, "Minutes of the Meeting of the Treasury Borrowing Advisory Committee of the Securities Industry and Financial Markets Association, February 3, 2009, http://www.bustedbudget.com/TBACminutes.htm.

12. Mark Knoller, "Bush Administration Adds $4 Trillion to National Debt," CBSNews.com, September 29, 2008, http://www.cbsnews.com/blogs/2008/09/29/couricandco/entry4486228.shtml.

13. Landon Thomas, Jr., "Treasury Boss Taking Fire in Europe Over Stimulus," *New York Times*, February 14, 2009, http://www.nytimes.com/2009/02/15/business/worldbusiness/15g7.html?ref=business.

14. See, for instance, Christine Romans, "Numb and number: Is trillion the new billion?" CNN.com, February 4, 2009, http://www.cnn.com/2009/LIVING/02/04/trillion.dollars/index.html; Barbara Kiviat, "How to Understand a Trillion-Dollar Deficit," Time.com, January 11, 2009, http://www.time.com/time/business/article/0.8599.1870699.00.html; and the Muser, "What's a Trillion, Grandpa?" GreatReality.com, updated January 2004, http://www.greatreality.com/DebtTrillion.htm.

15. See U.S. National Debt Clock at http://www.brillig.com/debt_clock/.

16. Kevin Hamlin, "Asia Needs Deal to Prevent Panic Selling of U.S. Debt, Yu Says," Bloomberg.com, September 25, 2008, http://www.bloomberg.com/apps/news?pid=newsarchive&sid=anZHfo6tQi60.

17. Andrew Batson and Andrew Browne, "Wen Voices Concern Over China's U.S. Treasuries," *Wall Street Journal,* March 14, 2009, http://online.wsj.com/article/SB123692233477317069.html.

18. Joe McDonald, "China 'worried' about US Treasury holdings," Associated Press, March 13, 2009, http://apnews.myway.com/article/20090313/D96T37FO0.html.

19. Lukanyo Mnyanda and Bob Chen, "Treasuries Drop as Stocks Gain, China Asks for Debt Assurance," Bloomberg.com, March 13, 2009, http://www.bloomberg.com/apps/news?pid=20601087&sid=aP7DPb6vb0Eo&refer=home.

20. Ibid.

21. Martin Hutchinson, "China is right to have doubts about who will buy all America's debt," *Daily Telegraph*, February 13, 2009, http://www.telegraph.co.uk/finance/breakingviewscom/4611408/China-is-right-to-have-doubts-about-who-will-buy-all-Americas-debt.html.

22. Keith Bradsher, "U.S. debt is losing its appeal in China," *International Herald Tribune*, January 8, 2009, http://www.iht.com/articles/2009/01/07/business/yuan.php.

23. Andrew Peaple, "Trade Off for China Could Hurt the U.S.," *Wall Street Journal,* February 11, 2009, http://online.wsj.com/article/SB123436917475673461.html?mod=rss_Heard_on_the_Street.

24. Henry Sender, "China to stick with U.S. bonds," *Financial Times*, February 11, 2009, http://www.ft.com/cms/s/0/ba857be6-f88f-11dd-aae8-000077b07658.html.

25. John Parry, "Depression risk might force U.S. to buy assets," Reuters.com, February 12, 2008, http://www.reuters.com/article/ousiv/idUSGOR27660220080212?ref=patrick.net.

26. Chairman Ben S. Bernanke, at the Greater Austin Chamber of Commerce, Austin, Texas, December 1, 2008, http://www.federalreserve.gov/newsevents/speech/bernanke20081201a.htm.

27. Bank of International Settlements, "Semiannual OTC derivative statistics at end-June 2008," http://www.bis.org/statistics/derstats.htm.

28. Tom Cahill, "Third of Hedge Funds Face 'Wipe Out' After Slump, Godden Says," Bloomberg.com, December 15, 2008, http://www.bloomberg.com/apps/news?pid=20601087&sid=agmxqxRJfrCI&refer=worldwide.

29. See http://www.deepcaster.com/.

30. Lisa LaMotta, "Merrill Can't Stop the Bleeding," Forbes.com, July 17, 2008, http://www.forbes.com/2008/07/17/merrill-lynch-earnings-markets-equity-cx_lal_0717markets35.html.

31. Associated Press, "Bank of America to purchase Merrill Lynch," MSNBC.com, September 15, 2008, http://www.msnbc.msn.com/id/26708958/.

32. "Bank of America gets another $20B," CNN.com, January 16, 2006, http://edition.cnn.com/2009/BUSINESS/01/16/boa/index.html.

33. Fox News, "Obama Warns of 'Catastrophe' Without Stimulus, Seeks Compromise," February 4, 2009, http://www.foxnews.com/politics/first100days/2009/02/03/republicans-block-billions-infrastructure-stimulus/.

34. For a nontechnical discussion of Keynesian economics applied to the Obama 2009 economic stimulus package, see Gary Wolfram, Business & Media Institute, "Econ 101: That Old-Time Keynesian Theory," BusinessAndMedia.org, January 21, 2009, http://www.businessandmedia.org/commentary/2009/20090121144938.aspx.

35. Jim Kuhnhenn, "Obama: Economic crisis 'not as bad as we think,'" Associated Press, March 12, 2009, http://www.breitbart.com/article.php?id=D96SP30G5&show_article=1.

36. Megan Davies and Walden Siew, "45 percent of world's wealth destroyed: Blackstone CEO," Reuters, March 10, 2009, http://www.reuters.com/article/wtUSInvestingNews/idUSTRE52966Z20090310.

37. Emily Kaiser, "U.S. household wealth falls $11.2 trillion in 2008," Reuters, March 12, 2009, http://www.reuters.com/article/domesticNews/idUSTRE52B58720090312?feedType=RSS&feedName=domesticNews&rpc=22&sp=true.

38. S. Mitra Kalita, "Americans See 18 percent of Wealth Vanish," *Wall Street Journal*, March 13, 2009, http://online.wsj.com/article/SB123687371369308675.html#mod=todays_us_nonsub_page_one.

39. David M. Dickson, "World loses more than $50 trillion," *Washington Times*, March 10, 2009, http://www.washingtontimes.com/news/2009mar/10/world-loses-over-50-trillion/.

40. Alexandra Twin, "Stocks crushed," CNNMoney.com, September 29, 2008, http://money.cnn.com/2008/09/29/markets/markets_newyork/index.htm?cnn=yes.

41. Susan Thompson, "Global stock market loses total $21 trillion," *Times Online*, February 11, 2009, http://business.timesonline.co.uk/tol/business/markets/article5705526.ece.

Chapter 2: The Mortgage Bubble Bursts

1. Robjert J. Shiller, *The Subprime Solution: How Today's Global Financial Crisis Happened, and What to Do about It* (Princeton and Oxford: Princeton University Press, 2008), p. 29.

2. William A. Fleckenstein with Frederick Sheehan, *Greenspan's Bubbles: The Age of Ignorance at the Federal Reserve* (New York: McGraw Hill, 2008).

3. "Open Market Operations," Federal Reserve Board, http://www.federalreserve.gov/fomc/fundsrate.htm.

4. "Federal Open Market Committee," Board of Governors of the Federal Reserve System, http://www.federalreserve.gov/monetarypolicy/fomc.htm.

5. Federal Funds Rates 1955–2009, Federal Reserve Statistical Release, on the website of the Federal Reserve Board, http://www.federalreserve.gov/releases/h15/data/Annual/H15_FF_O.txt.

6. Alan Greenspan, *The Age of Turbulence: Adventures in a New World* (New York: Penguin, 2007), pp. 224–25.

7. Ibid., p. 226.

8. Ibid., p. 229.

9. Ibid.

10. Federal Reserve Chairman Ben S. Bernanke, "The Community Reinvestment Act: Its Evolution and New Challenges," http://www.federalreserve.gov/newsevents/speech/Bernanke20070330a.htm.

11. Aaron Pressman, "Community Reinvestment Act had nothing to do with subprime crisis," *BusinessWeek,* September 29, 2008, citing Michael Barr, a professor of law at the University of Michigan, testifying before the House Committee on Financial Services in February 2008, http://www.businessweek.com/investing/insights/blog/archives/2008/09/community_reinv.html.

12. See, for instance, Doug Ross, "Charts: The tragic results of the 'Community Reinvestment Act,'" December 24, 2008, http://directorblue.blogspot.com/2008/12/charts-tragic-results-of-community.html.

13. CNBC, "House of Cards," first broadcast February 12, 2009, http://www.cnbc.com/id/28892719/.

14. CNBC, "Origins of the Financial Crisis 'Then and Now,'" Slideshow from the CNBC Special Report "House of Cards," Slide no. 11, "Wall Street Banks," http://www.cnbc.com/id/28993790/?slide=11.

15. Ibid., Slide no. 12, "Rating Agencies," http://www.cnbc.com/id/28993790/?slide=12.

16. Ibid., Slide no. 8, "The 'Refi' Years," http://www.cnbc.com/id/28993790/?slide=8.

17. Greenspan, *The Age of Turbulence*, p. 230.

18. Robert J. Shiller, *Irrational Exuberance*, 2nd ed. (Princeton, N.J.: Princeton University Press, 2006), pp. 12–20. See also "A History of Home Values," graph constructed to illustrate Robert Shiller's index of American

housing prices going back to 1890, *New York Times*, http://www.ny times.com/imagepages/2006/08/26/weekinreview/27leon_graph2.html.

19. Stephen Labaton and Edmund L. Andrews, "In Rescue to Stabilize Lending, U.S. Takes Over Mortgage Finance Twins," *New York Times*, September 7, 2008, http://www.nytimes.com/2008/09/08/business/08fannie .html.

20. Simon Atkinson, "US rescues giant mortgage lenders," BBC News, September 8, 2008, http://news.bbc.co.uk/1/hi/business/7505152.stm.

21. Deborah Soloman and Damian Paletta, "U.S. Near Deal on Fannie, Freddie," *Wall Street Journal,* September 6, 2008, http://online.wsj.com/ar ticle/SB122064650145404781.html?mod=hpp_us_whats_news.

22. Dan Gainor, "Journalists Convinced Government Bailouts Better Solution," Business & Media Institute, September 17, 2008, http://www .businessandmedia.org/commentary/2008/20080917073634.aspx.

23. David Frum, "David Frum on the demise of Fannie Mae and Freddie Mac," NationalPost.com, July 11, 2008, http://network.nationalpost .com/np/blogs/fullcomment/archive/2008/07/11/david-frum-on-the -demise-of-fannie-mae-and-freddie-mac.aspx.

24. "Franklin Raines: Fannie Mae," *BusinessWeek*, January 10, 2005, http:// www.businessweek.com/magazine/content/05_02/b3915646.htm.

25. Associated Press, "Ex-Fannie Mae Chief Ends Pay Dispute," *New York Times*, November 15, 2006, http://www.nytimes.com/2006/11/15/business/ 15fannie.html.

26. Associated Press, "Scandal to Cost Ex–Fannie Mae Officers Millions," *New York Times*, April 19, 2008, http://www.nytimes.com/2008/04/19/ business/19fannie.html?_r=2.

27. Anita Huslin, "On the Outside Now, Watching Fannie Falter," *Washington Post*, July 16, 2008, http://www.washingtonpost.com/wp-dyn/con tent/article/2008/07/15/AR2008071502827.html.

28. Byron York, "Is He or Isn't He?," "The Corner" blog, NationalReview .com, September 18, 2008, http://corner.nationalreview.com/post/?q=ND Y5MGQ1MWMwMjQzM2E5ODI0NzNiZmUyZDVkNGVkYTY=.

29. "McCain Charges Obama with Taking Advice from Raines," "The Trail" blog, *Washington Post*, September 19, 2008, http://voices.washington post.com/44/2008/09/19/_the_ad_obama_has.html.

30. "Written Testimony of Roger Barnes, former Manager of Financial Accounting, Deferred Assets in Fannie Mae's Controller Division," for the U.S. House of Representatives Committee on Financial Services, Subcommittee on Capital Markets, Insurance, and Government Sponsored Enterprises Hearings on "The OHFEO Report: Allegations of Accounting and Management Failure at Fannie Mae," October 6, 2004, http://financial services.house.gov/media/pdf/100604rb.pdf.

31. "The OFHEO Report: Allegations of Accounting and Management Failure at Fannie Mae," U.S. House of Representatives, Committee on Financial Services, Subcommittee on Capital Markets, Insurance, and

Government Sponsored Enterprises, Washington, D.C., October 6, 2004, http://commdocs.house.gov/committees/bank/hba97754.000/hba97754 _0f.htm.

32. Jayne O'Donnell, "Fannie Mae whistle-blower feels vindicated by SEC decision," *USA Today,* January 16, 2004, http://www.usatoday.com/ money/2004-12-16-barnes-cov_x.htm.

33. Glenn R. Simpson and James R. Hagerty, "Countrywide Friends Got Good Loans," *Wall Street Journal,* June 7, 2008, http://online.wsj.com/ article/SB121279970984353933.html.

34. Kathleen Day and Terence O'Hara, "False Signatures Aided Fannie Mae Bonuses, Falcon Says," *Washington Post,* April 7, 2005, http://www .washingtonpost.com/wp-dyn/articles/A32845-2005Apr6.html. Gorelick was never charged with, nor did she admit, wrongdoing in the matter.

35. Andrew C. McCarthy, "The Wall Truth," *National Review,* April 19, 2004, http://www.nationalreview.com/mccarthy/mccarthy2004041906 49.aso.

36. Bruno Waterfield, "European bank bail-out could push EU into a crisis," *Daily Telegraph,* February 11, 2009, http://www.telegraph.co.uk/finance/ financetopics/financialcrisis/4590512/European-banks-may-need-16.3- trillion-bail-out-EC-document-warns.html.

37. "Re: It's Official: The Crash of the U.S. Economy has begun," posted by "Mago," on RTVSLO.si, February 11, 2009, http://www.rtvslo.si/modload .php?&c_mod=forum&op=viewtopic&topic_id=23644&forum=122& post_id=1550163.

38. Edward Schatz, "Jim Cramer Responds to White House Criticism," Business & Media Institute, March 6, 2009, http://www.businessandmedia .org/articles/2009/20090306151603.aspx.

39. Ruth Simon, "Loan Delinquencies Rear Their Ugly Head Again," *Wall Street Journal*, September 20, 2008, http://online.wsj.com/articleSB 122186669697058789.html.

Chapter 3: Still Dependent on Foreign Oil

1. Julian Simon, *Hoodwinking the Nation* (New Brunswick, N.J.: Transaction, 1999), p. 1.

2. U.S. Department of Energy, Energy Information Administration, http:// www.eia.doe.gov/basics/quickoil.html.

3. "Crude Oil and Total Petroleum Imports Top 15 Countries," U.S. Department of Energy, Energy Information Administration, http://www .eia.doe.gov/pub/oil_gas/petroleum/data_publications/company_level_ imports/current/import.html.

4. "Short-Term Energy Outlook," U.S. Department of Energy, Energy Information Administration, http://www.eia.doe.gov/steo.

5. Emily Thornton, "The New Kings of Wall Street," *BusinessWeek*, January 10, 2008, http://images.businessweek.com/ss/08/01/0110_oil_wealth/ index_01.htm.

6. Michael F. Martin, "China's Sovereign Wealth Fund," Congressional Re-

search Service, January 22, 2008, Order Code RL34337, www.fas.org/sgp/crs/row/RL34337.pdf.

7.   Eric Dash and Andrew Ross Sorkin, "Citigroup Sells Abu Dhabi," *New York Times*, November 27, 2007, http://www.nytimes.com/2007/11/27/business/27citi.html?ref=business.

8.   Robin Sidel, "Abu Dhabi to Bolster Citigroup With $7.5 Billion Capital Infusion," *Wall Street Journal*, November 27, 2007, http://online.wsj.com/article/SB119613039399104832.html?mod=hps_us_whats_news.

9.   "The World's Billionaires: #13 Prince Alwaleed Bin Talal Alsaud," Forbes.com, March 8, 2007, http://www.forbes.com/lists/2007/10/07billionaires_Prince-Alwaleed=Bin-Talal-Alsaud_0RD0.html.

10. David Ellis, "Citi dodges bullet," CNNMoney.com, November 24, 2008, http://money.cnn.com/2008/11/23/news/companies/citigroup/index.htm.

11. Jack Healy and Chris Nicholson, "Bank Worries Send Stock Markets Falling," *New York Times*, February 20, 2009, http://www.nytimes.com/2009/02/21/business/economy/21markets.html?ref=business.

12. Stephen Labaton and Julia Werdigier, "Mild Reaction in Capitol to a Dubai Nasdaq Stake," *New York Times*, September 21, 2007, http://www.nytimes.com/2007/09/21/business/worldbusiness/21exchange.html?partner=rssnyt&emc=rss.

13. Chip Cummins, "Abu Dhabi Sets Investment Code," *Wall Street Journal*, March 18, 2008, http://online.wsj.com/article/SB120578487346142857.html

14. For a more comprehensive discussion of peak oil theories and the controversy between the biological origin of oil theories and abiotic oil theories, see Jerome R. Corsi and Craig R. Smith, *Black Gold Stranglehold: The Myth of Scarcity and the Politics of Oil* (Nashville, Tenn.: WND Books, 2005).

15. "International Petroleum (Oil) Reserves and Resources," Energy Information Administration, U.S. Department of Energy, http://www.eia.doe.gov/emeu/international/oilreserves.html.

16. "Petroleum: U.S. Data: Weekly Imports & Exports," U.S. Department of Energy, Energy Information Administration, http://tonto.eia.doe.gov/dnav/pet/pet_move_wkly_dc_NUS-Z00_mbblpd_w.htm.

17. "Country Energy Profiles," Energy Information Administration, U.S. Department of Energy, http://tonto.eia.doe.gov/country/index.cfm.

18. Ken Zweibel, James Mason, and Vasilis Fthenakis, "A Solar Grand Plan," *Scientific American*, December 2007, http://www.sciam.com/article.cfm?id=a-solar-grand-plan.

19. "Wind Energy Could Produce 20 Percent of U.S. Electricity by 2030," U.S. Department of Energy, May 12, 2008, http://www.energy.gov/news/6253.htm.

20. Matthew L. Wald, "Wind Energy Bumps Into Power Grid," *New York Times*, August 28, 2008, http://www.nytimes.com/2008/08/27/business/27grid.html.

21. Keith Stelling, "Calculating the Real Cost of Industrial Wind Power: An Information Update for Ontario Electricity Customers," Friends of Arran Lake Wind Action Group, Bruce County, Ontario, Canada, November 2007, http://www.wind-watch.org/documents/calculating-the-real-cost-of -industrial-wind-power/.

22. Reported in Susan S. Lang, "Cornell ecologist's study finds that producing ethanol and biodiesel from corn and other crops is not worth the energy," Cornell University News Service, July 5, 2005, http://www.news .cornell.edu/stories/July05/ethanol.toocostly.ssl.html.

23. "T. Boone Pickens takes to the skies," *Economist,* July 17, 2008, http:// www.economist.com/world/unitedstates/displaystory.cfm?story_id=1175 0614.

24. "Pickens Plan," PickensPlan.com, http://www.pickensplan.com/media/?b cpid=1640183817&bclid=1641831862&bctid=1651750502.

25. "T. Boone Pickens takes to the skies," *Economist.*

26. Associated Press, "Pickens orders $2 billion in wind turbines," MSNBC, May 15, 2008, http://www.msnbc.msn.com/id/24654895.

27. The Heartland Institute, http://www.heartland.org/.

28. S. Fred Singer, "Nature, Not Human Activity, Rules the Climate," Nongovernmental International Panel on Climate Change, Heartland Institute, March 2, 2008, http://www.heartland.org/policybot/results/22835 /Nature_Not_Human_Activity_Rules_the_Climate_pdf.html.

29. Intergovernmental Panel on Climate Change (IPCC), http://www.ipcc.ch/.

30. "Climate Change 2007, Synthesis Report," IPCC Fourth Assessment Report, Intergovernmental Panel on Climate Change, http://www.ipcc.ch/ ipccreports/ar4-syr.htm.

31. "Obama's $300 billion-a-year climate-change plan," World Net Daily, February 22, 2009, http://www.worldnetdaily.com/index.php?fa=PAGE .view&pageId=89729.

32. For a discussion of "cap-and-trade" by a proponent of the system, see Center for American Progress, "Cap and Trade 101," January 16, 2008, http://www.americanprogress.org/issues/2008/01/capandtrade101.html.

33. Statement of Peter R. Orszag, Director of the Office of Management and Budget, before the Committee on Finance, U.S. Senate, "Implications of a Cap-and-Trade Program for Carbon Dioxide Emissions," April 24, 2008, http://www.cbo.gov/ftpdocs/91xx/doc9134/04-24-Cap_Trade_Testimony .1.1.shtml.

34. "Who Pays for Cap and Trade," *Wall Street Journal, Opinion Journal,* March 9, 2009, http://online.wsj.com/article/SB123655590609066021 .html.

35. Tom LoBianco, "Obama climate plan could cost $2 trillion," *Washington Times,* March 18, 2009, http://www.washingtontimes.com/news/2009 mar/18/obama-climate-plan-could-cost-2-trillion/.

36. Julian Simon, "Will We Run Out of Oil? Never!," *Ultimate Resource 2* (Princeton, N.J.: Princeton University Press, 1996), pp. 162–81, at p. 165.

37. Paul and Anne Ehrlich, *The End of Affluence: A Blueprint for Your Future* (New York: Ballantine, 1974).

38. W. Stanley Jevons, *The Coal Question: An Inquiry Concerning the Progress of the Nation, and the Probable Exhaustion of our Coal-mines* (London: Macmillan, Limited, 1865), http://books.google.com/books?id=c UgPAAAAIAAJ&dq=stanley+jevons+%2B+the+coal+question&printsec =frontcover&source=bl&ots=FR5jis89QJ&sig=ObEbEGRBqAs0YrGR Qnu_ekOkvOw&hl=en&ei=1YShSZD6PIT6MqvviM8L&sa=X&oi= book_result&resnum=1&ct=result#PPR6,M1.

39. Simon, "Will We Run Out of Oil? Never!," p. 165.

40. Ibid., p. 177.

41. "Power struggle," *Economist*, December 4, 2008, http://www.econo mist.com/business/displaystory.cfm?story_id=12724850.

42. H. Stewart Edgell, "Basement tectonics of Saudi Arabia as related to oil field structures," in M. J. Rickard et al., eds., *Basement Tectonics 9, Proceedings of the Ninth International Basement Tectonics Symposium* (Dordrecht, Netherlands: Kluwer, 1992), pp. 163–93, http://pagesperso -orange.fr/brcgranier/gmeop/Edgell_1992.htm.

43. Giora Proskurowski, Marvin D. Lilley, Jeffery S. Seewald, Gretchen L. Früh-Green, Eric J. Olson, John E. Lupton, Sean P. Sylva, Deborah S. Kelley, "Abiogenic Hydrocarbon Production at Lost City Hydrothermal Field," *Science* 319, no. 5863 (February 2008): pp. 604–7, http://www .sciencemag.org/cgi/content/abstract/319/5863/604.

44. Thomas Gold, *The Deep Hot Biosphere: The Myth of Fossil Fuels* (New York: Copernicus, 1999).

45. Russell Gold, "In Gulf of Mexico, Industry Closes in on New Oil Source," *Wall Street Journal*, September 5, 2006, http://online.wsj.com/article/ SB115742365939953524.html?mod=home_whats_news_us.

46. "Mexico discovers 'huge' oil field," BBC News, March 15, 2006, http:// news.bbc.co.uk/2/hi/americas/4808466.stm.

47. "Cuba drills for oil off Florida," *Washington Post*, July 24, 2006, http:// washingtontimes.com/news/2006/jul/24/20060724-122242-7824r/.

48. Associated Press, "Offshore oil discovery could help make Brazil major petroleum exporter," *International Herald Tribune*, November 8, 2007, http://www.iht.com/articles/ap/2007/11/09/america/LA-FIN-Brazil-Oil .php.

49. "New Find Places Brazil on World's Top 10 Oil Producers List," *Brazil Magazine*, March 30, 2008, http://www.brazzilmag.com/content/view/ 9209/.

50. U.S. Department of the Interior, U.S. Geological Survey, "3 to 4.3 Billion Barrels of Technically Recoverable Oil Assessed in North Dakota and Montana's Bakken Formation—25 Times More than 1995 Estimate," April 10, 2008, http://www.usgs.gov/newsroom/article.asp?ID=1911.

51. "Technology-Based Oil and Natural Gas Plays: Shale Shock! Could There Be Billions in the Bakken?" U.S. Department of Energy, Energy Informa-

tion Administration, Office of Oil and Gas, Reserves and Production Division, November 2006.

52. "Dorgan Says U.S. Geological Survey's Bakken Shale Study Shows Dramatic Increase in Recoverable Oil," Press Release, Office of U.S. Senator Byron Dorgan (D.—North Dakota), April 10, 2008, http://dorgan.senate.gov/newsroom/record.cfm?id=295964.

53. "'Deep Trek' and Other Drilling R&D, U.S. Department of Energy, http://fossil.energy.gov/programs/oilgas/drilling/index.html.

54. "International Natural Gas Reserves and Resources," U.S. Department of Energy, Energy Information Administration, http://www.eia.doe.govemeu/international/gasreserves.html.

55. "Short-Term Energy Outlook," U.S. Department of Energy, Energy Information Administration, February 10, 2009, http://www.eia.doe.gov/steo.

56. "Liquefied Natural Gas," U.S. Department of Energy, Fossil Energy, http://fossil.energy.gov/programs/oilgas/storage/index.html.

57. "Liquified Natural Gas," Federal Energy Regulatory Commission, http://www.ferc.gov/industries/lng.asp.

Chapter 4: Exporting Jobs While Importing an Underclass

1. Lou Dobbs, *War on the Middle Class: How the Government, Big Business, and Special Interest Groups Are Waging War on the American Dream and How to Fight Back* (New York: Viking, 2006), p. 3.

2. Jim Gilchrist and Jerome R. Corsi, *Minutemen: The Battle to Secure America's Borders* (Los Angeles: World Ahead, 2006), p. 96.

3. Wayne M. Morrison, "China and the Global Financial Crisis: Implications for the United States," Congressional Research Service, RS22984, February 9, 2009, p. 1.

4. Wayne Morrison, "U.S.-China Trade Issues," Congressional Research Service, IB91121, updated May 16, 2006.

5. "Manufacturing: All Employees: Seasonally Adjusted: Employment, Hours, and Earnings from the Current Employment Statistics survey," Bureau of Labor Statistics, U.S. Department of Labor, http://data.bls.gov/PDQ/servlet/SurveyOutputServlet:jsessionid=f030ec8113e0sR$3F$0A.

6. Thomas Lum and Dick K. Nanto, "China's Trade with the United States and the World," Congressional Research Service, March 14, 2006.

7. Edward Wong, "Factories Shut, China Workers Are Suffering," *New York Times*, November 13, 2008, http://www.nytimes.com/2008/11/14/world/asia/14china.html.

8. Associated Press, "China's toy factory closing down: Causing insecure job security," *International Business Times*, October 20, 2008, http://www.ibtimes.co.in/articles/20081020/toy-factory-protest-global-slowdown-manufacturer.htm.

9. Don Lee, "China's bosses are abandoning ship," *Los Angeles Times*, November 3, 2008, http://articles.latimes.com/2008/nov/03/business/fi-factory3.

10. Senator Charles E. Schumer, "Senators Announce Bipartisan Effort to Force China to Stop Currency Manipulation," Press Release, September 9, 2003, http://schumer.senate.gov/SchumerWebsite/pressroom/press _releases/PR01993.html.

11. Senator Charles E. Schumer, "Schumer Details Plan to Get Tough on China in Wake of Mounting Manufacturing Job Losses," Press Release, October 20, 2003, http://schumer.senate.gov/SchumerWebsite/press room/press_releases/PR02116.html.

12. Nina Easton, "U.S. delegation's tiny China victories," *Fortune*, December 15, 2006, http://money.cnn.com/2006/12/15/news/international/easton _china3.fortune/index.html.

13. Heather Scoffield, " 'There will be blood': Harvard economic historian Niall Ferguson predicts prolonged financial hardship, even civil war, before the 'Great Recession' ends," *Globe and Mail*, February 23, 2009, http://www.globeinvestor.com/servlet/story/RTGAM.20090223.wfergu son0223/GIStory/.

14. Niall Ferguson, *The Ascent of Money: A Financial History of the World* (New York: Penguin, 2008), pp. 335–36.

15. Ibid., p. 337.

16. Jonathan Manthorpe, "Washington-Beijing economic ties are a top priority," *Vancouver Sun,* February 25, 2009, http://www.vancouversun .com/business/fp/Washington+Beijing+economic+ties+priority/1326514/ story.html.

17. Pankaj Mishra, "JPMorgan Chase to Increase India Outsourcing 25%," *Economic Times of India*, reprinted by *BusinessWeek*, March 9, 2009, http://www.businessweek.com/globalbiz/content/mar2009/gb2009039 _431274.htm?chan=top+news_top+news+index+-+temp_global+business.

18. Sharon Otterman, "TRADE: Outsourcing Jobs," Council on Foreign Relations, February 20, 2004, http://www.cfr.org/publication/7749/trade .html.

19. "Shaking Up Trade Theory," *BusinessWeek*, December 6, 2004, http:// www.businessweek.com/magazine/content/04_49/b3911408.htm.

20. Ibid.

21. "UC Berkeley study assesses potential impact of 'second wave' of outsourcing jobs from U.S.," University of California Berkeley, Haas School of Business, Press Release, October 29, 2003, http://www.haas.berke ley.edu/news/20031029_outsourcing.html.

22. Paul A. Samuelson, "Where Ricardo and Mill Rebut and Confirm Arguments of Mainstream Economists Supporting Globalism," *Journal of Economic Perspectives* 18, no. 3 (Summer 2004): pp. 135–46, at p. 135.

23. Declan McCullagh, "Gates wants to scrap H-1B Visa Restrictions," ZDNet.com, April 27, 2005, http://news.zdnet.com/2100-3513_22-142 533.html.

24. Stephen Foley, "Harvard drop-out to billionaire: Gates to retire from Microsoft," *Independent,* World Edition, June 16, 2006, http://www

.independent.co.uk/news/world/americas/harvard-dropout-to-billionaire
-gates-to-retire-from-microsoft-404266.html.

25. Moira Herbst, "Are H-1B Workers Getting Bilked?" *BusinessWeek*, January 31, 2008, http://www.businessweek.com/magazine/content/08_06b4
070057782750.htm.

26. Jeffrey S. Passel, Senior Research Associate, Pew Hispanic Center, "The Size and Characteristics of the Unauthorized Migrant Population in the U.S.: Estimates Based on the March 2005 Current Population Survey," Research Report, March 7, 2006, p. 9, http://pewhispanic.org/reports/
report.php?ReportID=61.

27. Steven A. Camarota, Director of Research, Center for Immigration Studies, "Dropping Out: Immigrant Entry and Native Exit From the Labor Market, 2000–2005," March 2006, Table 5, p. 12, http://www.cis.org/
articles/2006/back206.html.

28. Ibid., p. 13.

29. Ibid., p. 12.

30. Ibid., p. 15. Table D, pp. 25–33, presents detailed calculations of the immigrant share versus native-born share in 473 job categories.

31. Ibid., p. 6.

32. Ibid., p. 21.

33. David Hammer, "Mexican Consulate opens Monday," *Times-Picayune,* April 18, 2008, http://www.nola.com/news/index.ssf/2008/04/mexi
can_consulate_opens_monday.html.

34. Michael Cust and Alexander Moens, "Saving the North American Security and Prosperity Partnership: The Case for a North American Standards and Regulatory Area," Fraser Institute, March 18, 2008, http://www
.fraserinstitute.org/researchandpublications/publications/5244.aspx.

35. Suzanne Gamboa, "Administration to reinvent Mexican truck program," Associated Press, March 11, 2009, http://www.breitbart.com/article.php?
id=D96S48SO3&show_article=1.

36. Ibid.

37. Jerome R. Corsi, "Hundreds of safety violations documented for Mexican rigs," World Net Daily, December 5, 2007, http://www.worldnetdaily
.com/news/article.asp?ARTICLE_ID=59044.

38. Jerome R. Corsi, "Mexican truck drivers take English exam in *Spanish,*" World Net Daily, March 14, 2008, http://www.wnd.com/index.php/index
.php?pageId=58843.

39. Jerome R. Corsi, "Mexican rigs hitting U.S. pavement today," World Net Daily, September 7, 2007, http://www.worldnetdaily.com/news/article.asp?
ARTICLE_ID=57520.

40. Alison Sider, "Economics professor Austan Goolsbee appointed to two Obama committees," *Chicago Maroon,* February 12, 2009, http://
www.chicagomaroon.com/2008/12/2/economics-professor-austan-gools
bee-appointed-to-two-obama-committees.

41. Ewan MacAskill, "Obama raises Nafta renegotiation during first official

visit to Canada," *Guardian*, February 12, 2009, http://www.guardian .co.uk/world/2009/feb/19/barack-obama-stephen-harper-canada-visit.

42. North American Center for Transborder Studies, "North America Next: A Report to President Obama on Building Sustainable Security and Competitiveness," Arizona State University, released at the National Press Club, Washington, D.C., February 10, 2009, http://nacts.asu.edu/ Home. See also North American Center for Transborder Studies, "Press Release: Obama Administration Urged to 'Seize North American Opportunities' on Security and Competitiveness," Arizona State University, released in Washington, D.C., on February 10, 2009.

43. Foreign Trade Statistics, U.S. Census Bureau, "U.S. Trade in Goods (Imports, Exports and Balance) by Country," http://www.census.gov/ foreign-trade/balance/index.html.

44. Elana Schor, "China rejects U.S. textile protection," *Market Watch*, April 5, 2005, http://www.marketwatch.com/News/Story/Story.aspx?guid= {9CB9C807-838B-4FE1-BDBA-11D47969F7F9}&siteid=google&dist= google.

45. David Wessel and Bob Davis, "Pain From Free Trade Spurs Second Thoughts," *Wall Street Journal*, March 28, 2007, http://online.wsj.com/ article/SB117500805386350446.html?mod=todays_us_page_one.

46. Joseph R. Meisenheimer II, "The services industry in the 'good' versus 'bad' jobs dispute," *Monthly Labor Review* 121, no. 2 (February 1998), http://www.bls.gov/opub/mlr/1998/02/art3exc.htm.

47. 1968–2006 Annual Social and Economic Supplement, Current Population Survey (CPS), Bureau of Labor Statistics, U.S. Department of Labor.

48. David K. Shipler, *The Working Poor: Invisible in America* (New York: Knopf, 2004), p. 3.

49. Daniel E. Hecker, "Occupational employment projections to 2014," *Monthly Labor Review Online* 128, no. 11 (November 2005), http:// www.bls.gov/opub/mlr/2005/11/contents.htm.

50. Ibid., p. 71.

51. Kelly Evans, "Jobless Rate Tops 8%, Highest in 26 Years," *Wall Street Journal*, March 7, 2009, p. 1; also, the Labor Department data on structural unemployment was presented on the next page in "Behind the Numbers, As job loses reach historic levels . . . ," *Wall Street Journal*, March 7, 2009, p. 2.

52. Kenneth F. Scheve and Matthew J. Slaughter, "A New Deal for Globalization," *Foreign Affairs* 86, no. 4 (July/August 2007): pp. 34–47, http:// www.foreignaffairs.org/20070701faessay86403/kenneth-f-scheve-matthew -j-slaughter/a-new-deal-for-globalization.html.

53. U.S. Census Bureau, "Historical Income Tables—Households," http:// www.census.gov/hhes/www/income/histinc/h02AR.html.

54. Bob Davis, John Lyons, and Andrew Batson, "Globalization's Gains Come with a Price," *Wall Street Journal*, May 24, 2007, http://online .wsj.com/article/SB117994581454912387.html.

Part II: America for Sale
Chapter 5: Meet the Globalists

1. George Soros, *The Age of Fallibility: The Consequences of the War on Terror* (New York: PublicAffairs, 2006).
2. Christopher Booker and Richard North, *The Great Deception: The Secret History of the European Union* (New York: Continuum, 2003).
3. George Soros, *On Globalization* (New York: PublicAffairs, 2002), p. 2.
4. Ibid., p. 9.
5. Soros, *The Age of Fallibility*, p. 134.
6. Ibid., p. 129.
7. Ibid., p. 135.
8. Ibid., p. 69.
9. Ibid., "Prologue," p. xv.
10. Ibid., "Prologue," p. xi.
11. Ibid., p. 83.
12. Ibid., "Prologue," p. xvi.
13. Ibid., pp. 88–89.
14. Ibid., "Prologue," p. x.
15. Peter Wilson, "George Soros interview: A very good crisis," *Australian*, March 19, 2009, http://www.theaustralian.news.com.au/business/story/0.28124.25211027-5018061.00.html.
16. Zbigniew Brzezinski, *The Choice: Global Domination or Global Leadership* (New York: Basic Books, 2004), "Preface," p. ix.
17. Ibid., p. viii.
18. Ibid., p. 2.
19. Ibid., p. 137.
20. Ibid., p. 142.
21. Ibid.
22. Ibid., p. 143.
23. Ibid., p. 149.
24. Ibid., p. 222.
25. Ibid., p. 148.
26. Zbigniew Brzezinski, *The Grand Chessboard: American Primacy and Its Geostrategic Imperatives* (New York: Basic Books, 1997), "Introduction," p. xiv.
27. Zbigniew Brzezinski, *Between Two Ages: America's Role in the Technetronic Era* (New York: Viking, 1970), p. 56.
28. Ibid., p. 72.
29. Ibid., p. 74.
30. Peter Drucker, *Post-Capitalist Society* (New York: Harper Business, 1993), p. 11.
31. Peter Drucker, "The Global Economy and the Nation-State," *Foreign Affairs*, September/October 1997, http://www.foreignaffairs.com/print/53396.
32. Kenichi Ohmae, *The Borderless World: Power and Strategy in the Interlocking Economy* (New York: Harper Business, 1991).

33. Ibid., "Introduction," p. xvi.

34. Kenichi Ohmae, *The End of the Nation State: The Rise of Regional Economies* (New York: Free Press, 1995).

35. Ibid., "Preface," p. viii. Emphasis in original.

36. Ibid.

37. Ibid., p. 16.

38. Ibid., p. 17.

39. Ibid., p. 42.

40. Kenichi Ohmae, *The Invisible Continent: Four Strategic Imperatives of the New Economy* (New York: Harper Business, 2001), p. 5.

41. Ibid., p. 129.

42. Ibid.

43. Ibid., pp. 136–39.

44. David Rockefeller, *Memoirs* (New York: Random House, 2002), pp. 404–19.

45. Ibid., p. 405.

46. Ibid.

47. Joseph E. Stiglitz, *Globalization and Its Discontents* (New York: Norton, 2002), p. 5.

48. Ibid.

49. Joseph E. Stiglitz, *Making Globalization Work* (New York: Norton, 2007), p. 15.

50. Ibid., p. 21.

51. Stiglitz, *Globalism and Its Discontents*, pp. 21–22. Emphasis in original.

52. Stiglitz, *Making Globalization Work*, p. 21 and again at p. 269.

53. Ibid., p. 278.

54. Harvey Morris, "UN panel calls for council to replace G20," *Financial Times*, March 22, 2009, http://www.ft.com/cms/s/0/b43aedf2-172a-11de-9a72-0000779fd2ac.html.

55. Brzezinski, *The Choice*, p. 134.

56. Patrick Wood, Editor, "Obama: Trilateral Commission Endgame," *August Review*, January 30, 2009, http://www.augustreview.com/index2.php?option=com_content&task=view&id=110&pop=1&page=0&Itemid=5. For a list of Trilateral Commission members, see "The Trilateral Commission," *August Review*, http://www.augustreview.com/knowledge_base/getting_started_with_globalism/trilateral_commission_membership_-_2008_20081010103/.

57. See, for instance, Daniel Estulin, *The True Story of the Bilderberg Group* (Chicago: Independent Publishers, 2007), p. 23.

58. Rockefeller, *Memoirs*, pp. 412–13.

59. Chairs John P. Manley, Pedro Aspe, and William F. Weld; and Vice Chairs Thomas P. D'Aquino, Andres Rozental, and Robert A. Pastor, "Building a North American Community," Council on Foreign Relations, http://www.cfr.org/publication/8102/building_a_north_american_community.html?breadcrumb=default.

60. David Rothdopf, *Superclass: The Global Power Elite and the World They Are Making* (New York: Farrar, Straus & Giroux, 2008).

61. Ibid., p. 279.

62. Ibid.

63. Ibid., p. 280.

64. See, for instance, Timothy Garton Ash, "Davos man's death wish," *Guardian*, February 3, 2005, http://www.guardian.co.uk/world/2005/feb/03/globalisation.comment.

65. "EU-USA—Transatlantic Economic Council," http://ec.europa.eu/enterprise/international_relations/cooperating_governments/usa/usa_tec_en.htm.

66. Clarence K. Streit, *Union Now: The Proposal for Inter-Democracy Federal Union* (New York: Harper & Brothers, 1940).

67. "About Us," Streit Council for a Union of Democracies, http://www.streitcouncil.org/content/about_us/History/About%20Us.htm.

68. EU/US Summit: December 3, 1995, Madrid, Spain, "The New Transatlantic Agenda."

69. Transatlantic Policy Network, http://www.tpnonline.org/who.html.

70. Ira Straus, "Sarkozy, Merkel Revive Atlanticism," *Freedom and Union* 2, no. 2 (Fall 2007), http://www.streitcouncil.org/content/pdf_and_doc/Journal%20SC%20Fall%202007%20Straus.pdf.

71. Representative Jim Costa, "The Roadmap to a Common Market," *Freedom and Union* 2, no. 2 (Fall 2007), http://www.streitcouncil.org/content/pdf_and_doc/Journal%20SC%20Fall%202007%20Costa.pdf.

72. Senator Bob Bennett, "Institutionalizing a Barrier-Free Transatlantic Market," *Freedom and Union* 2, no. 2 (Fall 2007), http://www.streitcouncil.org/content/pdf_and_doc/Journal%20SC%20Fall%202007%20Bennett.pdf.

73. Domenec Ruiz Devesa, "From Atlantic Market to Atlantic Polity?" *Freedom and Unity* 2, no. 2 (Fall 2007), http://www.streitcouncil.org/content/pdf_and_doc/Journal%20SC%20Fall%202007%20Devesa.pdf.

74. "Completing the Transatlantic Market," Transatlantic Policy Network, February 2007, http://www.tpnonline.org/TPN%20transatlantic%20market%20paper%20FINAL.pdf.

75. Advisory Committee on International Economic Policy, U.S. Department of State, http://www.state.gov/e/eeb/adcom/aciep/index.htm.

76. Membership of the Advisory Committee on International Economic Policy, Current Membership, January 5, 2009, http://www.state.gov/e/eeb/adcom/85129.htm.

77. Fareed Zakaria, *The Post-American World* (New York: Norton, 2008).

78. Ibid., pp. 2–3.

79. Parag Khanna, *The Second World: Empires and Influence in the New Global Order* (New York: Random House, 2008).

80. Khanna borrowed "consumption binge" from Joseph Stiglitz, "The Roaring Nineties," *Atlantic Monthly*, October 2002.

81. Ibid., p.327.

82. Ibid.
83. Ibid., p. 328.
84. Ibid., p. 333.
85. Peter F. Drucker, "The Global Economy and the Nation-State," *Foreign Affairs*, September/October 1997, http://www.foreignaffairs.com/articles/53396/peter-f-drucker/the-global-economy-and-the-nation-state.
86. Thomas L. Friedman, *The World is Flat: A Brief History of the Twenty-First Century* (New York: Farrar, Straus & Giroux, 2005), p. 10.
87. "Transcript: Obama's Speech in Berlin," *New York Times*, July 24, 2008, http://www.nytimes.com/2008/07/24/us/politics/24text-obama.html.

Chapter 6: Here Come the Cheap Chinese Goods

1. World Trade Organization Director-General Pascal Lamy, quoted in "WTO sees 9% global trade decline in 2009 as recession strikes," Press Release, World Trade Organization, March 23, 2009, http://www.wto.org/english/news_e/pres09_e/pr554_e.htm.
2. "United States Balance of Trade," Trading Economics: Global Economics Research, TradingEconomics.com, http://www.tradingeconomics.com/Economics/Balance-of-Trade.aspx?Symbol=USD.
3. "Trade in Goods (Imports, Exports and Trade Balance) with China," U.S. Census Bureau, Foreign Trade Statistics, http://www.census.gov/foreign-trade/balance/c5700.html#2004.
4. "Goods and Services Deficit Decreases in January 2009," U.S. Census Bureau, March 13, 2009, http://www.census.gov/indicator/www/ustrade.html.
5. "WTO sees 9% global trade decline in 2009 as recession strikes," Press Release, World Trade Organization, March 23, 2009.
6. "Employment Situation Summary," Bureau of Labor Statistics, U.S. Department of Labor, March 6, 2009, http://www.bls.gov/news.release/empsit.nr0.htm.
7. Andrew Goetz and Sutapa Bandyopadhyay, Department of Geography and Intermodal Transport Institute, University of Denver, "Regional Development Impacts of Trade Corridors: Recent Experiences from the United States," presented at the Regina Gateway and Corridor Round-table, February 21, 2007, http://www.gateway-corridor.com/reginaroundtable/documents/papers/Goetz-RegionalDevelopment.pdf.
8. "Falling world trade: Going under," *Economist*, March 24, 2009, http://www.economist.com/finance/displayStory.cfm?story_id=13355727&source=features_box_main.
9. "China Bets on Yangsham Port to Ease Jam, Expand Trade," Bloomberg, December 10, 2005, http://www.bloomberg.com/apps/news?pid=10000006&sid=aYmVP7PFSEUU&refer=home.
10. "Post Panamax vessels: How big can they go?" Hong Kong Trade Development Council, http://info.hktdc.com/shippers/vol24_5/vol24_5_seafr03.htm.

11. Federal Highway Administration, U.S. Department of Transportation, "Public Private Partnerships," http://www.fhwa.dot.gov/PPP/.

12. John Quiggin, "New rationale, same old problems," *Australian Financial Review*, August 8, 2005, http://www.uq.edu.au/economics/johnquiggin/news/2005-08-08-AFR.htm.

13. Canada's Asia-Pacific Gateway and Corridor Initiative, Asia-Pacific Gateway and Corridor Research Consortium, Center for Transportation Studies, University of British Columbia, http://www.gateway-corridor.com/.

14. The video can still be seen at Jerome R. Corsi, "Port sparks NAFTA super-railway challenge," World Net Daily, September 19, 2007, http://www.worldnetdaily.com/index.php?pageId=43597.

15. "National Policy Framework for Strategic Gateways and Trade Corridors," Gateway Connects—A Building Canada Initiative, Transport Canada, Government of Canada, http://www.tc.gc.ca/GatewayConnectsdocs/NationalPolicyFramework.pdf.

16. Ibid.

17. Jafar Khondakar, International Trade Division, Statistics Canada, "Canada's Trade with China: 1997 to 2007," http://www.statcan.gc.ca/pub/65-508-x/65-508-x2007001=eng.htm.

18. "Governments of Canada, Ontario and Quebec to Develop the Ontario-Quebec Continental Gateway and Trade Corridor," Press Release, Transport Canada, July 30, 2007, http://www.tc.gc.ca/mediaroom/releasesnat/2007/07-h141e.htm.

19. "Backgrounder: Memorandum of Understanding for the Development of the Ontario-Quebec Continental Gateway and Trade Corridor," Transport Canada, July 30, 2007, http://www.tc.gc.ca/mediaroom/releasesnat/2007/07-h141e.htm; nsbg.

20. "CN celebrates opening of Port of Prince Rupert container terminal," Press Release, Canadian National, September 12, 2007, http://www.cn.ca/en/media-news-20070912.htm.

21. "Canadian Pacific announces agreement to acquire DM&E railroad," Press Release, Canadian Pacific, September 4, 2007, http://www8.cpr.ca/cms/English/Media/News/General/2007/CP+announces+agreement+to+acquire+DM+and+E+Railroad.htm.

22. Scott Deveau, "CP plans to buy U.S. railway to tap Wyoming coal basin," *Vancouver Sun*, September 6, 2007, http://www2.canada.com/vancouversun/news/business/story.html?id=b5b615cb-7304-4ac9-a737-cabfdc4eb53a.

23. Resolution No. 060343, Sponsor Council Member Barnes, March 24, 2006, recorded by Kansas City Office of the City Clerk, http://cityclerk.kcmo.org/LiveWeb/Documents/Document.aspx?q=%2bSOiLiH6CV0JIMnyTK6Jav6tMSRgrBqP1uJ3dflFWX3kFlAN%2bx9mJ7AQvJb3w%2bBs.

24. "Two Worlds . . . One Route," Kansas City SmartPort, http://www.kcsmartport.com/pdf/SmtPrtOneRoute.pdf.

25. "I-35 Trade Corridor Study Begins," I-35 Trade Corridor Study, Kansas, Missouri, Newsletter, vol. 1, Winter 1998, http://publications.iowa.gov/archive/00002975/01/i35study.pdf.

26. See, for instance, Jerome R. Corsi, "Southern border blurs for global trade," World Net Daily, June 1, 2006, http://www.worldnetdaily.com/news/article.asp?ARTICLE_ID=50451.

27. "TxDOT to Change Highway Network Plan," Associated Press, January 6, 2009.

28. "Texas Corridors," on "Keep Texas Moving," website maintained by the Texas Department of Transportation, http://www.keeptexasmoving.com/index.php/texas_corridors.

29. Christopher Hayes, "The NAFTA Superhighway," *Nation*, August 9, 2007, http://www.thenation.com/doc/20070827/hayes. Also Gretel C. Kovach, "Highway to Hell?," *Newsweek*, December 10, 2007, http://www.newsweek.com/id/73372.

30. North American's SuperCorridor Coalition, Inc., http://www.nascocorridor.com/. See also Jerome R. Corsi, "Name changed to hide 'Superhighway'?," World Net Daily, September 2, 2007, http://www.worldnetdaily.com/news/article.asp?ARTICLE_ID=57444.

31. "Union Pacific Begins Construction of $90 Million State-of-the-Art Intermodal Terminal in Southwest Bexar County," Press Release, Union Pacific, August 22, 2007, http://www.uprr.com/newsinfo/releases/capital_investment/2007/0822_sanantonio.shtml.

32. Reported in Jerome R. Corsi, "San Antonio developing NAFTA inland port," World Net Daily, August 28, 2007, http://www.wnd.com/news/article.asp?ARTICLE_ID=57347.

33. "Union Pacific begins development of local rail port," *San Antonio Business Journal*, August 22, 2007, http://www.bizjournals.com/sanantonio/stories/2007/08/20/daily20.html.

34. Michael S. Bomba, Center for Transportation Research, University of Texas at Austin, "Shifting U.S.-China Maritime Logistical Patterns: The Potential Impact on U.S. Gulf Ports," August 1, 2004, http://www.trb.org/Conferences/MTS/4C%20BombaPaper.pdf#search=%22percent%20of%20Chinese%20imports%20headed%20for%20east%20coast%22.

35. Bill Geroux, "Smooth sailing ahead? Port has become economic engine but road congestion could hamper its growth," *Virginia Business*, September 2005, http://www.gatewayva.com/biz/virginiabusiness/magazine/yr2005/sep05/port.shtml.

36. "Gateway Florida: Our History," website of FTAA Florida, http://web.gatewayflorida.org/site/content/view/39/55/.

37. "Fourth Summit of the Americas, Mar del Plata, Argentina, November 4–5, 2005," Summits of the Americas Information Network, http://www.summit-americas.org/NextSummit_eng.htm.

38. Laura Carlsen, "Timely Demise for Free Trade Area of the Americas," *Upside Down World*, November 30, 2005, http://upsidedownworld.org/main/content/view/124/54/.

39. "Cargo Gateway of the Americas," Port of Miami, http://www.metro-dade.com/portofmiami/cargo.asp.

40. "Cargo Statistics," Port of Miami, http://www.metro-dade.com/portofmiami/stats_25_countries.asp.

41. Marla Dickerson and Ronald D. White, "Mexico plans big splash with new Baja Port," *Los Angeles Times*, March 25, 2008, http://articles.latimes.com/2008/mar/25/business/fi-mexport25.

42. Diane Lindquist, "Plans being drawn up, Baja governor says," *San Diego Union Tribune,* March 7, 2007, http://www.signonsandiego.com/news/mexico/tijuana/20070307-9999-1b7colonet.html.

43. CANAMEX Corridor Coalition, http://www.canamex.org/.

44. Hutchison Ports Holdings, http://www.hph.com.hk/webpg.aspx?id=87.

45. Hutchison Whampoa Limited, http://www.hutchison-whampoa.com/eng/about/overview.htm.

46. "Complaint Requesting an Investigation of Hutchison Whampoa, Ltd.'s Actions to Gain Controlling Interest in Global Crossing Ltd., and Former Defense Secretary William S. Cohen's Activities as A Director of Global Crossing, Ltd," Judicial Watch, February 27, 2002, http://www.judicialwatch.org/cases/85/globalwhampoa.htm.

47. Ibid.

48. See "Nathan M. Hansen's Blog," http://www.nathanmhansen.blogspot.com/.

49. "Non-Binding Letter of Intent," dated February 19, 2007, between Savi Networks, LLC and North America's SuperCorridor Coalition, http://www.hansenlawoffice.com/nasco/NASCODocumentsPart10.pdf.

50. Mary Louise Kelly, "China's Military Threat In Focus After Naval Incident," National Public Radio, *Morning Edition,* March 26, 2009, http://www.npr.org/templates/story/story.php?storyId=102371127.

51. Jonathan Medalia, "Terrorist Nuclear Attacks on Seaports: Threats and Response," Congressional Research Service, January 24, 2005.

52. Leonard Gilroy, Robert Poole, Peter Samuel and Geoffrey Segal, "Building New Roads Through Public-Private Partnerships: Frequently Asked Questions," Reason Foundation, March 1, 2007, http://www.reason.org/news/show/1002866.html.

53. Daniel Schulman and James Ridgeway, "The Highwaymen," *Mother Jones*, January/February 2007, http://www.motherjones.com/politics/2007/01/highwaymen.

54. "U.S. Trade Balance as a Percentage of GDP," Data360.org, http://www.data360.org/dsg.aspx?Data_Set_Group_Id=270.

55. "Sink or swim," *Economist*, March 27, 2009, http://www.economist.com/business/displaystory.cfm?story_id=13381514.

56. See, for instance, William M. Welch, "Illegal immigrants might still get stimulus jobs, experts say," *USA Today,* March 10, 2009, http://www.usatoday.com/money/economy/employment/2009-03-08-immigrant-jobs_N.htm.

Chapter 7: The Plan to Destroy the Dollar

1. Benn Steil, "The End of National Currency," *Foreign Affairs*, May/June 2007, http://www.foreignaffairs.com/articles/62614/benn-steil/the-end-of-national-currency.

2. Peter B. Kenen and Ellen E. Meade, *Regional Monetary Integration* (New York: Cambridge University Press, 2008), p. 41.

3. See, for instance, "World Currency," The Works of Robert A. Mundell, at http://www.robertmundell.net/Menu/Main.asp?Type=5&Cat=09&ThemeName=World%20Currency.

4. Robert Mundell, "What the Euro Means for the Dollar and the International Monetary System," U.S.A. Distinguished Address, presented at the Forty-Fifth International Atlantic Economic Conference, Rome, Italy, March 14–21, 1998, published in *Atlantic Economic Journal* 26, no. 3 (September 1998): pp. 227–37, http://www.springerlink.com/content/67 15561141781038/.

5. Ibid., p. 232.

6. Ibid.

7. Steil, "The End of National Currency."

8. Herbert G. Grubel, "The Case for the Amero: The Economics and Politics of a North American Monetary Union," Simon Fraser Institute, Vancouver, British Columbia, Canada, 1999, http://oldfraser.lexi.net/publications/critical_issues/1999/amero/

9. Ibid., "Executive Summary," http://oldfraser.lexi.net/publications/critical_issues/1999/amero/section_02.html

10. Ibid., "The Institutions of a North American Monetary Union," http://oldfraser.lexi.net/publications/critical_issues/1999/amero/section_03.html

11. Ibid., "Efficiency Gains from Monetary Union," http://oldfraser.lexi.net/publications/critical_issues/1999/amero/section_05.html

12. Ibid., "What is in it for the Americans?," http://oldfraser.lexi.net/publications/critical_issues/1999/amero/section_07.html

13. Herbert Grubel, "Fix the Loonie," *National Post*, January 31, 2008. The article is no longer posted on the newspaper's website, although it is referred to here: Drew Hasselback, "Exchange-rate debate: Herbert Grubel," *Financial Post*, January 31, 2008, http://network.nationalpost.com/np/blogs/fpcomment/archive/2008/01/31/exchange-rate-debate-herbert-grubel.aspx.

14. Jane Lewis, "Stephen Jarislowsky—the Canadian Warren Buffett," *Money Week*, December 12, 2005, http://www.moneyweek.com/investment-advice/how-to-invest/stephen-jarislowsky—the-canadian-warren-buffett.aspx.

15. Steven Chase, "Consider a continental currency, Jarislowsky says," *Globe and Mail*, November 23, 2007, http://www.theglobeandmail.com/servlet/story/LAC.20071123.RDOLLAR23/TPStory/?query=%22Steven+Chase%22.

16. Duncan Hood, "Invest like the ultra-rich: a Q&A with Stephen Jaris-

lowsky, *Canadian Business OnLine*, November 2005, http://www
.canadianbusiness.com/my_money/investing/article.jsp?content=2005112
8_111228_4548, reprinting an article from *MoneySense* magazine, November 2005.

17. "#512 Stephen Jarislowsky," Forbes.com, 2006, http://www.forbes
.com/lists/2006/10/CMUH.html.

18. Stephen A. Jarislowsky, *The Investment Zoo: Taming the Bulls and the
Bears* (Montreal: Transcontinental, 2005).

19. Jarislowsky Fraser Limited Investment Counsel, http://www.jfl.ca/Contact
.html.

20. Jerome R. Corsi, "Economist longs for creation of amero," World Net
Daily, January 24, 2008, http://www.wnd.com/news/article.asp?
ARTICLE_ID=59832.

21. Drake Bennett, "The amero conspiracy," *Boston Globe*, November 25,
2007, http://www.boston.com/bostonglobe/ideas/articles/2007/11/25the_
amero_conspiracy/.

22. Vicente Fox, *Revolution of Hope: The Life, Faith, and Dreams of a Mexican President* (New York: Viking, 2007).

23. "Interview with Vicente Fox," Transcript, *Larry King Live*, aired October 8, 2007, http://transcripts.cnn.com/TRANSCRIPTS/0710/08/lk1.01
.html.

24. Elaine Ayala, "Mexico's Fox touts EU-like integration for the Americas,"
March 28, 2009, http://www.mysanantonio.com/news/Mexicos_Fox
_touts_EU-like_integration_for_the_Americas.html#.

25. "Nobel-prize winner backs world currency," *Australian*, March 11, 2009,
http://www.theaustralian.news.com.au/story/0.25197.25173126-12377
.00.html, reporting an article originally published by Agence France-
Presse.

26. See "Mundell: China should keep currency peg," *China Daily*, June 3,
2005, http://www.chinadaily.net/english/doc/2005-06/03/content_448457
.htm; Profile, "Robert A. Mundell," Forbes.com, http://people.forbes
.com/profile/robert-a-mundell/25100; "Mundell: China Should Keep
Currency Peg," Beijing official website, September 7, 2006, http://www
.ebeijing.gov.cn/feature_2/Nobel_Prize_Forum/News_Events/t920737
.htm; "People in Economics: Ahead of His time," International Monetary
Fund, September 2006, http://www.imf.org/external/pubs/ft/fandd/2006/
09/people.htm.

27. Ira Iosebashvili, *Moscow Times*, March 17, 2007, http://www.the
moscowtimes.com/article/600/42/375364.htm.

28. "China's plan to end the dollar era," *Financial Times*, March 24, 2009,
http://www.ft.com/cms/s/0/26884cle-18ab-11de-bec8-0000779fd2ac
.html?nclick_check=1.

29. Patrice Hill, "Geithner gaffe roils markets," *Washington Times*, March
26, 2009, http://www.washingtontimes.com/news/2009/mar/26/geithner
-gaffe-on-dollar-roils-stock-bond-markets/.

30. Ibid.

31. Joe Murray, "China Coup: Dollar Marked for Extinction," *Bulletin*, March 27, 2009, http://thebulletin.us/articles/2009/03/27/business/doc 49cc5ee8b71ef627774698.txt.

32. Alex Davidson, "Strauss-Kahn backs the greenback, but says he understands China's position," Forbes.com, March 27, 2009, http://www .forbes.com/2009/03/27/imf-dollar-china-markets-economy-dollar.html.

33. Jason Webb, "Dollar crisis looms, China ponders reform: Mundell," Reuters, June 3, 2008, http://www.reuters.com/article/reutersEdge/idUSL 0221460620080603.

34. Harvey Morris, "UN hears calls to end dollar's reserve status," *Financial Times*, March 27, 2009, http://www.ft.com/cms/s/0/a8abd170-1a6f -11de-9f91=0000779fd2ac.html.

35. Federal Reserve Bank of New York, Press Release, "New York Fed Issues Tentative Operation Schedule, FAQs for Treasury Purchases, Updated FAQs for Agency Debt and Agency MBS Purchases," March 24, 2009, http://www.newyorkfed.org/newsevents/news/markets/2009/ma090324 .html.

36. John Williams, "Fed's Effort at Dollar Debasement Had Some Immediate 'Success,' " ShadowStats.gov, Newsletter Alert, March 23, 2009, http:// www.shadowstats.com/article/alert-14.

37. Kim-Mai Cutler, "U.K. Bond Auction Fails for First Time Since 2002," Bloomberg, March 25, 2009, http://www.bloomberg.com/apps/news ?pid=20601087&sid=aQGG.mWeZ4eU&refer=worldwide.

38. Deborah Solomon, "Geithner Banks on Private Cash," *Wall Street Journal*, March 23, 2009, http://online.wsj.com/article/SB1237764744316 08981.html.

39. "Abu Dhabi Firm Buys 9.1% of Daimler," *Wall Street Journal,* March 23, 2009, http://online.wsj.com/article/SB123776367498808703.html.

40. Jeffrey McCracken and Tamara Audi, "Las Vegas Property Venture Is in Peril," *Wall Street Journal*, March 24, 2009, http://online.wsj.com/ar ticle/SB123783663634216785.html.

41. Simeon Kerr and Roula Khalaf, "Dubai outlines plan to escape doldrums," *Financial Times*, March 29, 2009, http://www.ft.com/cms/s/0/ fa8229c6-1c7d-11de-977c-00144feabdc0.html.

42. "Discontinuation of New Investment Series," contained in the press release titled "Foreign Direct Investors' Outlays to Acquire or Establish U.S. Businesses Increased in 2007," Bureau of Economic Analysis, U.S. Department of Commerce, June 4, 2008, http://www.bea.gov/news releases/international/fdi/2008/fdi07.htm.

43. Yu Qiao, "How Asia can protect itself from a dollar default," *Financial Times,* April 1, 2009, http://www.ft.com/cms/s/0/18f4530c-1e54-11de -830b-00144feabdc0.html.

Part III: Fighting the New World Order, Surviving a Global Depression, and Preserving U.S.A. Sovereignty

1. "Reserve Board Finds Action Unnecessary," *New York Times*, October 30, 1929, http://www.nytimes.com/library/financial/103029crash-fed.html.

2. "China sells 790,000 vehicles in January," China View, XinhuaNet.com, February 5, 2009, http://news.xinhuanet.com/english/2009-02/05/content_10769550.htm.

3. "2009 U.S. Vehicles Sales Fall to 10.7 Million Units, Polk Forecasts," Edmunds Auto Observer, February 10, 2009, http://www.autoobserver.com/2009/02/2009-u-s-vehicle-sales-fall-to-107-million-units-polk-forecasts.html.

4. Laurie Whalen, "More new-car dealers to close," *Arkansas Democrat Gazette,* January 4, 2009, http://www.nwanews.com/adg/Business/248548/.

Chapter 8: Say "No!" to the Global New Deal

1. "Brown: World needs 'global New Deal,' " CNN.com, February 22, 2009, http://edition.cnn.com/2009/WORLD/europe/02/22/germany.financial.summit/index.html.

2. "Leaders Statement: The Global Plan for Recovery and Reform," G20, London, April 2, 2009, Publications: Communiqués, http://www.g20.org/pub_communiques.aspx.

3. Ambrose Evans-Pritchard, "The G20 moves the world a step closer to a global currency," *Daily Telegraph,* April 7, 2009, http://www.telegraph.co.uk/finance/comment/ambroseevans_pritchard/5096524/The-G20-moves-the-world-a-step-closer-to-a-global-currency.html.

4. Ron Paul, *The Revolution: A Manifesto* (New York: Grand Central, 2008), p. 98.

5. Frank Gaffney, "Lawfare and Obama's Transnationalist," March 30, 2009, http://townhall.com/columnists/FrankGaffney/2009/03/30/lawfare_and_obamas_transnationalist?page=full&comments=true.

Chapter 9: Strategies for Middle-Class Survival in Economic Hard Times

1. Paul Krugman, *The Return of Depression Economics and the Crisis of 2008* (New York: Norton, 2008), p. 181.

2. "Grandparents Day 2007: Sept. 9," U.S. Census Bureau, Press Release, July 9, 2007, http://www.census.gov/Press-Release/www/releases/archives/facts_for_features_special_editions/010321.html. See generally, U.S. Census Bureau, American Community Survey (ACS), http://www.census.gov/acs/www/.

3. "Children in Single-Parent Households and Stepfamilies Benefit Most Socially From Time With Grandparents," American Psychological Association, Press Release, February 23, 2009, http://www.apa.org/releases/grandparents.html.

4. Tom Leonard, "Struggling US towns print their own currency," *Daily Telegraph*, April 8, 2009, http://www.telegraph.co.uk/news/worldnews/northamerica/usa/5126185/Struggling-US-towns-print-their-own-currency.html.

5. "What are BerkShares?" BerkShares, Inc., http://www.berkshares.org/whatareberkshares.htm.

6. Emily Lambert, "Funny Money," Forbes.com, February 14, 2006, http://www.forbes.com/2006/02/11/local-currencies-ithaca_cz_el_money06_0214local.html.

7. "The Story of Bay Bucks: Printing Money, Making Change," http://www.baybucks.org/about/?id=39.

8. See, for instance, Greg Spotts, *Wal-Mart: The High Cost of Low Price* (New York: Disinformation Company, 2005).

9. "What are Ithaca Hours?," http://www.ithacahours.org/.

10. "Local Currencies," E. F. Schumacher Society, http://www.smallisbeautiful.org/local_currencies.html.

11. See, for instance, Swiss America Trading Corporation, http://www.swissamerica.com/. Craig R. Smith, founder and chief executive of Swiss America, is coauthor, with Jerome Corsi, of *Black Gold Stranglehold: The Myth of Scarcity and the Politics of Oil* (Nashville, Tenn.: WND, 2005).

Chapter 10: The Rise of Twenty-First-Century American Patriots

1. Jim Gilchrist and Jerome R. Corsi, *Minutemen: The Battle to Secure America's Borders* (Los Angeles: WND, 2006).

2. National Security and Homeland Security Presidential Directive, NSPD-51, HSPD-20, White House Press Release, May 9, 2007, http://www.fas.org/irp/offdocs/nspd/nspd-51.htm.

3. U.S. Code, Section 1621, "Declaration of national emergency by President; publication in Federal Register; effect on other laws; superseding legislation," Cornell University Law School, http://www.law.cornell.edu/uscode/50/usc_sec_50_00001621—-000-.html.

4. Harold C. Relyea, "National Emergency Powers," Congressional Research Service, updated August 30, 2007, http://www.fas.org/sgp/crs/natsec/98-505.pdf.

5. Jerome R. Corsi, "Lawmakers in 20 states move to reclaim sovereignty," World Net Daily, February 6, 2009, http://www.worldnetdaily.com/index.php?fa=PAGE.view&pageId=88218.

6. Leslie Eaton, "More States Look to Raise Taxes," *Wall Street Journal*, April 9, 2009, http://online.wsj.com/article/SB123923448796803135.html.

7. Dan Walters, "Worst deficit news waits around the corner," *Sacramento Bee*, December 9, 2008, http://www.sacbee.com/walters/story/1459183.html.

8. George Skelton, "Illegal immigrants are a factor in California's budget math," *Los Angeles Times*, February 2, 2009, http://www.latimes.com/news/columnists/la-me-cap2-2009feb02.0.418500.column.

9. "California Budget Meltdown Would be Lessened by Combating Increases in Illegal Immigration," Reuters, February 6, 2009, http://www.reuters.com/article/pressRelease/idUS268071+06-Feb-2009+PRN20090206.

10. All statistics in this paragraph are drawn from "The Tax Capital of the World," *Wall Street Journal*, April 11, 2009, http://online.wsj.com/article/SB123940286075109617.html.

11. "Santelli's Tea Party," CNBC Video, February 29, 2009, http://www.cnbc.com/id/15840232?video=1039849853.

12. Michael P. Mayko, "Activists vent at AIG executives," *Connecticut Post*, March 24, 2009, http://www.connpost.com/ci_11968393.

13. Ben Hall and Esther Bintliff, "French unions vow to keep up pressure," *Financial Times*, March 19, 2009, http://www.ft.com/cms/s/0/fa2fea66-1481-11de-8cd1-0000779fd2ac.html.

14. "Paris in the spring," *Economist*, March 19, 2009, http://www.economist.com/world/europe/displayStory.cfm?story_id=13348655&source=features_box_main.

15. Ben Hall, "French workers stage strike in protest at job losses and reforms," *Financial Times*, January 29, 2009, http://www.ft.com/cms/s/71c25576-eda6-11dd-bd60-0000779fd2ac.Authorised=false.html?_i_location=http%3A%2F%2Fwww.ft.com%2Fcms%2Fs%2F0%2F71c25576-eda6-11dd-bd60-0000779fd2ac.html&_i_referer=.

16. Leila Abboud and David Gauthier-Villars, "In France, Oui to Bailout, Non to Layoffs," *Wall Street Journal*, March 19, 2009, http://online.wsj.com/article/SB123742034399078391.html#mod=todays_us_nonsub_page_one.

17. Angelique Chrisafis, "Sacked French Sony workers release boss from captivity," *Guardian*, March 13, 2009, quoting a report from Agence France-Presse, http://www.guardian.co.uk/world/2009/mar/13/sony-france-boss-hostage.

18. William Maclean and Kate Holton, "G20 protestors smash windows and clash with police," Reuters, April 2, 2009, http://uk.reuters.com/article/UKNews1/idUKTRE53101020090402.

19. State Foreclosure Prevention Working Group, "Data Reports," Conference of State Bank Supervisors, http://www.csbs.org/Content/NavigationMenu/Home/StForeclosureMain.htm.

20. Alan Choate, "Proposals for homeless include tent city acreage, forced aid," *Las Vegas Review-Journal*, March 19, 2009, http://www.lvrj.com/news/41483592.html.

21. Suzanne Hurt, "California 'tent city' for homeless to be closed," Reuters, March 20, 2009, http://www.reuters.com/article/topNews/idUSTRE52J0FK20090320?feedType=RSS&feedName=topNews.

22. Stacy Forster, "While lawmakers problem-solve, examples of a chronic concern seek shelter beneath their feet," March 18, 2009, http://www.jsonline.com/news/statepolitics/41472052.html.

23. Haya El Nasser and Paul Overberg, "No one home: 1 in 9 housing units

vacant," *USA Today*, February 13, 2009, http://www.usatoday.com/money/economy/housing/2009-02-12-vacancy12_N.htm.

24. John Leland, "With Advocates' Help, Squatters Call Foreclosures Home," *New York Times*, April 9, 2009, http://www.nytimes.com/2009/04/10/us/10squatter.html.

25. Ed Gillespie and Bob Schellhas, eds. *Contract with America: The Bold Plan by Rep. Newt Gingrich, Rep. Dick Armey, and the House Republicans to Change the Nation* (New York: Random House, 1994), pp. 3–5.

26. Ibid., p. 5.

27. Jerome R. Corsi, "Hunter wants 'fence' back in 'Secure Fence Act,' " World Net Daily, January 25, 2008, http://www.worldnetdaily.com/news/article.asp?ARTICLE_ID=59877.

Conclusion: Taking America Back

1. Joseph Farah, *Taking America Back: A Radical Plan to Revive Freedom, Morality and Justice* (Nashville, Tenn.: WND, 2003), p. 41.

2. See the Reform Institute, http://www.reforminstitute.org/. The Reform Institute is a nonprofit 501(c)(3) organization.

3. The Soros-Kerry funding connection with McCain was first exposed by Ed Morrissey at the "Captains Quarters" blog in 2005. See "Inside McCain's Reform Institute," March 9, 2005, http://www.captainsquartersblog.com/mt/archives/004026.php. Subsequently, David Horowitz's DiscoverTheNetworks.org website gave renewed attention to the Reform Institute's funding ties. See "John McCain Gets Soros Cash," March 10, 2005, http://www.discoverthenetworks.org/moonbatcentral/2005/03/john-mccain-gets-soros-cash.html. Michelle Malkin's blog has also covered the issue. See "Meet the open borders family: McCain, Hernandez, Soros, and the 'Reform Institute,' " January 25, 2008, http://michellemalkin.com/2008/01/25/meet-the-open-borders-family-mccain-hernandez-soros-and-the-reform-institute/.

4. Todd Shields, "Report: McCain Took Cablevision Money," *Mediaweek*, March 8, 2005, http://www.allbusiness.com/services/business-services-miscellaneous-business/4762529-1.html: the story was originally reported by the Associated Press; see "McCain group got big donation while he promoted Cablevision policy," March 7, 2005, http://www.kvoa.com/Global/story.asp?S=3043288&nav=HMO6XGD1.

5. Mail Foreign Service, " 'I'm having a very good crisis,' says Soros as hedge fund managers make billions off recession," *Daily Mail*, March 25, 2009, http://www.dailymail.co.uk/news/worldnews/article-1164771/Im-having-good-crisis-says-hedge-fund-manager-1billion-world-plunged-recession.html.

6. George Soros, *The New Paradigm for Financial Markets: The Credit Crisis of 2008 and What It Means* (New York: PublicAffairs, 2008), "Introduction," p. vii.

7. Reuters, "U.S. Recovery Is Far Off, Banks Are 'Basically Insolvent': Soros," April 6, 2009, published on CNBC.com.

8. "Barack Obama: Top Contributors, 2008 Election Cycle," OpenSecrets .org, http://www.opensecrets.org/pres08/contrib.php?cycle=2008&cid=N0 0009638.

9. "John McCain: Top Contributors, 2008 Election Cycle," OpenSecrets .org, http://www.opensecrets.org/pres08/contrib.php?cycle=2008&cid=N0 0006424.

10. Kenneth P. Vogel, "W.H. team discloses TARP firm ties," Politico, April 3, 2009, http://www.politico.com/news/stories/0409/20889.html.

11. Ibid.

12. Jim McElhatton, "Obama adviser lobbied to protect Fannie," *Washington Times*, November 18, 2008, http://washingtontimes.com/news/2008/ nov/18/obama-adviser-lobbied-to-protect-fannie/. According to the *Washington Times,* however, "Mr. Donilon wasn't involved in the accounting irregularities that ultimately prompted OFHEO to seek more than $100 million that Fannie Mae paid out in compensation to Mr. Raines and two other top officials."

13. Robert Scheer, "Obama's Toxic Advisers," *Nation*, March 25, 2009, http:// www.thenation.com/doc/20090406/scheer.

14. Ibid.

15. John D. McKinnon, "Obama Team's Finances Released," *Wall Street Journal*, April 6, 2009, http://online.wsj.com/article/SB123897383971909 73.html.

16. Jerome R. Corsi, "Will Obama take a pay cut, too?," World Net Daily, January 22, 2009, http://www.worldnetdaily.com/index.php?pageId=86846.

INDEX

Bank of America, 36–37, 55, 104, 260, 261
Bank of Canada, 190, 191–92
Bank of International Settlements, 33
Banking Committee, U.S. Senate, 43, 59, 71
bankruptcy
  as alternative to bailout, 219, 254, 264
  and "America for sale," 130
  in automotive industry, 244, 264, 265
  and bursting bubbles, 33–36
  and currency issues, 196
  and derivatives, 36–37
  and entitlement programs, 22
  and global Economic Panic (2009), 22
  and globalism, 41
  of life-insurance companies, 229
  and need for market remedy, 216
  and Obama's optimism, 39–40
  overview about, 21–22, 40–41
  and saying no to global New Deal, 216, 219, 220, 221
  and state budget deficits, 244
  and stimulus plan, 37–39
  and trillions of dollars, 22–25
  of U.S., 21–41, 65, 130, 220, 254
  See also debt, U.S deficit
banks. *See* central banks; financial institutions; *specific institution*
Banque AIG, 32
Bardhan, Ashok Deo, 106
Barnes, Roger, 60–61
Barroso, Jose Manuel, 150, 151
Bay Bucks, 226
BBC News, 58
Bear Stearns, 3, 104, 260
Bennett, Robert, 152–53
BerkShares, 226
Bernanke, Ben, 26–27, 32–33, 49, 55, 101, 103, 263
Bernhard (prince of Netherlands), 145
Biden, Joseph, 262–63
Bilderberg Group, 145, 147, 149, 261
bin Laden, Osama, 25
bin Talal, Alwaleed, 71
biofuels, 74, 76–78, 82
Black Thursday (1929), 209–10
Blackstone Group, 39
Blackwill, Robert, 146
Blair, Dennis C., 146
Bliley, Thomas, 59
Blinder, Alan S., 120–21, 129
Blitzer, Wolf, 196
Bloomberg News, 35
Bodman, Sam, 102
Boehner, John A., 85
Boeing Corporation, 154
Bomba, Michael, 176
"Bonus Army," 248
Booker, Christopher, 133

Borrowing Advisory Committee (TBAC), U.S. Treasury Department, 27
Borse Dubai, 71
Boston Tea Party, 237
Brascan brokerage, 91–92
Brazil
  oil in, 91–92
British Petroleum, 92
Brogdon, Randy, 181–82, 241
Brown, Gordon, 198, 213, 214
Brzezinski, Zbigniew, 136–38, 142, 145, 150, 158, 183
bubbles. *See type of bubble*
budget, U.S.
  balancing of, 253–54
  and "cap-and-trade" carbon emissions tax, 84
  deficits of, 22–27
  and Obama administration, 27, 225, 230, 240, 264
  and rise of patriots, 253–54
  and social welfare programs, 254
  See also bankruptcy; debt, U.S deficits
budgets, state, 243–44, 251, 252–53
Buffett, Warren, 191
bumblebee analogy, 10–11
Bureau of Economic Analysis, U.S., 3
Bureau of Labor Statistics, U.S., 99, 122, 123–24
Burges, Judy, 242
Burlington Northern Santa Fe, 172
Burns, Kyle, 175
Bush, George H.W., 1, 146, 150, 161, 181, 206, 234
Bush (George W.) administration
  and "America for sale," 14
  and China's unfair advantages, 100, 101–2
  and conservatives, 238
  and currency issues, 193, 194
  deficits of, 12, 14, 27, 266
  and free trade, 5, 6, 113–15, 118, 176–77, 207
  and FTAA initiative, 176–77
  and globalism, 135–36, 146–47, 148, 150–51, 153, 266
  and government takeover of Fannie Mae and Freddie Mac, 57–58
  and homeownership, 44, 46–47, 54, 64
  and Medellín case, 115–16
  and Mexican-truck demonstration, 9, 117, 118
  and mortgages, 44
  Obama compared with, 266
  optimism of, 18
  and presidential powers, 238–39, 240
  and public-private partnerships, 167, 181, 206
  and regulation of financial institutions, 58
  and social welfare programs, 12, 266